W9-AWK-671

The
Essential
Guide to
O'ahu

The
Essential
Guide to
O'ahu

ISLAND HERITAGE
Honolulu, Hawaii

Many people assisted with this project by providing information. It is impossible to name them all, but those we wish to thank for being particularly helpful to us are:

John Alford, Sandy Beach Surf Design Hawaii; Marlene Among, Polynesian Voyaging Society; Alan Awana, KCCN Hawaiian Radio; Pat Bacon, Bernice Pauahi Bishop Museum; Joe Balantine; Penny Barr, Hilton Hawaiian Village; Lindy Boyes, Hawai'i Visitors Bureau; Russ Brown, Turbo Surf Designs; Leon Bruno, Hawai'i Museums Assocation; Michaelyn Chou, Hamilton Library, University of Hawai'i; John Clark; Agnes Conrad, Hawai'i Museums Association; John Gray, Pacific Outdoor Adventures; Sarah Gray, Little Hawaiian Craft Shop; Nanci Hersh, The Pegge Hopper Gallery; Carol Hopper, Waikiki Aquarium; Ruth Horie, Bernice Pauahi Bishop Museum Library; Hoku Fenn, Sheraton-Waikiki; Brickwood Galuteria, KCCN Hawaiian Radio; Hawaii Hotel Association; Hawai'i State Library; Hawai'i Visitors Bureau; Emily Hawkins, Indo-Pacific Languages, University of Hawai'i; Tommy Holmes, Hawai'i Maritime Center; Kamehameha Schools/Bishop Estate; Fritz Luden, Dances We Dance; Ed Michaelman, State of Hawai'i Office of Hawaiian Affairs; Joseph Morgan, Geography Department, University of Hawai'i; Michael Nacapuy, Musicians' Association of Hawaii; Carol Naish, Naish Hawaii; Mike Niederer; Harry Rubello, Aloha Beach Service; Ann Pinkerton, Hilton Hawaiian Village; Robert Schmidt, Hawai'i State Department of Business and Economic Development; Robert Smith; Myron Thompson, Polynesian Voyaging Society; John Kaha'i Topolinski; Christine Valles, State of Hawai'i Office of Hawaiian Affairs.

COPYRIGHT © 1988 ISLAND HERITAGE
All Rights Reserved

Please address orders and
editorial correspondence to:

ISLAND HERITAGE PUBLISHING
A division of The Madden Corporation
99-880 Iwaena Street
Aiea, Hawai'i 96701
(808) 487-7299

SECOND EDITION, FIRST PRINTING–1991
PRINTED IN HONG KONG

Produced by:
THE MADDEN CORPORATION

Published by:
ISLAND HERITAGE
A Division of The Madden Corporation

Written by:
RUTH GURNANI-SMITH

1991 Editors:
PENNY PENCE SMITH
DIXON J. SMITH

Production Assistant:
JANE K. MORITA-SIBLEY

Research Assistant:
SYLVIA MORRIS

Original Hotel & Restaurant Rating System:
JERI BOSTWICK

Art Direction/Production:
THE BAPTISTA GROUP

Page Layout/Photo Editor:
SCOTT RUTHERFORD

Cartography:
ANDREA HINES

Original Cover Artwork by:
MARK A. WAGENMAN

TABLE OF CONTENTS

INTRODUCTION

Geography
Climate and weather
Cultural background
Language

INTRODUCTION

Most people think of Hawai'i as ... " The telling part of this familiar phrase is that most people do, indeed, think of Hawai'i. There would be few—at least in the Western world—who have not heard of it. Hawai'i has been immortalized and publicized in song, in print and in film—to say nothing of just plain advertising—until it has become a global legend.

Can its reality live up to its myth? Despite the changes in this once-Polynesian-kingdom, few of the more than five million tourists who visit these islands each year go away disappointed. Some don't go away at all. Many return again and again; nearly half Hawai'i's tourists are repeat visitors.

GEOGRAPHY

The name *Hawai'i* evokes in the minds of most people images of a tropical paradise in an idealized 'South Pacific'. In fact, Hawai'i is an island group in the North Pacific, uniquely isolated at about a thousand miles from its nearest neighbors—the Line Islands to the south and the Marshall Islands to the southwest. Nothing but open ocean lies between Hawai'i and southern California, 2390 miles [3846km] to the east-northeast; Japan, 3850 miles [6196km] to the west-northwest; and Alaska, 2600 miles [4184km] to the north. The Marquesas—from which at least some of the early Polynesian migrants came—are 2400 miles [3862km] to the south-southeast.

The archipelago spans 1523 miles [2451km] and includes 132 islands, reefs and shoals strewn across the Tropic of Cancer—from Kure Atoll in the northwest to underwater seamounts off the coast of the island of Hawai'i in the southeast. All are included in the state of Hawai'i except the Midway Islands, which are administered by the US Navy. This southernmost of the United States lies between latitudes 28° 15' and 18° 54'N and between longitudes 179° 25' and 154° 40'W, reaching almost as far west as Alaska's

Aleutian Islands. Hawai'i's major islands share their tropical latitudes with such urban centers as Mexico City, Havana, Mecca, Calcutta, Hanoi and Hong Kong. The 158th meridian west, which passes through O'ahu's Pearl Harbor, also crosses Point Barrow on Alaska's north coast, Atiu Island in the South Pacific's Cook Islands and Cape Colbeck near the edge of Antarctica's Ross Ice Shelf.

Though Hawai'i's land surface adds up to only 6425 square miles [16,642 sq km] (at that still larger than Connecticut, Delaware or Rhode Island), the archipelago, including its territorial waters, covers a total of about 654,500 square miles [1,695,155 sq km]—an area considerably bigger than Alaska and more than twice the size of Texas.

There are eight main islands in the Hawaiian chain, one of which—Kaho'olawe—is not inhabited because it is used by the military for target practice. The tiny island of Ni'ihau is privately owned and can be visited by non-residents only at the invitation of its owners—an honor rarely bestowed on anyone. This island—due to its fierce protection from outside influence—

Late afternoon on O'ahu's North Shore.

is the last stronghold of Hawaiian culture (its entire population [226] is of at least part-Hawaiian blood), and it is the only place on the planet where Hawaiian is still spoken as the mother tongue. Scenic helicopter flights over the island may touch down to a designated area for up to twenty minutes, but no contact with the residents is permitted.

That leaves visitors to Hawai'i the islands of Kaua'i, O'ahu, Moloka'i, Lāna'i, Maui, and Hawai'i (familiarly known as 'the Big Island')—in that order, north to south and chronologically in age—to play with. And there's much fun to be had!

TIME AND DAYLIGHT

Because of Hawai'i's tropical position, the length of daylight doesn't vary greatly from one time of year to the next—only around three or four hours—so that Hawaiians have never felt any need to save it. Thus Hawaiian Standard Time is in effect year-round, and the time differences between Hawai'i and places that do save daylight varies by an hour when daylight saving is in effect elsewhere.

Hawaiian Standard Time is five hours behind New York, four hours behind Chicago, three hours behind Denver and two hours behind San Francisco; it is also eleven hours behind London, nineteen hours behind Tokyo, twenty hours behind Sydney, and twenty-two hours behind Auckland and Suva. Add an hour to all these for daylight time.

The popular local phrase 'Hawaiian time' simply means 'late'.

INTRODUCTION

Exploring tidepools at sunset near Portlock Point.

4

CLIMATE AND WEATHER

Hawai'i is blessed with a pleasant and equable climate—that is, it doesn't change much throughout the year—at sea level. The temperature ranges between a daytime high near 90°F [around 30°C] in 'summer' and a nighttime low near 60°F [around 18°C] in 'winter'.

There really are no distinct seasons as such. Even in 'winter' the daytime temperature is usually in the 80s. The comfort factor that this involves depends on what you're used to: where you've come from and how long you've been here. People do acclimatize. Those of us who live here start to shiver and bundle up when the mercury plummets to 75°F [24°C]. The coldest months are February and March and the hottest August and September.

Despite this lack of strong seasonal variation, Hawai'i is home to an extraordinary diversity of microclimates—from desert to rainforest. Temperature drops about 3°F for every thousand feet of increased altitude, a factor which produces seasonal snow on the upper slopes of the Big Island's Mauna Kea. Rainfall varies dramatically in different parts of each island—from a mere ten inches annually in some leeward areas to more than forty feet at the summit of Kaua'i's Mount Wai'ale'ale (the wettest spot on Earth), where it virtually never stops raining. The State's heaviest rains are brought by storms and fall between October and April. A lot of rain is needed to water all this lush tropical foliage, and drought in some areas of the islands is not unheard-of.

Fortunately, most of our local rainshowers are short if heavy. Downtown Honolulu, for example, has on rare occasions had as much as seventeen inches of rainfall in a single day, though its annual average is only twenty-four inches. There are, of course, occasions when it rains all day, but these are rare, except in the upper reaches of valleys where the rainclouds never leave for long. The windward areas get far more rain than their leeward counterparts.

The Waikīkī district, on Oʻahu's south shore, has amongst the fairest weather patterns in the islands—a fact which has, no doubt, contributed greatly to its popularity (see Especially Waikīkī below). There have been few damaging storms or tsunami (seismic sea waves) in Hawaiʻi. If you would like information about Civil Defense Warnings and procedures, refer to the front section of the White Pages of the local telephone directory.

CULTURAL BACKGROUND

Hawaiian history has been aptly divided by some into two categories: BC—Before Cook, and AD—After Discovery. Very recent archaeological findings suggest that Hawaiʻi was, in fact, settled by humans much earlier than had been believed: in the centuries BC (Before Christ) rather than the mere fifteen hundred years ago previously postulated. Details of this evidence have yet to be published.

There is no doubt, though, that voyaging Polynesians did arrive deliberately from the islands of Tahiti and the Marquesas around 500 AD (Anno Domini) and again around 1100. Some 'experts' claim that the name Hawaiʻi doesn't actually mean anything in Hawaiian; others see it as an obvious variation of the name of the legendary homeland claimed by *all* Polynesians: Hawaiki, and the term Hawaiʻi Nei (literally, Hawaiʻi here, this Hawaiʻi) as their way of making a clear distinction in speech between a reference to their present homeland and one to its legendary namesake.

Another interesting theory now rejected by most modern historians is that the first European to discover these islands was not the famed Captain Cook in 1778—as is generally supposed—but the Spanish navigator Gaetan who,

according to early explorers such as Dixon and La Perouse, passed by *en route* from the Philippines to Mexico in 1542 and named them the King's Islands. The alleged Spanish visit is dismissed as being, in any case, insignificant and without any lasting effect on the islands' culture as it was not repeated. This line of reasoning might lead us far from the truth. The first English visitors noted distinctly Caucasian features in the faces of some of the natives they encountered. There are local legends also that allude to white men coming to live amongst the people of these islands in the distant past. The most apparent evidence in support of this hypothesis is, however, the existence in Hawaiʻi—but nowhere else in Polynesia—of armor-like, crested, helmet-shaped headgear and ceremonial cloaks, in the royal colors of Spain; some consider this all together unlikely to be coincidence. These magnificent garments were made from many thousands of tiny feathers plucked from small, predominantly black native birds, which were trapped, relieved of their few brightly colored feathers and released to produce a new supply—an early example of ecologically efficient management of natural resources. It thus took many years—often generations—to

large cloak. These richly textured, velvet-like artifacts were, and are, priceless.

Be that as it may, Captain Cook did arrive, and with him such sweeping change that Hawaiian culture was shaken to its very foundations. The first and perhaps the most powerful influence to take hold in the Islands was the intro-duction of European diseases. Hawaiians died in droves. The ambitious young Kamehameha quickly adopted and promoted the technologies of European warfare. With these, his resident English advisors, and his own intelligence and determination, he not only unseated his cousin Kiwala'o, the hereditary ruler of his home island, Hawai'i, but also conquered the rest of the islands, which previously had been governed by a family of chiefs—Kahekili, his son Kalani-kupule, his brother Ka'eokulani, and *his* son Kaumuali'i—to whom the 'Great' Kamehameha was also related, though himself of less exalted lineage.

Trade flourished under the guiding hand of Kamehameha, and the Islands were swept inexorably into the Western world of the nineteenth century. The old rules no longer applied. For millenia the Hawaiian people had been gov-erned by a complex system of *kapu* or restrictions that effectively regulated everything from manage-ment of the local ecosystems, through the details of daily life, to the most intimate aspects of spiritual and religious practice. These areas were not demarcated in the world of the Hawaiians. All was one—life was life. Some of the native laws appeared meaningless and merciless to the European mind, and many laws were sus-pended for immigrant foreigners—

men from visiting ships. The Hawaiian people saw this and worried, and wondered why the gods did not intervene.

The loudest death knell for the Hawaiian way of life was rung inadvertently by the powerful Ka'ahumanu, a widow of Kamehameha. At his death he had created for her the title *kuhina nui* and set her up as co-regent with his son and heir, Liholiho. Ka'ahumanu abolished the law prohibiting men and women from dining together, which she found both inconvenient and incompatible with her esteemed position, by persuading Liholiho— Kamehameha II—to sit down and eat with her and his mother, Keopuolani, at a public banquet— an act which produced no response from the gods. She had not realized that the whole *kapu* system would thus come crashing down around the heads of her people, and she had nothing to offer in its place. Their world was shattered—their gods had abandoned them—and the Hawaiians were dazed and spiritually adrift when the first missionaries arrived from New England in 1820. The Hawaiians had already torn down many of their own temples and chased their priests into hiding. These new invaders met no resistance from the local religion, for there was none. It was the traders and other white residents of the Islands who howled loudly in protest, over moralistic meddling.

As the newcomers acquired more land, as their trading and planting ventures flourished and grew, and as the native population continued to decline, cheap agricultural labor was brought to the islands, first from China then from Japan, Europe, the Philippines

the islands, first from China then from Japan, Europe, the Philippines and elsewhere. Thus began the famed Hawaiian 'melting pot'. In Hawai'i today, there is no ethnic majority; this is probably the only place in the world where *everyone* belongs to a minority group. All these people naturally brought with them the languages and customs of their native lands, and with them have enriched the cultural life of Hawai'i.

As a result of the powerful influence the missionary establishment exercised through members of the ruling [*ali'i*] class of Hawaiians (particularly a few powerful women), and of the 'guidance' of foreign 'advisors' to Hawaiian kings, the Hawaiians—not at all grasping the full implications of Western concepts such as property and ownership—signed away their 'rights' and virtually gave their homeland to the newcomers. These rulers of the local economy—mostly Americans and many missionary-descended—eventually wrested the government as well from the Hawaiian royal line, with the help of representatives of the US government, and set themselves up as the new government of a 'Republic of Hawai'i' until they were able to persuade the US Congress to annex them outright—after which they continued to lobby for statehood. None of these sweeping decisions had much to do with the actual preferences of the Hawaiian people who were, by now, a minority.

This exceedingly brief account of Hawaiian history leaves out, of course, details and differing viewpoints of the diverse interest groups involved (see RECOMMENDED READING). Nonetheless, the result

is the same.

Hawai'i was granted statehood and admitted as a fully fledged member of the United States of America in 1959, and is now squarely in the mainstream of modern American life. Its capital, Honolulu, is a thriving business and academic center—the gateway for commerce and cultural exchange with Asia, Australia and the South Pacific. Throughout the islands which can be visited, all the modern conveniences of contemporary American life are readily available—yet it is still possible to 'get away from it all'. Hawai'i as a resort has something for almost everyone.

7

Lei-draped King Kamehameha I.

LANGUAGE

The common language of Hawaiian commerce became English very early in the era of immigration and economic investment by Americans and other foreigners. And so it remained. The missionaries made sweeping and now irreversible changes in the Hawaiian language when they hurriedly transliterated and transcribed it for print in order to produce bibles. Subsequent efforts to stamp out the native tongue were very successful. There are only a thousand or two native speakers left—most either very old or from the private island of Ni'ihau, but a strong grassroots movement to save the language has taken hold in recent years and is gaining widespread support. Virtually everyone in the islands today speaks the American variety of English, with a few local variations on the theme. Some of these should be noted because they are so common that tourists must be aware of them or stay lost.

Perhaps most important is the local way of giving directions. Nobody ever uses the cardinal points of the compass. On an island these are far less relevant than the obvious 'toward the mountain' and 'toward the sea'. A contracted form of the Hawaiian words for these directions is universally used in Hawai'i. 'Toward the upland[*uka*]' is *mauka*; 'toward the sea [*kai*]' is *makai*. For the other directions, major landmarks are used. In Honolulu, the common directional features are 'Ewa (referring to 'Ewa Plantation, just past Pearl Harbor) and Diamond Head. Thus, you may be told to walk *mauka* two blocks and Diamondhead a block to find the building you want on the *makai-*

'Ewa corner. If you go past the named landmark, another takes its place. For instance, in Kāhala, the Diamondhead direction is the same as 'Ewa, and the other way is called Kokohead, because Koko Head lies in that direction. On the windward side, the standard directions are Makapu'u (the southeast tip of the island) and Hale'iwa (a town near the northwestern tip). It makes perfect sense.

The other major obstacle, for some, to comfortable getting around is the ubiquitous use of Hawaiian placenames and streetnames. The Hawaiian language is beautiful and only *looks* intimidating to non-Polynesians because they are not accustomed to seeing so many vowels in a row. **Basically, if you just pronounce all the letters one by one, you'll be fine.** In fact you might, at that, be pronouncing Hawaiian more correctly than a lot of people who are used to it. The 'glottal stop' (written ') is the hard sound created by stopping between vowel sounds, like the English 'oh-oh', rather than a sliding from one vowel to the next, as is usual. In Hawaiian, this is called '*okina*. Just stop talking then start again immediately. The macron (written as a - over a vowel), called *kahakō* in Hawaiian, simply means that vowel is held a little longer—as if it were written twice, which it occasionally is. Consonants are pronounced the same as in English except that *w* sometimes sounds like *v* , as when it immediately precedes a final single vowel (as in 'Ewa). Vowels are pronounced as in Spanish or Italian (*ah, eh, ee, oh, oo*). The vowel combinations *ai, ae, ao, au, ei, eu, oi* and *ou* are stressed on the first

A chameleon casts its shadow on a palm frond.

member and basically sounded as single units, though the second vowel in the set is truly pronounced and not lost in the combination as with English diphthongs. Otherwise, stress (accent) is almost always on the next-to-last syllable. No matter how many times you hear it along the tourist trail, the very special and wonderfully soft Hawaiian word *aloha* is NOT correctly pronounced with the stress on the last syllable.

You will often see Hawaiian words written without the *kahakōs* and *'okinas*. This was the custom of the English-speaking people who first transcribed the language and was common practice until fairly recently. The markings are necessary for correct pronunciation of many words, and for discerning between similarly spelt words with quite different meanings. Government policy is now to insert the correct markings in all Hawaiian words on street and road signs as they are replaced. At the moment, outside the Waikīkī-Downtown area, you may see them either way. The other feature of local language that visitors are bound to encounter is our own brand of pidgin English. It is spiced with words from the rich linguistic heritage brought by people of many lands, but basically, it is English with a bit of Hawaiian, and if you listen carefully, you'll catch on. The idiom and the lilt are peculiar to Hawai'i, but the pronunciation of most words is recognizable. Lists of commonly used Hawaiian and pidgin words, with their meanings and pronunciations, can be found at the back of this guidebook.

INTRODUCTION

THE FLAG

Most first-time visitors to Hawai'i are intrigued to note the British Union Jack in the corner of the Hawaiian State Flag. This same flag has served kingdom, republic and state and was designed prior to 1816 for King Kamehameha I. The Union Jack honors Hawai'i's early ties with Britain; the eight horizontal stripes represent the archipelago's eight main islands. Hawai'i's State Anthem, 'Hawai'i Pono'ī', is its former national anthem and was composed by King Kalākaua.

O'AHU IN PARTICULAR

O'ahu is the capital isle, but this was not always so. In ancient times, the Big Island—Hawai'i—was preeminent in island affairs, both in contemporary life and in legend and oral tradition. The conquering Kamehameha was from that island and ruled his newly unified kingdom from there much of the time. In the 1820s, the nation's official capital was established at Lahaina, Maui, where the Pacific fleets of the whaling industry based their activities. The seat of national government was moved to Honolulu, O'ahu in 1845 and this city was officially declared the capital in 1850.

Contrary to modern myth, the name O'ahu does not mean 'gathering place'. The name is so ancient that both its origin and its meaning are lost in the mists of time. It is best not to attempt a translation and simply to accept it as the name given this island by the ancients. O'ahu is, though, in modern Hawai'i, definitely a gathering place, being the focal point of most of the State's educational, artistic, business and social activities. The University of Hawai'i's main campus (Mānoa) is on this island, as are four of its associated community colleges; there are several small, private universities and a large number of secondary and primary schools, both private and public. Most of the State's museums, libraries, art galleries, theatres and other entertainments are here, as well as the greatest number and diversity of restaurants. Major festivals, concerts and sporting events are frequent on Oʻahu. The third largest of the Hawaiian Islands—about 607 square miles [1570 sq km]—Oʻahu is home to nearly 817,000 people (80% of the State's population), about half of whom live in Honolulu. Military personnel and their dependents comprise nearly 15% of the State's population, and almost all of them reside on Oʻahu (less than .4% on the other islands). Ninety percent of Oʻahu's hotels are in Waikīkī, so there are still a lot of agricultural and undeveloped countryside, even on this most populous island, and a great deal of spectacularly beautiful scenery.

Though Oʻahu's—indeed Hawaiʻi's—main source of revenue is now tourism, with military expenditure in second place, agriculture is still important, the principal crops being sugar cane and pineapple, on Oʻahu as on the other principal islands. The movie industry provides notable revenue and local employment as our islands offer such a variety of popular film locations, even for stories that are set elsewhere. Classic feature films shot here include *Bird of Paradise, Waikiki Wedding, From Here to Eternity, Hawaiʻi, In Harm's Way* and *Tora! Tora! Tora!*; fun films such as *Gidget Goes Hawaiian* and *Goin' Surfing* are well remembered, and *North Shore, Tour of Duty, Karate Kid II* and made-for-television mini-series movies *War and Remembrance* and *Blood and Orchids* were shot on Oʻahu. Major successful and long-running television series have been Oʻahu-based: *Adventures in Paradise, Hawaiian Eye, Hawaii Five-0, Magnum P.I.* and *Jake & the Fat Man.*

Outrigger canoes slice through the warm waters surrounding Oʻahu.

ESPECIALLY WAIKĪKĪ

Waikīkī has always been popular. Prior to the arrival of Europeans, it was the center of power for the ruling chiefs of O'ahu. Its reefs provided fish, shellfish, octopus, sea urchins and other marine delicacies; the marshy inland floodplain provided perfect conditions for wetland agriculture; the wide sandy shoreline was perfect for beaching canoes; its surf was ideal for the most Hawaiian of recreations; and its weather was idyllic.

With the advent of European trade via large deep-draught sailing ships, Waikīkī—where these behemoths had to anchor offshore in sometimes heavy surf conditions—was left to the farmers, and commerce and government shifted toward Honolulu Harbor—where European vessels could dock with ease in calm, sheltered waters.

Waikīkī remained, however, a favored spot for the local aristocracy to escape the bustle of 'urban' life, and well-heeled immigrant merchants and planters followed suit. Cottages and, later, more substantial dwellings became clustered along the Waikīkī shoreline, and some of these eventually began to offer paid lodging to visitors. Waikīkī's first resort hotel—the now venerable Moana—opened its doors to guests in 1901, followed in 1927 by the 'pink palace' of the Royal Hawaiian. The pair were, for decades, the second most prominent feature in the district, both dwarfed by the looming brow of Lae'ahi, now called Diamond Head.

The most substantial changes to the face of Waikīkī were made possible by the construction of the Ala Wai Canal, a drainage channel

Waikīkī Beach with Diamond Head beyond.

Sunset off Waikīkī.

that converted the former marshes *mauka* of Kalākaua Avenue into terra firma. Waikīkī's centuries-old agricultural system had been made possible by the Ku'ekaunahi, 'Āpuakēhau and Pi'inaio Streams, flowing to the sea from the Pālolo, Mānoa and Makiki Valleys and crossing the beach at points near the present end of 'Ōhua Avenue, between the Moana and Royal Hawaiian Hotels and at the present site of Fort DeRussy Beach Park.

The man-made peninsula that is now known as Waikīkī has become a self-contained metropolis where most of O'ahu's transient population resides. An ordinary day finds more than 93,000 people dwelling on this 450 acres (smaller in area than Honolulu Airport's reef runway), about seventy percent of whom are visitors. The remaining thirty percent—Waikīkī's 'permanent' population—are overwhelmingly Caucasian (64%) newcomers (72% having lived in their present

dwelling for under five years) who were born outside Hawai'i (81%). Most are unmarried (63%) and live in high-rise buildings (98%). These statistics are not typical of Hawai'i or O'ahu in general. Nothing about Waikīkī is typical.

Waikīkī has always been a special place with special appeal. The nature of this appeal has changed radically over the years, but it hasn't diminished. The glitz and the glamour in this languorous tropical paradise provide a dreamlike context for vacationers from all over the world. The Waikīkī lifestyle is not the normal routine. A most unlikely and eclectic mix of humanity throngs its streets in blissful harmony: honeymooners, teenagers, conventioneers, businessmen, retirees, beach bums, even local residents out for a night on the town, the cast of thousands constantly changing. Waikīkī is a fantasy world—exciting and relaxing, fleeting and eternal.

Warm smiles from lovely kama'aina.

IN TRANSIT

Getting here
Bookings
Tours and rentals
Getting around

GETTING HERE

P lanning a trip to Hawai'i usually starts as a dream—or, at least, a fantasy. Happily, transforming that dream into reality has become very easy and not all that expensive. This section discusses the several practical considerations involved in making your Hawaiian dream come true, and offers options you may wish to consider.

Because of the vast difference in time and expense involved, most people choose air travel over sea travel, but the latter is still available; details are discussed below under Bookings. When to come is anytime, depending on your own schedule and preferences. The largest crowds usually gather in February and August.

CHOOSING LOCATION

The first order of business in planning your stay is to choose your preferred location.

O'ahu has both throbbing urban glamour and idyllic rural retreat, both upscale luxury and rustic camping—and lots of offerings in between. Most of O'ahu's hotels are in Waikīkī, many of its condominiums are not, and none of its bed-and-breakfast homes or its campsites are. Honolulu and Waikīkī, the most populated areas, are on the island's South Shore; the rest of the island—with the exception of the largely military residential suburbs in the area surrounding Pearl Harbor, and the Kailua-Kāne'ohe town area on the Windward side—is relatively undeveloped.

SELECTING LODGING

Hotels are by far the most popular type of accommodation for visitors, especially those who wish to be pampered during their holiday. Most of our hotels are staffed by friendly, accommodating people, and most are near where the action is.

Some visitors—especially those traveling with children—prefer the self-contained apartment facilities available at condominium resorts. This option is usually less expensive and offers more privacy and independence. Housekeeping services can be arranged at many of these resorts to relieve vacationers of the drudgery of housework; laundromats are usually available and many resorts offer pools and other recreational facilities.

Bed-and-breakfast accommodation in private homes is an increasingly popular option for budget-minded travelers and for those wishing to avoid crowds, and exclusive use of private homes is also available for longer-term visits. The latter option is popular with families visiting for the summer months.

Another family favorite is camping, either in rustic rural cabins or in tents.

Specific places that offer these various types of lodging are described in detail under ACCOMMODATION.

16

Day's end, Waimea Bay.

IN TRANSIT/Getting Here

18

WHAT TO BRING

In this land of perpetual spring and summer, apparel known elsewhere as 'summer clothing' is worn all year, and the usual attire is casual. Shorts are acceptable almost anywhere, though many businesses require customers to wear shoes (rubber thongs will usually suffice). Comfortable walking shoes are a must. Sleeveless or short-sleeved shirts are usually best for day wear, but long sleeves—or even a jacket or sweater—may be needed for cool winter evenings and air-conditioned buildings (most restaurants fall into this category).

Some deluxe restaurants and nightclubs have a dress code requiring men to wear jackets, though usually not ties.

PERMITS AND LICENSES

Some activities in which visitors may choose to participate require licenses or permits. The most obvious and common is driving. Any visitor who drives in Hawai'i must have a valid license from another state or a Canadian province or a current international driver's license issued in another country. All car rentals require the presentation of a driver's license and major credit card. Bicycles must be registered, so if you bring your own and it isn't licensed elsewhere you must obtain a local permit (Division of Motor Vehicles and Licensing 1455 S Beretania Street 943-3324); proof of ownership is required for issuance.

Camping permits are required for public parks that allow camping; these are detailed in the Camping subsection under AC-COMMODATION. All hunting requires a license, as does freshwater fishing; none is required for shore fishing and recreational boat fishing. Further details of these sporting licenses are discussed under relevant headings in the SPORTS & RECREATION section.

Those wishing to indulge in the romance of tropical nuptials also need a license—which can be obtained from the Honolulu City Marriage License Office in the State Health Department Building (1250 Punchbowl Street 548-5862 8am-4pm), or from a marriage license agent. Numerous local companies specialize in wedding services, including renewal of vows; these services and popular wedding venues are described in the Nuptials subsection of OTHER SERVICES. No vaccinations or innoculations are required for entry into Hawai'i.

Diamond Head from Waikīkī Beach.

BOOKINGS

The next order of business is to book your air or cruise tickets, your lodging, and any tours you may wish to arrange in advance. For any and all of this, we recommend using the services of a travel agent. You could spend days chasing specifics and comparing prices, and you may want to, but travel agents have most of the information you're likely to need at their fingertips—or a phone call away—and they know their sources well. It costs you no more as the agent's commission is paid by the provider, not the customer; and in many cases the agent can offer you a better deal than you could get if you booked directly by shaving their profit and passing that saving on to you. Many airlines and hotels also give priority to bookings made through agents as they are generally less likely to be canceled.

Airlines

Though our island state is accessible only by air or sea, it is such a popular destination that airfares are kept low through volume and competition. There are many airlines serving the Hawaiian Islands, most landing at Honolulu International Airport.

Flight times are roughly five hours from California, nine hours from Chicago, eleven hours from New York, eight hours from Tokyo and nine and a half hours from Sydney.

Domestic carriers providing service to and from the US mainland are **America West, American Airlines, Continental, Delta,** **Hawaiian Airlines, Northwest Airlines, Pan Am, TWA** and **United Airlines.** Foreign carriers currently serving Honolulu are **Air New Zealand, Canadian Airlines International, China Airlines, Garuda Indonesian, Japan Air Lines, Korean Air, Philippine Airlines, Qantas,** and **Singapore Airline.** Please note, however, that these lists are subject to change without notice. Your travel agent will have all the latest details and schedules.

For direct flights from the US mainland to Maui, Hawai'i and Kaua'i and for interisland air service information, see OUTER ISLANDS.

Cruise lines

It's not easy to come to Hawai'i by cruise ship these days. Most of the cruise lines that make stops at our islands—**P & O Lines, Princess Cruises, Royal Viking Line, Cunard Line** and other European-based cruise operators—are of foreign registry and are forbidden by US law from transporting American citizens from one US port to another US port. This law—the Jones Act—was passed in 1896. Thus, if you board a foreign vessel in New York or California, you may visit Hawai'i, but cannot make it or any other US port your final destination.

You may, if you board ship in another country, make Hawai'i or another American port your final destination, but most cruise operators today don't encourage one-way traffic. Still, it is possible, and there really is no more beautiful way to arrive here than by sea. **American Hawai'i Cruises** has two ships, the SS *Constitution* and SS *Independence*, that cruise the Hawaiian island chain on a weekly basis. They make a few trips a year to the ports of Seattle, San Francisco and Los Angeles. If your determined dream is to come here by ship, your travel agent will be able to provide dates of upcoming trans-Pacific voyages by these US-registered vessels, or contact American Hawai'i Cruises. For details of interisland cruises, see GETTING AROUND.

Tours

There are so many tours and tour operators on O'ahu that it would be impossible to list them all or to keep up with their continually changing schedules and fees. Your travel agent will be able to book tours for you through the larger companies, if you want your trip precisely planned.

Many visitors, though, prefer to book tours after arrival and a bit of scouting around, and many of the best tours are offered by small operators not linked by telex to Mainland or foreign cities.

There is no danger of not being able to get onto a tour to where you want to go—because so much is available—so we have chosen to describe a selection of tours and tour companies under GETTING AROUND.

Zen archery in Kapi'olani Park.

AIRPORT

Honolulu International Airport, serving as gateway between East and West, is one of the busiest airports in the world. Passengers arriving from the US mainland or from other countries emerge from the catacombs of this vast complex on the ground level of the main terminal building. Monitors with arrival information are located throughout the area. The airport's second level services Mainland and overseas departures and includes ticket counters for reservations and check-in, monitors with departure information, and all departure gates.

From the second level an escalator takes passengers leaving from the most distant gates up to a third level where free Wiki Wiki (Hawaiian for 'quick') buses, stopping every fifteen to twenty minutes, twenty-four hours a day, transport them to the far ends of the terminal. Most arriving and departing interisland flights service passengers from the interisland terminal, located next to the main terminal building at the 'Ewa end.

Adjacent to the main terminal is a large parking lot with easy access to and from both ground and upper levels. Car rental agencies (see Transportation below) are located on the ground level; their rental return areas are in the same vicinity as the lei stands, a vital airport facility unique in the nation.

Customs and immigration

All passengers arriving from other countries must pass through Customs and Immigration, located in the International Arrivals Center at the 'Ewa end of the main terminal building. All foreign nationals except Canadians require visas for entry into the United States. After clearance by customs and quarantine inspectors, these passengers exit the airport on the ground level, as do US mainland arrivals.

Quarantine

Quarantine regulations in Hawai'i are amongst the strictest in the world, and all arriving passengers must declare any plants or animals or their products they are bringing to the Islands. Failure to do so is punishable by law and the penalties are severe.

The Hawaiian Islands are free of many plant and animal diseases that cause problems in other parts of the world, and our quarantine laws are designed to prevent the introduction of those problems here. The importation of live animals is strictly prohibited except by permission; this includes all household pets, which must be boarded at the State's quarantine station for a period of 120 days. If you wish to import live plants to Hawai'i, contact the Hawai'i Department of Agriculture, Plant Quarantine Inspection at 701 Ilalo Street, Honolulu 96813 548-7175 for details and permits. For information about importing domestic animals, contact the Animal Quarantine division at 99-770 Moanalua Road, Aiea 96701 488-8462.

IN TRANSIT/Getting Here

22

Amenities

Honolulu's airport has all the standard conveniences: restaurant, coffee shop, cocktail lounge, duty free shops, currency exchange, barber shop, shoe shine, and newsstand. It is worth noting that everything is more expensive at the airport, so it is best to do most of your shopping elsewhere (see SHOPPING).

For people with late flights who've spent the day at the beach or who, for some other reason, need a shave, a wash or a nap, **The Shower Tree** offers showers and/or private, Pullman-like sleeping compartments for a very modest fee. A new Pacific Aerospace Museum is located in the main concourse area.

Finding your way out

Within the airport, free Wiki Wiki buses transport people from faraway gates to the escalators leading to the baggage claim areas on the lower level. Buses also transport people between the main terminal and the interisland terminal from 7am-10pm, every twenty to twenty-five minutes.

Arriving passengers pour forth from the terminal building's ground level, having collected their belongings from one of the many baggage claim areas.

All tour-booked passengers are greeted here or at the gates with flower leis, sometimes accompanied by a quick hula.

Central O'ahu's dense pineapple fields.

Honolulu International Airport is four miles from downtown and eight miles from Waikīkī. Public and private buses, taxis and limousines provide airport service, and several car rental agencies have offices at or near the airport. Limited helicopter transfer service is also available.

For more details about transportation and tours, see GETTING AROUND.

Public bus

The public buses on Oʻahu are called TheBus. These yellow and white leviathans (sometimes with orange) bus passengers all over the island for sixty cents.

The #19 and #20 buses, labeled 'Waikiki Beach and Hotels' when inbound and 'Airport' when outbound, stop at the second level of the main terminal about every ten minutes during the day.

Passengers on city buses are not allowed to carry on anything that will not fit onto their laps.

Private bus

Several private bus operators offer airport service. The **Gray Line Airporter** (834-1033) is the largest; look for a huge bus with a red hibiscus blossom on it, or a man in a red and blue shirt holding a sign; if neither is in sight, have a Gray Line representative paged from the information booth. The fare is eight dollars one way,

23

Local greeting at a Makaha Beach canoe regatta.

and the buses operate from 6 am to 11:30 pm daily. Outbound passengers are requested to make reservations a day in advance.

The **Airport Bus** (942-2177) transports passengers between the airport and the hotels in Waikīkī. For visitors departing O'ahu, they request advance notice of at least a day. The fare is five dollars each way, and their white vans operate from 5am-12m daily.

Airport Motorcoach (926-4747) offers outbound airport service for four dollars from 6:30am-10:30pm. These bus services handle your luggage at no extra cost.

Automobile

Sida has the **TAXI** concession for the arrival area of the airport and offers transportation in both ordinary cars and limousines. There is an extra charge for each piece of luggage. The cost of the metered journey to Waikīkī averages around fifteen dollars.

A number of **CAR RENTAL** agencies have service desks fronting the baggage claim areas on the ground level of the main terminal building. Many others have offices near the airport and courtesy phones in the baggage claim area. Those not on the premises will pick up customers at the terminal.

Private **LIMOUSINE** service is provided for arriving guests of some luxury hotels and tour companies, or you can arrange to be met by a chauffered Cadillac limousine or a Rolls Royce.

Weddings, Hawaiian style.

GETTING AROUND

T here are so many ways of getting around O'ahu that it's impossible to describe them all in detail. Basically, you can get around on land, by sea, or in the air; you can use many kinds of public and private transportation; you can be escorted, or can explore on your own. Addresses of tour companies and rental agencies are listed in alphabetical order at the back of this book in the APPENDIX Section.

TOURS AND RENTALS

The guided tours you can take are legion. There are well over two hundred companies listed under Tours in the O'ahu Yellow Pages. There are numerous modes of self-guided touring, and several modes of transportation you can rent to enhance your mobility.

There are also many packages that combine different types of touring; see the tour desk in your hotel for the smorgasbord, or visit the brochure racks at the Hawai'i Visitors Bureau (Kalākaua at Seaside Avenue 8th Floor 923-1811).

Air tours

Scenic flights are not inexpensive, but they offer good value for the price. A few companies offer air tours around the island chain with stops along the way—usually in Maui, Kaua'i and the Big Island—and various fly/drive combinations where a rental car awaits sightseers for terrestrial investigations.

Two such companies are **Panorama Air Tour** (836-2122) and **Scenic Air Tour Hawaii** (836-0044); their prices are comparable. Hawaiian Airlines' all-day 'Islands in the Sky' (537-5100) package covers a lot of territory, including the Big Island's Kohala coast, Maui's Haleakalā, Moloka'i's north shore and Kalaupapa Peninsula, Kaua'i's Nā Pali coast and Waimea Canyon, and O'ahu's surfing beaches. Their Dash 7s fly low enough to provide spectacular views of inaccessible places.

Papillon Hawaii Pacific Helicopters (836-1566) offer tours around O'ahu and Moloka'i, flying from

Diving Hawaiian waters.

Honolulu International Airport. Their Waikīkī tours consist of short flights above Waikīkī, Diamond Head and longer excursions to Hanauma Bay, Pearl Harbor and two covering the whole island, rates climbing with flight time; tours originating from Turtle Bay include short excursions to the North Shore, Sacred Falls (weather permitting), and another entire-island flight covering Pearl Harbor, Punchbowl, Hanauma Bay and Nuʻuanu Pali.

All flights are narrated. Also offered are airport transportation, charter and photography services.

Land tours

There are myriad options for getting around on land. Buses come in several varieties; numerous types of private vehicles can be rented; pedicabs ply the streets of Waikīkī and environs, as does the Waikiki Trolley; and, of course, there are lots of places to go on foot.

Buses

Oʻahu has a good public bus system and almost every available variety of tour bus. The huge buses that hold half a hundred people each are good for keeping large tour groups together, and they are air-conditioned. Several smaller sizes of buses are also used by tour companies, and these, though not always air-conditioned, afford a more intimate atmosphere for the passengers. Best of all are the increasingly popular mini-buses or large vans that are used by many local tour companies. These allow the most personalized service of all.

Guided group

Tours of Oʻahu follow two basic routes: **Circle Island** (around the eastern tip of the island, all the way up the Windward coast, around the North Shore, across the Leilehua Plateau and back to Waikīkī via the freeway), and **Little Circle Island** (around the eastern tip, up the Windward coast to Kailua and through the Pali Highway tunnel back to town, stopping off at the Nuʻuanu Pali lookout). These routes can be followed in reverse, of course, and sometimes are, though the former direction is most common. Considering how few roads there are on the island, the variety of tours is amazing. This is because there are so many good places to stop along the way that no single tour stops at all of them; to do so would take a week rather than the customary day for the full circle. The short circle eliminates most of the drive through rural countryside, but still includes so many points of interest that it could take all day, though it is usually a half-day tour. Visits to the **Polynesian Cultural Center** or **Waimea Falls Park** can also easily occupy half a day as there is so much to see. Shorter tours take in selected spots such as **City/Chinatown/ʻIolani Palace/Punchbowl, Hanauma Bay/ Sea Life Park**, or **Pearl Harbor/ Arizona Memorial**.

The best tours are those using the smaller conveyances, though this extra quality and service also costs more. **E Noa Tours** (599-2561) offers many different routes to most popular destinations, plus a special ʻNa ʻIke' tour that takes interested vistors off the beaten tourist track. **Trans Hawaiian Services** (735-6467) offers a variety of good trips

ing an 'Above and Below' tour that includes a helicopter flight followed by a cruise in a glass-bottomed boat—great for photo buffs.

Polynesian Adventure Tours (922-0888) uses vans and mini-buses to transport sightseers to the full gamut of localities, offering an excellent selection of both short and long excursions. **Akamai Tours** (922-6485 or 800 922-6485) also runs small bus/van tours, and they cover all the main attractions, concentrating on friendly, personalized service. **Gray Line Hawaii** (834-1033) and **Roberts Hawaii** (947-3939) can accommodate those interested in the general sightseeing routes on big buses.

Almost all Hawai'i's tour bus drivers and guides are well informed—many having voluntarily taken courses in Hawaiiana—and are sincerely eager to share their knowledge of the islands with interested visitors. Feel free to ask questions of any of them. This is easier on a small bus, but the drivers of big buses are as friendly as those driving vans.

Most tour operators offer reduced prices for children. Advance reservations should be made for all tours; most hotels have courtesy desks in their lobbies where these can be arranged quickly and easily.

Public bus

If you know where you're going or have the time for leisurely exploring, no cheaper transportation can be found than **TheBus** (531-1611). This is the name of the public bus system on O'ahu. It is not only the least expensive way to go—sixty cents to anywhere—but also can be just as interesting as a guided tour

Nu'uanu Pali overlooks windward O'ahu.

because TheBus is hardly used by tourists except between Waikiki and downtown, and you'll come face to face with a cross-section of the local population.

The information center for TheBus is located on the street level of Ala Moana Center, and bus route information from any departure point to any destination can be found by telephoning 531-1611. Buses operate all day from 4:30am to 1am. Passengers cannot wear wet bathing suits, and the only baggage allowed must be carried on the lap or under the seat. Valid transfers are accepted when a passenger is changing from one route to another and traveling in one general direction via the most direct route, and bus operators are generally helpful in telling visitors which buses to catch to reach their destinations.

Limousines

If you prefer a private excursion, there are limousines at your service, all charging hourly rates.

The leaders on O'ahu are **Elite Limousine Service** (735-2431), offering formal and stretch Cadillacs and Lincolns, **Aloha Amenities** (955-3886), with Mercedes stretches. **Executive Limousine Service** (941-1999) and **Americabs** (521-6680) offer Cadillacs and Continentals. **Cloud 9** (524-7999) is known for Rolls Royce service in a Phantom or a Silver Cloud—manned by a tuxedo-clad chauffeur who can double, if you ask questions, as a well-informed island guide; cellular telephones are available.

All the limousine services will drive you anywhere on the island at any time for as long as you like.

Surfers 'talk story' at Moana Beach.

Private vehicles

If you wish to drive yourself around the island, you may choose almost any kind of car, a motorcycle or a moped, or even a bicycle. To rent a motor vehicle, you must present a valid driver's license from any US mainland state or Canadian province, or a current international driver's license issued outside the United States.

Driving tips

O'ahu has more cars per capita than anywhere else in the nation. Between 6:30 and 8:30am and 3:30 and 5:30pm, it appears that all of them are trying to drive into or out of Honolulu. Visitors are well advised to avoid driving in urban areas during those hours if possible.

Friday and Saturday nights in Waikīkī are also traffic-packed. A lot of locals are courteous, letting fellow drivers into lanes or allowing others to make a left turn where oncoming traffic makes it seemingly impossible to do so. Horn honking is uncommon. There are many joggers, bikers and pedestrians in park-like or residential areas, and they have the right of way. There are also many low-speed mopeds on the roads, often impeding the traffic flow.

When sightseeing at a slow pace, particularly along the two-lane highways outside the metropolitan area, it's customary and courteous to pull off the road occasionally to let others pass.

Car rental

O'ahu has more than five dozen car rental agencies, all with substan-

Waikīkī's famous strip, Kalākaua, at sunset.

tial fleets, so you will be able to get a car if you want one. You will also be able to get virtually any kind of car you want. Most of the agencies provide current standard American and Japanese models—sedans, compacts, convertibles, station wagons, even vans—most automatic with air conditioning. However, if your fancy runs to Jeep or other four-wheel-drive vehicles, or to the likes of Corvette, Porsche, Ferrari, Maserati or Mercedes, your wish will be granted—for a price. There are even a couple of Rolls Royces for rent, though if you want a Phantom or Silver Cloud, you'll have to allow yourself to be driven around by the chauffeur that comes with it.

In addition to the license requirement, renters of cars must be at least twenty-one years of age; those under twenty-five must also hold a major credit card.

Most agencies have courtesy phones in the baggage claim area at the airport and will collect customers in a van, transporting them to their offices to complete appropriate paperwork. Customers already in Waikīkī can be picked up from their hotels, though most agencies are within walking distance as Waikīkī is not that big.

Budget Rent-A-Car (922-3600), along with global giants **Hertz** (836-2511) and **Avis** (834-5536), are well established in Hawai'i, as is another large car rental agency, Hawai'i's own **Tropical Rent-A-Car** (836-1176).

Others are **Aloha Funway Rentals** (942-9696), **Dollar Rent A Car** (926-4200), **Alamo Rent A Car** (834-4080), **Odyssey Rentals** (947-8036), **National Car Rental** (831-3800/Waikiki 922-3331), **Thrifty Rent-A-Car** (836-2388) which, despite its name, rents very nice

cars. A complete listing of the above companies' toll-free numbers and locations can be found at the back of this book.

Only a few companies rent luxury and sports cars.

Aloha Funway Rentals (942-9696) offers Corvette, Mercedes, Porsches, and Mustang convertibles. **Odyssey** (947-8036) adds Jaguar and BMW to the list.

Numerous other car rental companies are available with rates and types of cars covering the gambit. Hotel concierges can be of assistance if you need a single-day rental or have other questions.

Motorcycles and mopeds

For the more casual, outdoor touring experience, you can motor along on two wheels. Renters of motorcycles or mopeds must be licensed and over the age of eighteen. Those not holding major credit cards must leave cash deposits. Only **Aloha Funway Rentals** (942-9696) rents motorcycles; they feature Kawasakis. They are also the leading agent for moped rentals. Another major moped agency is **Island Bicycle Adventure** (734-0700). There are lots of small enterprises renting mopeds located along Waikīkī's side streets.

Mopeds are very popular with young beach-going visitors in particular. Drivers of mopeds should be especially aware of other vehicles on the roads and should move to the side of the road allowing cars and trucks to pass. They should also stay off main thoroughfares whenever possible and avoid bumpy surfaces and loose gravel.

Waikane Valley and the Ko'olau Mountains, windward O'ahu.

Bicycles

Pedaling along under your own steam provides an even closer experience of the natural beauty of O'ahu's tropical environment. The loop trip (135 miles) around the island mostly hugs the coastline and is the easiest island loop in the state. In fact, aside from walking, this is the only way you can go all the way around the perimeter of O'ahu as the nine miles of rough, unpaved track around Ka'ena Point is impassable by car; it's really a bit rough for cycling, too, but it's popular. Virtually the entire route is peppered with beautiful and accessible beaches, so it's easy to stop for a refreshing ocean plunge.

A slightly shorter loop (108 miles) circles only the Ko'olau Mountain range, cutting across the Leilehua Plateau, through fields of pineapple and sugar cane, and eliminating the rough Ka'ena segment as well as the entire Leeward coast. To avoid head-winds, it is best to travel counter-clockwise and, in any case, much of the journey is more scenic when taken in this direction.

Traffic in rural areas is generally light and poses little hazard to alert cyclists, but traffic in Honolulu is very heavy indeed, and cycling in the city and Waikīkī is not recommended particularly during rush hours (see Driving Tips above). To accommodate the increasing popularity of bicycling in Honolulu, a series of 'bikeways' has been created. A current booklet called 'Bicycle Regulations and Illustrated Safety Tips', published by the City and County of Honolulu, is available from the Department of Transportation Services (650 S King Street 4th Floor 527-5009) and from most bike shops.

Touring bicycles can be rented from **Aloha Funway Rentals** (942-9696) and from the **University Cyclery** (944-9884) near Ala Moana. **Island Triathlon and Bike** (732-7227) also rents bikes and services visitors in nearby Waikīkī. It is also cheap and easy to bring your own (see Permits and Licenses under GETTING HERE) as excess baggage; most airlines provide cartons and some require that handlebars be rotated and pedals removed for transport.

If you need emergency repairs, the following Honolulu shops offer service in a half day to a day, depending on the problem and on how busy they are at the time: **Eki Cyclery** (847-2005), **The Bike Shop** (531-7071), **The Bike Way** (538-7433), **University Cyclery** (944-9884) and **McCully Bicycle** (955-6329). If you happen to be on the Windward side when trouble strikes, try **Kailua Bike Shop** (261-9213); on the Leilehua Plateau, check in at **Wahiawa Bicycle Shop** (622-5120). If you break down on the Leeward coast, you've got a problem; the nearest bike shop is **Waipahu Bicycle** (671-4091) near Pearl City. Try any service station.

For further information and handy hints about cycling in Hawai'i contact the Hawaiian Bicycling League (P.O. Box 4403 Honolulu 96812 Phone: 988-7175).

Pedicabs

To get someone else to do the pedaling for you, hop aboard one of the myriad pedicabs—a cross between a tricycle and a rickshaw. Although they do not journey the busy main streets of Waikiki, they are a pleasant way to explore other parts of the town.

Mostly powered by sun-bronzed Mainland youth, these quaint vehicles will ferry you through the snarl of traffic at a snail's pace and can tell you where to find whatever you're looking for.

The oldest and largest of the few pedicab companies is **Paradise Pedicabs** (922-8161) with a fleet of 140 pedicabs and fully licensed drivers ready to give knowledgeable personalized tours, or merely to transport you slowly from Point A to Point B. Rates are higher for tours than for plain transportation. (A taxi is cheaper than a pedicab.) There are a few independently owned and operated pedicabs, usually easily distinguished from the others by their customized appearance.

Waikiki Trolley

This picturesque open-air conveyance is reminiscent of the old Waikiki Trolley that once linked downtown Honolulu with rural Waikīkī—three miles away. The original trolley was mule-drawn. This modern version—a charming, self-propelled replica—makes a round-trip journey through Waikīkī from Kapi'olani Park to Fisherman's Wharf with twenty-nine stops along the way; you can get off and on as many times as you like during the circuit.

This fully narrated tour can be heard all day; one way passes are also available (approximate hours: daily 9am-5pm).

Walking

For the not-quite-so-hardy or the less than athletically inclined, there are many delights to be savored by just plain walking around, especially in the historic districts of our city. The **Hawaii Geographic Society** (PO Box 1698 Honolulu 96806 538-3952 leave message) conducts walking tours that include historic downtown and Chinatown. The tours are led by Executive Secretary of the Society and university Instructor Willis H. Moore. Reservations should be made in advance by writing to the above address. The **Chinese Chamber of Commerce** (42 N King Street 533-3181) has been leading walking tours of Chinatown for years; they begin on Tuesday mornings at the Chamber building and end at the famous Wo Fat Restaurant (lunch is optional). The tour lasts two to three hours and the cost is minimal. Advance reservations are requested. The **East-West Center** tour (944-7691) begins with a short video presentation explaining the work of this federally funded agency, and covers the grounds of the Center, adjacent to the campus of the University of Hawai'i at Mānoa, including the Japanese Garden, Thai Pavilion, and Burns Hall. Reservations are not necessary for the hour and a half tour, which commences in the basement of Jefferson Hall at the Friends Desk (Tu-W-Th 1:30pm).

Self-guided tours of Honolulu's historic districts are also easy and rewarding. To facilitate and inform such a leisurely stroll, the buildings described under Historic Sites and Buildings in the SIGHT-SEEING section of this book have been listed in a sensible geographical sequence.

Outside the urban environment, the **Hawaii Geographic Society** also conducts archaeological tours to significant sites in the Nu'uanu Valley, including a drive to a *heiau* near Kailua; to *heiau* sites at Pōka'i Bay and Mākaha Valley; and to *heiau* and other archaeological sites on the North Shore, including the Waimea Valley (see Heiau and Parks and Gardens under SIGHT-SEEING).

33

Skyward palm trees.

Water tours

Lastly, but certainly not insignificantly in an island environment, are tours by various vessels that ply the waves off our lovely shores. Dinner Cruises are listed under ENTERTAINMENT. Muscle-powered and small, wind- or water-driven craft are listed under SPORTS & RECREATION. Here we detail those that offer less adventure and more information and entertainment.

Short excursions

Three-hour narrated tours by boat to and around Honolulu Harbor, Pearl Harbor and Waikīkī are offered daily from Kewalo Basin by **Hawaiian Cruises** (947-9971). They also offer one-hour narrated tours around the waters off Diamond Head in their glass-bottomed boats four times a day; both tours are modestly priced. **Paradise Cruises** (536-3641) also has excursions in Pearl Harbor. Visitors should be aware that US Navy regulations prohibit any private craft landing at the Arizona Memorial, so if you want to board this famous floating monument, you must go on an official tour (see · Memorials under SIGHTSEEING).

Leahi Catamaran (922-5665) takes passengers on an hour-long sail to Diamond Head buoy, departing every hour and a half from the beach in front of the Sheraton-Waikiki. They also have a Mai-tai Sunset Sail from 5pm-7pm that goes to Diamond Head, Honolulu Harbor and back to Waikīkī. Similar beach-based catamaran tours are run from Waikīkī aboard the Hyatt Regency's *Manu Kai* (923-1234/Ext. 6300).

On the Windward side, **Kaneohe Bay Cruises** (235-2888) has forty-five- to fifty-minute excursions in a glass-bottomed boat, leaving from He'eia Pier approximately hourly. **Atlantis Submarines** (522-1710) offers one of the most fascinating water excursions in Hawaii with its high-tech, deep water look at the flora and fauna off Waikiki. Tours leave from the Hilton Hawaiian Village starting at 8 am daily.

Charters

Tradewinds Sailing Charters (533-0220 or 533-7734) has the most to offer, with monohull sailing boats in several sizes and classes—from thirty to seventy feet—operating out of Ke'ehi Lagoon, a fifty-foot trimaran at the Ala Wai Yacht Harbor, and a sixty-five foot ketch at Kāne'ohe Bay on the Windward side. They will accommodate almost any request, but certain of their suggested cruises are especially popular.

Topping the list is an all-day private excursion to Hanauma Bay, which includes snorkeling equipment and a gourmet lunch and provides easy access to this fabulous underwater park while avoiding the crowds. (Share-trip snorkeling excursions are also available; see Sailing under SPORTS & RECREATION).

Another popular all-day trip takes the Kāne'ohe-based ketch out for a bit of blue-water sailing as well as snorkeling in and around Kāne'ohe and Kualoa. The Ala Wai-based trimaran accommodates up to thirty-eight people and is very popular for parties and weddings (see Nuptials under OTHER SERVICES). Tradewinds' experienced crews are also interested in and knowledgeable about whales, and during the January to April season when humpback whales

Sailing in Ala Moana Harbor.

swim south for their annual tropical Island holiday, special emphasis is placed on watching and photographing these magnificent creatures—forty to fifty feet long and weighing many tons—some of whom will come right up to the boat. On all their cruises, Tradewinds invites and encourages the active participation of passengers in trimming the sails, steering the boat

and other maritime adventures. If you prefer to be pampered on an expensive excursion with a gourmet lunch, **Cloud 9 Limousine Service** (524-7999 or 800 992-9918) offers three- and six-hour cruises along O'ahu's South Shore for up to six people aboard a forty-five foot sailing vessel; the substantial price includes transportation to and from Ke'ehi Lagoon in a Rolls Royce.

IN TRANSIT/Getting Around

Interisland cruise ship docked in Honolulu Harbor.

Extended cruises

For seven-day cruises around the Hawaiian island chain aboard luxurious ships, contact **American Hawaii Cruises** (550 Kearny Street San Francisco, CA 94108 800 227-3666). They run the two historic, thirty thousand-ton sister ships, SS *Constitution* and SS *Independence*, built in 1951.

The *Constitution* was re-christened in 1982 by Her Royal Highness Princess Grace of Monaco, who sailed aboard the ship in 1956 with her wedding party. The two ships were refurbished in 1980 and have been serving Hawai'i ever since. They occasionally make trans-Pacific voyages between Honolulu and Seattle, Los Angeles or San Francisco, but are usually found cruising warm Hawaiian waters. Originating in Honolulu, the ships make similar rounds visiting the islands of Hawai'i, Kaua'i and Maui, with ports of call at Hilo, Kona,

Nāwiliwili and Kahului, where they cross paths. Shipboard accommo-dations—cabins, staterooms and suites—range in size, location and price and determine the overall cruise fare. Besides an abundance of food, entertainment and recrea-tional facilities, the optional, planned activities on board and shore excursions will keep energetic passengers bustling.

For the even more energetic—who want to cruise in a smaller vessel with functional sails on it and to actually participate in the sailing process—**Tradewinds** (see Charters above) also offers interis-land trips; these are most com-monly run to Maui, Moloka'i and Lāna'i, and require a minimum of three days. All amenities are in-cluded, depending on the needs and preferences of the customer. These cruises are popular with both couples and groups. Longer excursions and trips to farther islands can be arranged.

EXPLORING

SIGHTSEEING

T here are many ways of seeing the sights and many sights to be seen. Here we present an overview of the types of places you may want to visit and the ways of getting about. Descriptions follow a counterclockwise sequence around the island. Be on the lookout along the roads for the 'Hawaiian warrior' signs that indicate points of interest and other places. O'ahu has a variety of sights worthy of visitor attention: scenic areas, historic and sacred buildings and sites, museums and galleries, parks and gardens, and special attractions—even some factories are of interest. An alphabetical listing of places of interest can be found in the APPENDIX Section at the back of this book.

SCENIC AREAS

There are few places in Hawai'i—even on O'ahu—that are not scenic, so we draw attention here to those that offer sweeping vistas or spectacular natural features. All the beaches are scenic, but because there are so many, they are dealt with under a separate heading, BEACHES.

The view from **Diamond Head** (an extinct volcanic crater previously known to Hawaiians as Lae'ahi), provides a 360° panorama of Waikīkī, downtown, Punchbowl (Pu'uowaina) crater, the **Wai'anae and Ko'olau mountain ranges,** Koko Head and, of course, the vast Pacific.

Three lookout points along Diamond Head Road also afford views over the sea where you can watch surfers on the offshore breaks. This is a good spot, in summer, to watch the end of some sailing races and long-distance outrigger canoe races (see LOCAL FESTIVALS/CALENDAR OF EVENTS). A 147-foot automatic lighthouse stands sentinel on the *kiawe*-covered hillside.

The parking area above **Hanauma Bay,** off the Kalaniana'ole Highway, offers a splendid view of that broken, flooded crater with its reefs and palm-fringed beach. For those inclined to more active viewing, the underwater scenery is also spectacular. On a clear day, the island of Moloka'i can also be seen from this lookout, or from another lookout point farther down the road.

Hanauma Bay.

Hālona Blowhole is a lava tube inside the cliff face that, when waves enter it with force, sends a spout of water shooting into the air. There are no official statistics on the upper limits of this event; locals variously report having witnessed heights of fifty to a hundred feet when the sea is rough. This scenic lookout also affords distant views of Lāna'i and Moloka'i on clear days.

The vista along the **coastline** when you round **Makapu'u Point** heading **to**ward **Waimānalo** is stunning. There is a lookout point here so that the pleasure can be prolonged. Makapu'u Beach is below, on the right, and Sea Life Park is on the left (see Popular Attractions below). The drive along this stretch of coastline in this direction is the prettiest on the island.

He'eia State Park occupies a grassy knoll overlooking Kāne'ohe Bay and the ancient He'eia fishpond, and provides lovely views of the bay and of the coast up to Kualoa Point and Mokoli'i Island (also known as Chinaman's Hat). Mokoli'i can be better seen from the shore along Hōkūle'a Beach at Kualoa Regional Park.

Behind Kāne'ohe, toward the mountains, are the beautiful **Haikū Gardens** and **Valley of the Temples**. Formerly a private estate, Haiku Gardens, just off Kahekili Highway on Ha'ikū Road, features acres of exotic plant life, highlighted by lily ponds, and a restaurant (see Parks and Gardens below). The Valley of the Temples, with its tranquil gardens, pools, statues and temple replica is actually a cemetery (see Sacred Sites below).

Along the **coast to Lā'ie**, there are many lovely stretches of shoreline and beachfront that are beside or near the road. (Also at Lā'ie is the famous Polynesian Cultural Center; see Popular Attractions below.) Most of the beaches along the famous **North Shore—**

Byodo-In Temple, Valley of the Temples Memorial Park.

from Kawela to Hale'iwa—are also near the road and, in winter when the surf is high, the enormous breaking waves provide some of the most spectacular ocean vistas anywhere (see BEACHES). Opposite Waimea Bay is the entrance drive to **Waimea Falls Park** (see Popular Attractions below). Above the Bay stand the ruins of **Pu'u o Mahuka** *heiau* (see *Heiau* under Sacred Sites below).

It is possible to drive farther up the **coast past Hale'iwa to Mokulē'ia**, where rocky coastline is punctuated with patches of sandy shore, but not all the way to Ka'ena Point. That excursion requires a hardy hike (see SPORTS).

From Hale'iwa, the drive **across the island** to the Pearl City interchange passes O'ahu's largest **pineapple and sugarcane fields**. Fields of pineapple and sugar cane are not spectacular sights, but are usually of great interest to those who've never seen them. To enhance the experience, stop at the Del Monte Pineapple Variety Garden (see Parks and Gardens below) and at the nearby Dole Pineapple Pavilion (see Popular Attractions below). Helemano Plantation, next door, offers a special and unusual experience most people (even residents) don't know about (see Popular Attractions below).

From the Pearl City interchange, you can follow the signs marked **Wai'anae** to drive along O'ahu's **Leeward coast toward** the other side of **Ka'ena Point**. There are some lovely stretches of shoreline and some popular beach parks in this district, along with some interesting historic and sacred sites. The road stops at **Yokohama Bay**; a long, hot track continues around the Point.

Most visitors choose to turn townward at Pearl City. There are a couple of easily accessible and quite spectacular scenic lookouts on the mountains above downtown Honolulu. Most famous of these is the **Nu'uanu Pali Lookout**, with unbeatable views of the Windward side. The edge of this precipice

Makapu'u Beach and windward O'ahu.

undoubtedly wins honors also for being the windiest place on the island.

Not far away, just Diamondhead of the Pali Highway, the **scenic view from** the edge of **Punchbowl crater** (above the cemetery) is also worthy of note. Even more spectacular vistas can be enjoyed by following the long winding drive that leads past the National Memorial Cemetery and passes over the hill called **Tantalus**, where the cool height enticed wealthy residents to build some of Hawai'i's finest homes. There are some excellent hiking trails up here (see Hiking under SPORTS & RECREATION). Proceeding in the same direction, the road winds down a lower hill called Round Top (and the street name changes from Tantalus to Round Top Drive). 'Ewa of the road about halfway down is the entrance to a park called **Pu'u 'Ualaka'a**, which also offers a spectacular vista over the city and toward the Wai'anae Mountains.

Sunset from Magic Island, near Ala Moana Park.

The sacred site Kūkaniloko–the Royal Birthing Stones–in central O'ahu.

HISTORIC SITES AND BUILDINGS

For ancient Hawaiians, virtually all natural features of the landscape had meaning. In a culture rich with oral tradition, the symbolic significance of every cave, crater, pinnacle and headland was passed from generation to generation, giving life and immediacy to the historic and mythic legends of gods and heroes. This abundant lore fills volumes, but here we offer a sampling to provide a glimpse of the way the Hawaiians of old related to the land that nurtured them.

Ka'ena Point is associated with many legends and traditions, and was considered the point from which the souls of the dead departed this world for the next. The large boulder off the Point is known as **Pōhaku o Kaua'i** [rock of Kaua'i]. The demigod Māui once stood on this headland and, in an attempt to draw together the islands of O'ahu and Kaua'i, threw across the intervening channel his special fishhook, Mana i ka Lani [divine power of heaven], which he had already used to fish up islands all over the Pacific. Giving a mighty tug, he succeeded only in dislodging a boulder, which flew across the channel and landed in the water at his feet. It is still there. The hook flew far behind him and landed in Pālolo Valley where it gouged Ka'au Crater (see Hiking under SPORTS & RECREATION). Mana i ka Lani was attached to a line made from the 'ie'ie vine, thus the channel separating the two islands has since been known as Ka'ie'ie.

Above Mākua Beach, not far from Yokohama Bay, is a huge cavern called **Kāneana**, which was carved from the rock by sea action more than 150,000 years ago when the present coastline was submerged. According to one legend, Māui once lived here with his grandmother; in another, the cave was once the home of Nanaue, son of the shark god Kamahoali'i. Nanaue's dual nature gave him the unfortunate ability to turn from a shark into a man and back again, and while a shark, he was fond of eating humans. Luring people to his home as a person, he then became a shark and sacrificed them on the white rock slab altar at the back of one of the cavern's small chambers before devouring them. He was killed by his neighbors when they at last discovered his ruse.

Near Wahiawā on the Leilehua Plateau of central O'ahu is a sacred site called **Kūkaniloko**, also known as the **Royal Birthing Stones**. *Ali'i* women were brought to these large stones, believed to have been established in the twelfth century, to give birth ceremonially in this consecrated setting. Use of the site declined and eventually stopped with the arrival of Europeans in the Islands. Surrounded by coconut

43

Petroglyphs on the Royal Birthing Stones.

EXPLORING/Sightseeing

is reached by a dirt road off Kamehameha Avenue just north of Wahiawā, opposite Whitmore Avenue.

Of great historic significance is the cliff at the end of Honolulu's Nu'uanu Valley, known as the **Nu'uanu Pali**. This is *the* Pali, and is the one meant when someone on O'ahu says 'the Pali' (which actually means 'cliff' or 'precipice', so there are lots of them). In the 1795 Battle of Nu'uanu, the invading Kamehameha and his men drove the defending forces of Kalani-ikupule up this valley and, at the *pali*, many of the defenders jumped to their deaths rather than be captured and sacrificed by Kamehameha to his war god, Kūka'ilimoku. Thus the invader gained control of O'ahu and its modern history began. The old road, now dilapidated and unused,

story of Hawai'i after European contact. There will inevitably be some overlap between this and the following subsection as some buildings of historic interest have been converted to use as museums.

The crown jewel and focal point of Honolulu's historic buildings is **'Iolani Palace**. Inspired by his travels, King David Kalākaua commissioned the construction of this comparatively small European-style palace, which was completed in 1882, as the royal residence for himself and his queen, Kapi'olani. It is said that he had stones brought to Honolulu from Ki'i *heiau* on the Big Island and used in the palace's foundations. After Kalākaua's death, 'Iolani Palace was occupied by his sister and successor, Queen Lili'uokalani, until the Hawaiian monarchy was overthrown in 1893. The new government auctioned off

Honolulu's 'Iolani Palace at night.

its furnishings and converted it to use as their headquarters, and it remained a government office building through a succession of types of government until 1969 when the new State Capitol was completed. The State Senate met in the dining room and the House of Representatives in the throne room. It has since been restored and stands as a grand memorial to Hawai'i's days as a

can still be seen to the right of the scenic lookout. Until 1955, this was the main artery connecting the island's Windward side with the thriving port of Honolulu.

Many buildings in Honolulu—old and new—are significant in the

Polynesian nation. Tours are available by reservation (523-0141) Wednesday through Saturday (admission).

The small **Coronation Pavilion** on the palace lawn was originally built at the foot of the main stairs for

The Hawai'i State Capitol Building, completed in 1969.

built at the foot of the main stairs for Kalākaua's belated coronation ceremony in 1883 (he had then been king for eight years), and was surrounded by a temporary amphitheatre to seat nine thousand people. The pavilion was later moved to its present location where it served as a bandstand. The Royal Hawaiian Band still gives free concerts here at noon most Fridays (922-5331). The roof is the original, but severe termite damage to the wooden structure necessitated its replication in concrete. Behind the pavilion is the coral block **'Iolani Barracks**, built by Kamehameha V near the site of the present State Capitol. To make way for that construction, it was moved and reassembled on the palace grounds where it now houses a small museum display and the Palace's ticket office and gift shop. On the other side of the palace is the **State Archives**, built in 1954. The small building in front of it, the original

Archives building, dates from 1906, and has just been renovated. *Makai* of this is a fenced mound which marks the site of the original Royal Mausoleum, built for King Kamehameha II and his Queen Kamāmalu, who died of measles in England in 1824. Other members of the ruling family were also interred here until the present Royal Mausoleum in Nu'uanu was built, and all royal remains were ceremonially transferred there. The leaves of ti plants such as those surrounding the mound are traditionally used in most Hawaiian spiritual and sacred ceremonies.

Outside the *mauka* palace gate stands a statue of Queen Lili'uokalani, Hawai'i's only reigning queen and the last monarch of the Kingdom of Hawai'i.

The imposing structure *mauka* of the palace is the **Hawai'i State Capitol Building**. Designed with a great deal of attention to symbolic detail and speaking proudly of

Hawai'i's island nature, it rises from reflecting pools as from the sea, supported by columns that resemble stately royal palms. The central court contains a sea-like mosaic floor and is flanked by two conical towers, reminiscent of volcanoes, that house the legislative chambers. The House chamber is furnished in the colors of earth and fire, the Senate chamber in the colors of sea and sky. The flared, crater-like roof is open to the sky. The top level houses the offices of the Governor and Lieutenant Governor, and their koa-paneled reception areas, with welcome signs in Hawaiian and English at the doors, display portraits of famous Hawaiians and works of island artists. Both entrances to the

Hawaiian version of Brittania) from the Capitol is **Washington Place**, which has been the Governor's residence since 1922. It was built in 1846 by merchant sea captain John Dominis, who soon disappeared at sea. His widow rented rooms to the American commissioner to Hawai'i, who hoisted his flag and presumed to name the building in honor of George Washington. Captain Dominis's son, also John Dominis, later married the future Queen Lili'uokalani and was Governor of O'ahu. Upon his death, the Queen inherited the house and, after her release from nine months' imprisonment in a room of the palace following an unsuccessful attempt to restore her to the throne, she lived at Washington Place until her death in 1917. In downstairs rooms, which are open only for official receptions, a few of the Queen's possessions are displayed, including her koa grand piano.

Washington Place, the Governor's official residence.

building are hung with huge bronze medallions bearing the State Seal, an edited version of the Hawaiian royal coat-of-arms. At the Beretania Street entrance to the capitol stands a statue of Father Damien.

Across Beretania Street (the

Beside the palace grounds, in the same block, is the **State Library**, built in 1913, with wings added in 1929. The area around its open central courtyard provides a lovely, pleasant spot to read up on local history. The library has a large collection of illustrated Hawaiian and Pacific books that make for good browsing, as well as more informational tomes.

The pretty Spanish colonial building across Punchbowl Street from the State Library is **Honolulu Hale** ('Honolulu House'—the Hawaiian equivalent of City Hall), built in 1929. Its open-roofed internal courtyard, patterned after that of a thirteenth century Florentine palace and often used for art shows and concerts, features a grand staircase, massive bronze chandeliers and doors, terra cotta tiles and cast stone sculpture. The building's coffered ceilings are decorated with Hawaiian frescoes.

The cluster of colonial red brick buildings near Honolulu Hale are known as the **Mission Memorial Buildings**, originally erected to honor the Congregational missionaries that wrought their handiworks in Hawai'i; they now house city and county offices.

The **Mission Houses**, on King Street diagonally opposite Honolulu Hale, are the original buildings (after the thatch houses) that served as both home and administrative center for the leaders of the American Protestant mission in Hawai'i during the nineteenth century. Built on land granted to the missionaries

The Mission Houses in Honolulu, now a museum.

by Kamehameha III, they are now a museum (see Museums below). The frame house, prefabricated in Boston and sent around Cape Horn in 1821, is the oldest European structure in the islands. The adjacent stone buildings are made of coral blocks quarried from the bedrock, as is their **Kawaiaha'o Church** (see Sacred Sites below) next door, built beside an ancient sacred spring known as *ka wai a Ha'o* (the waters of Ha'o, a legendary *ali'i* who bathed there).

Directly opposite the palace on King Street is **Ali'iolani Hale**. Originally designed as a palace for King Kamehameha V and completed in 1874, it never became a residence. Though King Kalākaua used it occasionally at night for receptions and balls, it has always housed government offices: originally the Supreme Court, the legislature and several ministries. It has been the home of the Judiciary since the change of government in 1893 when the other offices of the republican government were transferred to 'Iolani Palace.

In front of Ali'iolani Hale and facing 'Iolani Palace is a statue of King Kamehameha I (see Monuments below). On his right, beside Ali'iolani Hale, is the **Kekūanaō'a**

47

Building, which houses federal offices. Its facade still bears the inscription 'Territorial Office Building', for which it was built in 1926. The dome of its rotunda features a cut glass rendition of the Hawaiian coat-of-arms surrounded by American flags. Between the two buildings are some noteworthy banyans. Beside Ali'iolani Hale, on Kamehameha's left, is the beautiful Spanish Colonial **Old Federal Building**, with its loggias, courtyard garden, towers and red-tiled roofs. Built in 1922 to house the Post Office, Courthouse, Customs House and federal offices, it is now occupied by the Post and Customs Offices and a few state agencies. Diagonally opposite this wonderful bit of old-world graciousness is the 1927 **Hawaiian Electric Building**, designed by the same architects and fronted by a pillared arcade with vaulted, handpainted ceilings. Facing the palace grounds on Richards Street is the 1927 **YWCA**, also Spanish colonial, in keeping with the architectural mood of the neighborhood. Completing the ring of historic buildings around the palace is another, even grander, Mediterranean structure, built in 1928, which houses the headquarters of the **Hemmeter Corporation**, Hawai'i's resort development giant.

A couple of blocks 'Ewa, along Bishop Street, some of Hawai'i's finest old landmark buildings can be found. Just *makai* of Hotel Street where Bishop meets Union Mall, is the Ali'i Bishop Building. Though not in itself significant, the foyer of this building displays the most interesting series of **historical wall murals** in town. Executed in mono-chromatic tones suggesting old photographs, its life-size figures and scenes portray downtown Honolulu

as it might have looked in November 1876. If historical perspective interests you, this is an excellent introduction to a walking tour of the downtown district.

The block-long, neo-classical building on Bishop between King and Merchant Streets was built in 1925 to house the Bishop Trust Company and Bishop Bank, and is now occupied by that banks's descendant, **First Hawaiian Bank**. Diagonally opposite, occupying the block of Bishop between Merchant and Queen is the splendid **Alexander and Baldwin Building**, built in 1929 as corporate headquarters for this youngest of Hawai'i's 'Big Five' sugar factors (all now widely diversified). Diagonally opposite, running from Queen Street to Ala Moana Boulevard, is the grand 1929 Italian Renaissance **Dillingham Transportation Building**.

The ten-story **Aloha Tower**, on the waterfront at the foot of Fort Street, once dominated the city skyline. This historic landmark was built in 1926 as the harbor control tower and, with its welcoming word *aloha* on all four faces, became a primary symbol of greeting for visitors arriving by ship. The tower now houses on its ninth floor a small museum (see Museums below) operated by the Hawai'i Maritime Center; the tenth floor observation deck (open daily 8am-9pm) affords unobstructed panoramic views of Honolulu Harbor.

Mauka of Aloha Tower and Irwin Park, at the beginning of the Fort Street Mall, stands the hacienda-like 1930 **C. Brewer Building**, corporate headquarters of the smallest of the 'Big Five', and last to be built. One block *mauka*, at the *makai*-Diamond-head corner of Fort and Merchant, stands the **Judd Block**, and adjacent

century **Stagenwald Building**. The towering height of this six-story masterpiece was not exceeded in Honolulu for half a century.

A little farther 'Ewa on the *makai* side of Merchant stand the 1896 Romanesque Revival bluestone **Bishop Estate Building** and, swathed in stucco, an 1878 brick Italian Renaissance building that was once home to the Bishop Bank. Next, on the Bethel corner, is the 1854 coral block **Melchers Store**. Opposite, on the *mauka* corner, is Hawai'i's first post office, the 1871 **Kamehameha V Post Office**, presently standing vacant. The old **Yokohama Specie Bank** once occupied the other *mauka* corner; the terra cotta brick and friezes trimming the arched entry now usher one into the offices of *Honolulu* magazine. Next door is

the 1887 **Friend Building**, originally the offices of Hawai'i's first periodical, the *Friend of Temperance and Seamen*, a missionary publication. The last corner here, indeed the entire block, is occupied by the grand 1931 Spanish Colonial Honolulu Police Station, later converted to a courthouse and now occupied by government offices.

The Merchant-Nu'uanu intersection has been dubbed '**Merchant Square**' by the restaurateurs clustered at and near it. On the *mauka*-Diamondhead corner, the old **Waterhouse Warehouse** now houses Murphy's Bar & Grill, a friendly, trendy tavern. Next door, on Nu'uanu, is the 1916 **Wing Wo Tai Building**. Directly opposite is the 1896 bluestone home of the *Hawaii Times*, which prior to the bombing of Pearl Harbor went by its Japanese

49

Aloha Tower, built in 1926, no longer dominates Honolulu's skyline.

name, **Nippu Jiju**, as emblazoned on the front of the building. The corner **T.R. Foster Building**, an ordinary office building when erected in 1891, is today considered quite decorative. Named for the founder of the Inter-island Steamship Navigation Company, it is now the home of O'Toole's, Honolulu's Irish pub.

The area bounded by King, Nu'uanu, and Beretania Streets and Nu'uanu Stream is Honolulu's historic '**Chinatown**', though the ethnic origin of its residents has always been mixed. The district now has few residents of any sort, but the businesses are largely Chinese with a recent influx of Indochinese and upscale artsy enterprises such as galleries and the offices of architects and interior designers. The entire area was twice razed by fire, in 1886 and again in 1900. Many of the subsequent buildings are being restored and renovated, and several have been named to the Hawai'i Register of Historic Places. A Chinatown landmark is **Wo Fat**, Honolulu's oldest Chinese cafe. Established in 1882, its present flamboyant building, at the corner of Hotel and Maunakea Streets, was erected in 1936. Maunakea Street has more lei shops per linear foot than any other on the island.

On the corner of Kukui Street at Nuuanu stands the Taoist **Lum Sai Ho Tong** temple and the Shinto **Izumo Taishakyo** shrine, both of which are described under Sacred Sites below. At the end of River Street, across Vineyard, are the Buddhist **Kuan Yin Temple** and **Foster Botanic Gardens**.

Just beyond Chinatown and 'A'ala Park, on King Street at Iwilei, is the **Old O'ahu Railway Station**, built in 1925 as the terminus for the narrow gauge railway that ran around the island to Kahuku and its sugar mill until 1947. This grand Spanish mission style building now houses the Kalihi-Palama Community Center. A little further 'Ewa on King Street is the historic **Kaumakapili Church**.

Not far outside the downtown

area on the Diamondhead side, at the corner of Ward and Beretania, is the wonderful 1927-vintage **Honolulu Academy of Arts**. **Hānaiakamalama**, better known as the **Queen Emma Summer Palace**, is located on Pali Highway a couple of miles *mauka* of Downtown. This gracious white frame home, built in 1843, was purchased as a summer retreat for Queen Emma, consort of Kamehameha IV, and became her principal residence after the king's death in 1863. Furnished with Emma's possessions and displaying many of the royal *kahili* and *lei hulu*, it is maintained as an historic house by the Daughters of Hawai'i. (daily 9am-4pm 595-3167 admission)

The **Bernice Pauahi Bishop Museum & Planetarium** is a world center for the study of Pacific island cultures, and for marine research. Its galleries display and interpret artifacts and customs from throughout Polynesia, Micronesia and Melanesia and describe Hawaiian culture and history in detail. The collections on display include gourd utensils, ceremonial pieces carved from indigenous woods and rare items such as Hawaiian featherwork and barkcloth—both crafts lost generations ago—as well as more recent historical items. Demonstrations of contemporary craft-making, and performances of music and dance, enliven the displays. A planetarium show explains how the ancient Polynesians navigated by the stars. (Open daily 9am-5pm 1525 Bernice Street 848-4129 admission)

At the back of St Augustine's Church in Waikīkī, the small but fascinating **Damien Museum and Archives** chronicles the life of the 'martyr of Moloka'i'. Included in the displays are some of Father Damien de Veuster's possessions and correspondence, photos of the priest and his charges at Kalaupapa, and a twenty-minute video depicting the history of the Kalaupapa Settlement. (M-F 9am-3pm Sa 9am-12n 130 'Ōhua Avenue 923-2690)

The **Hawai'i Maritime Center** is one of the finest of its kind in the world, with some of its features unique in the world. Its present showpiece is the *Falls of Clyde*, moored at Pier 7 on the downtown waterfront, at the foot of Bishop Street. This historic vessel was active in Hawaiian waters during a significant portion of its career, and is the world's last remaining fully

rigged four-masted sailing ship and the world's only remaining sailing tanker. Near the *Falls of Clyde* is berthed the *Hokule'a*, a modern replica of an ancient Polynesian voyaging canoe. *Hokule'a* has made world headlines in recent years by retracing legendary migration routes of the early Polynesians using no navigational instruments. It has made three major voyages, the most recent, from which it returned in May 1987, being a two-and-a-half-year journey from Hawai'i to New Zealand and back, touching at all the major island groups along the way and proving irrefutably that these voyages—even the difficult west-to-east leg from Sāmoa to Tahiti against the prevailing winds—could have been deliberate and purposeful rather than accidental, as some sceptics have held (see Kualoa Regional Park under BEACHES).

The Maritime Center incorporates the museum of **Aloha Tower**, a room on the ninth floor displaying photographs and other memorabilia of Honolulu Harbor history, and containing a small reference library on the subject.

The **Honolulu Academy of Arts** is noted for its fine collections of oriental art, and it also holds a number of world-renowned American and European masterpieces, both paintings and sculptures. The exhibits in the thirty galleries are superbly presented, beautifully enhanced by the building itself, and the Academy offers lectures, films and concerts on a regular basis. (Tu-Sa 10am-4:30pm Su 1-5pm. closed Monday. 900 S. Beretania Street 538-1006 Garden Cafe 531-8865)

Honolulu's **Contemporary Arts**

Museum resides in the historic Spaulding House on Makiki Drive overlooking the city skyline and the Pacific Ocean. Sparkling galleries, a permanent David Hockney Pavilion, a popular cafe and gift shop blend Hawaii's gracious tradition with today's newest art forms. (Mon, Wed-Sat 10am-4 pm; Sun 12pm-4pm, closed Tues. 2411 Makiki Heights Drive 526-1322 admission)

'Iolani Palace, former residence of the last Hawaiian monarchs, and subsequent center for republican, territorial and state governments prior to 1969, is described under Historic Sites and Buildings above.

The **Mission Houses Museum**, run by the Hawaiian Mission Children's Society (whose members are descendants of the missionaries), interprets and explains the history of the Mission Houses buildings (see Historic Buildings above) and the lives and work of the people who lived there. The buildings are furnished much as they would have been at the time they were in domestic use, and some of the actual belongings of the early residents are on display. A fascinating diorama in the entry hall depicts this section of Honolulu as it appeared in the early nineteenth century. (M-Sa 9am-4pm 553 S King Street 531-0481 admission)

The **Queen Emma Summer Palace**, former retreat for King Kamehameha IV and his consort, Queen Emma, and later the widowed Emma's principal residence, is described under Historic Sites and Buildings above.

An unexpected pleasure is the **McDonald's Royal Hawaiian Collection** of works by living Hawaiian artists. Consisting of paintings, drawings, carving, featherwork, and sculpture in wood and stone, this fine representative collection of contemporary Hawaiian art is on display in the upper level dining room of the McDonald's restaurant at the Royal Hawaiian Shopping Center.

The **Tennent Gallery**, a private museum run by the Tennent Art Foundation, is devoted entirely to the works of Madge Tennent. Tennent has become to Hawai'i what Gaugin was to Tahiti, her distinctive style evoking the essence of the native Hawaiians she found so admirable and so endearing. Her primary subject was Hawaiian women and she painted them larger than life; her monumental images evoke the beauty, power and grace innate in these women without reducing them to calendar-girl postures and proportions. Her audacious use of bold, bright color and surface texture bring her canvases vibrantly alive and are the hallmark of her paintings, most of which are very large.

The hand and eye of Tennent are also unmistakable in her monochrome paintings, watercolors, and sketches and washes in various media—all depicting the distilled essence of her beloved Hawaiians. The gallery also displays a small selection of Tennent's early works, illustrating the evolution of her mastery and individuality. (M-F 10am-12n Su 2-4pm special appointments accepted 203 Prospect Street 531-1987)

The **US Army Museum of Hawai'i** is part of the military's Fort DeRussy reserve and recreation complex. It occupies the former Battery Randolph, from which a shot was never fired in anger. When it had outlived its potential usefulness, it proved almost impossible to destroy the solid structure with its twenty-two foot thick walls; the blasts required to do so would also have damaged every building in the Waikīkī district. Thus the Army turned it into a museum, displaying paraphernalia and memorabilia from wars all over the place including the American Revolution (which predates European discovery of these islands!). Some enemy artifacts are also exhibited, such as a Japanese mini-submarine captured at the Panama Canal. (Tu-Su 10am-4:30pm Kālia Road 543-2639).

The **USS *Arizona* Memorial Museum** is included in the description of the Arizona Memorial (see Memorials under Sacred Sites below).

SACRED SITES

Sacred sites of interest to visitors include memorials and cemeteries as well as distinctive houses of worship of a diversity of religious and spiritual traditions. The houses of worship mentioned in this section are of particular historical or architectural interest. A more complete list of churches, temples, synagogues and shrines can be found in the APPENDIX Section at the back of this book. Honolulu's lower Nu'uanu Valley, just *mauka* of the downtown area, has a striking and concentrated assemblage of churches and temples of all types and styles, making a survey of them a fairly simple excursion.

53

Christian

Kawaiaha'o Church, the oldest Christian house of worship in Hawai'i, stands at the corner of King and Punchbowl Streets, adjacent to the Mission Houses Museum. It was built in 1842 by the original Protestant missionaries to Hawai'i under the patronage of

Sunday services in Kawaiaha'o Church.

Kamehameha III. The simple coral block and wood structure was a focal point for religious and state ceremonies involving Hawaiian royalty, until the fall of the kingdom—indeed, King Lunalilo chose the grounds of Kawaiaha'o rather than the Royal Mausoleum as his final resting place. (M-F 8am-4pm 538-6267)

The second oldest church and the oldest remaining building downtown is the 1843 **Our Lady of Peace Cathedral** at the top of Fort

Street Mall. Originally a coral block rectangle with a steeple, it has been embellished over the years with towers, *lānai*, vaulted ceilings, balconies and other additions and, in 1893, a statue of Mary was placed in the courtyard near the stump of Hawai'i's parent *kiawe* [mesquite] tree, planted by a visiting priest in 1828. (daily 7am-8pm 536-7036)

St Andrew's Cathedral, at the corner of Queen Emma and Beretania Streets, was begun in 1867 by Queen Emma, widow of King Kamehameha IV, and his brother and successor Kamehameha V.

Kamehameha IV, an ardent Anglophile, made a special request to the English crown for the establishment of an Anglican diocese in Hawai'i, and was married in an Anglican ceremony, though the Bishop did not arrive from England in time to officiate. The King died in 1863 on the feast day of St Andrew, and the church was named to commemorate this event. The first services were held in 1886, but the building was not completed until 1958, so it is a conglomerate of architectural and decorative styles. A statue and fountain fronting the church depict St Andrew and his fishes. (M-F 8am-4pm 524-2822)

Kaumakapili Church, at 766 N King Street in Kapālama, was built in 1911 by missionaries and features unusual curved pews as well as Romanesque and Gothic architectural details. Located in an area once popular for 'town' houses of aristocracy and the well-to-do, it, too, has been prominent in Hawai'i's public affairs. (M-F 8am-4pm 845-0908)

The **Makiki Japanese Christian Church** and the associated building compound, on Pensacola near Kapi'olani, are modeled after a sixteenth-century Japanese castle. The only sign of its true function is the cross on the front of it. (M-F 8am-4pm Sa 8am-3pm 829 Pensacola Street 538-6664)

Nowhere near the Nu'uanu Valley is the **Mormon Temple**, located at Lā'ie, on the far side of the island. This handsome white edifice was erected by the Church of Jesus Christ of Latter Day Saints in 1919, and is the spiritual center for the 25,000 Mormons living in the area. The Church also runs the nearby Polynesian Cultural Center. Non-Mormon visitors are not generally allowed inside the temple, but are welcome to stroll the beautifully landscaped grounds. (daily 9am-8pm 55-600 Naniloa Loop [off Kamehameha Hwy] 293-2427)

Buddhist

The beautiful and typically Chinese **Kuan Yin Temple** is conveniently located right next to the entrance to Foster Botanic Gardens on Vineyard Boulevard. Dedicated to Kuan Yin, the goddess of mercy, this temple is very popular with local adherents of the faith, some of which are in the temple, leaving offerings and burning incense, most of the time. The respectful presence of visitors is welcomed. Incense and candles may be purchased at the temple. (daily 8:30am-2pm 170 N Vineyard Blvd 533-6361)

The Japanese **Soto Zen Temple** at 1708 Nu'uanu shows strong Indian influence in its external architecture while its pew-filled sanctuary is reminiscent of churches. Between 9am and 10am a priest is on hand to explain in English the basic beliefs and practices of Zen Buddhism. (hours vary M-F 8am-6pm 537-9409)

Near the *mauka* end of Nu'uanu Avenue in a quiet lane called Kawānanakoa Place is the lovely red-lacquered and green-roofed **Hsu Yun Temple** of the Chinese Buddhist Association of Hawai'i. (daily 8am-3pm 42 Kawānanakoa Place 536-8458)

The elegant, understated religious hall at the **Tenrikyo Mission**, 2236 Nu'uanu, sits in an exquisite Japanese garden that exudes tranquility. Here and at the **Tenrikyo Temple**, 2920 Pali Highway, Shinto and Buddhist practices are combined in an eclectic blend. (daily 6am-8pm 595-6523)

Impossible to miss, at 1727 Pali Highway, is the vast and imposing, Indian-inspired **Honpa Hongwanji Temple**, home of the Shinsu sect in Hawai'i. Dedicated chiefly to the Amida Buddha of infinite wisdom and compassion, the temple was constructed in 1918, of concrete, and was the first in Hawai'i to adopt features of church sanctuaries, like pulpit, pews, pipe organ and choir. Sunday morning services are in English. (M-Sa 8am-8pm Su 8am-4:30pm 536-7044)

The **Byodo-In Temple**, a beautifully rendered concrete replica of the famous temple of that name in Kyoto, Japan, is located in the Valley of the Temples (see Cemeteries below). It contains no altar and is not used in religious ceremonies except, at special request, funeral services.

Shinto

Shinto is the ancient religion of Japan and involves acknowledging and honoring the spirits of nature.

Hawai'i's oldest Shinto shrine, **Izumo Taishakyo**, was built in 1923 by a master carpenter from Japan using the traditional method of construction with no nails. It has the protruding horns and barrels atop the roof ridge traditional to Shinto shrines, and the *torii* (gate) and handwashing basin at the

entrance. Originally located in nearby Leleo Lane, this shrine was relocated to the McCully district after World War II then was moved to its present site beside Nu'uanu Stream in 1969. There is no schedule for services, the priest performing them at random; he is usually there on weekday mornings, and does not speak English. (irregular hours 215 North Kukui Street 538-7778)

Taoist

The **Lum Sai Ho Tong** temple, mostly used by members of the Lum clan, is dedicated to their most illustrious ancestress.

In addition to the altar, the temple contains a very large and intricate gilded carving depicting

important episodes in the family's long history.

This temple is located upstairs over a shop on the edge of the Chinatown district beside Nu'uanu Stream. (daily 7am-5pm 1315 River Street 536-6590)

EXPLORING/Sightseeing

Heiau

Heiau are the sacred sites where Hawaiians ceremonially honored their gods. The remains of many of these can be seen, though some have been completely destroyed. While official use of all *heiau* ceased more than a century and a half ago, fresh offerings are often found at the ruins. As these sites are still considered sacred by many of Hawaiʻi's people, please treat them with due respect.

There are no extant *heiau* in the Honolulu urban area. The easiest to reach is **ʻUlupō**, off Kailua Road (a continuation of the Pali Highway) near the Kailua YMCA, and it is in fairly good condition. Tucked away behind some houses and the Y's recreation yard, this stone platform is so ancient that Hawaiians believed it to have been built by

Menehune, a legendary race of small people who lived in these islands before the known migrations from southern Polynesia. It was used by these later arrivals to honor and cajole the gods of agriculture. Though it can actually be seen from the highway, it can't be reached from there. Turn down the street just *mauka* of the site, then take the first right, drive to the end then turn right again. You'll be in the Y's parking lot. Walk down the path between the Y and the adjacent residences for a few hundred feet and the *heiau* is there on your left.

A little farther from Waikīkī, but also easy of access is **Keaīwa Heiau** State Recreation Area, at the end of ʻAiea Heights Drive in ʻAiea (ʻEwa of the airport). Near the remains of

The view from Puʻu o Mahuka Heiau, above Waimea Bay.

this *heiau ho'ola*, which was dedicated to the healing arts, is an exhibition garden of medicinal plants used by *kahuna lapa'au*, ancient Hawaiian medical practitioners. Said to date from the time of the great chief Kākuhihewa, around the fifteenth century, the *heiau* had been partly dismantled and its stones taken away by the time it was rededicated as part of the park in 1951. (May through September 7am-7:45pm; October through April 7am-6:30pm)

The *heiau* site with the most splendid setting is **Kū'īlioloa** at Kāne'īlio Point, at the edge of Pōka'ī Bay on O'ahu's Leeward coast. Built in the fifteenth or sixteenth century, nothing now remains but the several terraces of the former 'temple'. When in use, and with its buildings,

altars, oracle tower and carved images of the gods intact, it must have been spectacular, jutting as it does out into the sea, with commanding views in and from all directions.

An even more commanding view is that from **Pu'u o Mahuka**, above Waimea Bay. The site is reached by a bumpy dirt track off Pūpūkea Road, on the hill behind St Peters & Paul Church. The largest remaining *heiau* on O'ahu, it has three distinct enclosures. The two largest are about 150 feet wide and well over 500 feet long. Atop the main terraced enclosure sits an altar-like stone structure which is frequently flanked by modern *kapu* sticks—poles topped with balls covered in red or white cloth—as well as holding the more usual offerings of

An offering, once a fresh lei, (left) at Ku'ilioloa Heiau on the edge of Poka'i Bay, and the terraces that compose it (above), looking toward Ka'ena Point.

stones wrapped in ti leaves—a modern practice (the ancients offered food).

A most moving experience is a visit to **Kāne'ākī** *heiau* in the Mākaha Valley. This thrill, however, takes some effort. The only fully restored *heiau* on the island— rebuilt entirely by hand using only traditional materials and containing all the appropriate wood and thatch structures—it is located on private land. When it is open to the public, a mile and a half drive followed by a

short walk is required to reach the secluded glade. Originally an agricultural *heiau* dedicated to Lono, it may have been converted by Kamehameha I to the worship of Kūka'ilimoku, his war god. The altar is usually laden with fresh offerings of ti-wrapped stones and food, and the site and the area surrounding it are well guarded and meticulously maintained. (hours vary Tu-Su 10am-2pm; for information telephone 695-9511 after 10am and ask for guest services)

Cemeteries

The cross-shaped **Royal Mausoleum** was built in 1865 to house the remains of the ruling families and their retainers once the original Royal Mausoleum on the grounds of 'Iolani Palace became inadequate (see Historic Sites and Buildings above). The coral block Gothic building was converted to use as a chapel in 1922 after the royal remains had been buried in crypts around the grounds. (M-F 8am-5pm except holidays 2261 Nu'uanu Ave 537-1716)

Nearby **Honolulu Memorial Park** is a beautifully kept cemetery with a diversity of individual monuments and memorials, but is most noted for its replicas of Japan's treasures—the **Sanju Pagoda** of Nara and the **Golden Pavilion** (Kinkakaku-ji) of Kyoto. (daily 7:30am-3:30pm 22 Craigside Place 538-3925)

The **National Memorial Cemetery of the Pacific** (commonly known as Punchbowl) is located in the caldera of the ancient volcanic crater known to the Hawaiians as Pu'u o Waina, Hill of Sacrifice. Some *haole* saw in the shape of the hill a resemblance to an inverted

punchbowl; the name stuck and that is how it is now known. The vast floor of the caldera is filled with more than 30,000 graves of American war dead from World War I, World War II, the Korean War and the Vietnam War, and those servicemen's families. Each year on Memorial Day every grave bears a flag and at least one lei. This is the number one visitor attraction in all Hawai'i. Above the cemetery on the crater's rim is a lookout with sweeping panoramic views of the city below and the sea beyond. (daily 8am-6:30pm 2177 Pūowaina Drive 541-1430)

Located in the lovely 'Āhuimanu Valley behind Kāne'ohe on O'ahu's Windward side, the **Valley of the Temples Memorial Park** provides a peaceful and powerful setting for its main feature, a beautifully wrought concrete replica of Kyoto's classic Byodo-In Temple, mirrored in a two-acre reflecting pool filled with hundreds of carp.

The temple is not used for worship, but funeral services are held there on request. (daily 8:30am-4pm 47-200 Kahekili Hwy 239-8811 admission)

An aerial perspective of the USS Arizona *and the Memorial.*

Memorials

Located in the National Memorial Cemetery of the Pacific (see Cemeteries above), the monumental 'Courts of the Missing' lists on marble slabs the names of 28,745 servicemen missing in war action. The massive tablets lead to a thirty-foot statue called Columbia that represents a mother looking over her lost children.

The second most visited attraction in the State is the **Arizona Memorial**, a radiant white structure that straddles the sunken hulk of the USS *Arizona* and marks the watery grave of the 1102 men who went down with it and remain entombed there. The names of the 1177 sailors and marines killed in the surprise attack are engraved on a marble wall. Before being shuttled by boat to the memorial, visitors are shown a film which recounts the *Day of Infamy*, December 7, 1941.

A museum room in the Visitor Center displays two models of the *Arizona*—as it was in 1941 and as it is today—and other exhibits relating to Pearl Harbor and the attack. Memorial: Daily 8am-3pm; Visitor Center/Museum: Daily 7:30am-5pm One Arizona Memorial Place [off Hwy 90] 422-0561 children under 45" not allowed, no bare feet or swimming apparel)

Near the Arizona Memorial Visitor Center is the USS *Bowfin*, a World War II submarine also open for tours. (daily 8am-4:30pm 11 Arizona Memorial Drive 423-1341 admission)

The **War Memorial Natatorium**, on the beach opposite Kapi'olani Park, was built in 1927, and plaques in front of the entrance list the 'honor roll' of local lads who died in World War I.

The Natatorium was for many years the scene of lively swimming contests featuring such Olympic greats as Duke Kahanamoku, Buster Crabbe and Johnny Weismuller. The structure has deteriorated badly and is closed to use, but it is still picturesque. Across Beretania Street from the State Capitol is a nine-foot free-form sculpture in copper and brass, by Bumpei Akaji, that holds an eternal flame honoring those service men and women who died in **World War II**.

MONUMENTS

The only Hawaiians who have thus far been honored with public statuary are the nation's first monarch and its last. The gilt and bronze statue of **King**

Kamehameha I that stands facing 'Iolani Palace in front of Ali'iolani Hale is a duplicate of the original work, commissioned by the Hawaiian Legislature in 1878. Carved by American artist Thomas Gould, whose studio was in Florence, the statue was cast in Paris and shipped from Bremen, but lost at sea when the ship carrying it sank off the Falkland Islands. The duplicate was unveiled in its present location during the coronation celebrations of King Kalākaua in 1883. The gilt bronze figure is impressive, especially on Kamehameha Day (June 11), and for the next few days, when the neck and arms of the figure are draped with dozens of leis up to thirty feet long. The original statue was recovered in later salvage operations and taken to the island of Hawai'i where it now stands in front of the old Kapa'au courthouse on the Kohala Peninsula near Kamehameha's birthplace.

An eight-foot bronze statue of Hawai'i's last monarch, **Queen Lili'uokalani**, the work of Boston sculptress Marianna Pineda, was placed in 1982 on the opposite side of 'Iolani

Queen Lili'uokalani.

Palace, at the *mauka* gate facing the new State Capitol building. In her left hand, the Queen holds two documents: her new Constitution of 1893, the planned declaration of which provoked her downfall, and her most famous musical composition, the melancholy farewell song, 'Aloha 'Oe'. Though there is no official day set aside to honor her, her extended right hand often bears a fresh flower lei.

The only other statue honoring a person notable in Hawai'i's history is that of **Father Damien**, the beloved leper priest of Moloka'i, which stands at the *mauka* entrance to the capitol facing Beretania Street. Venezuelan sculptress Marisol Escobar wrought the likeness from a photograph of Damien taken shortly before his death in 1889 when his features had become disfigured by the disease. This statue is also honored annually with a lei-draping ceremony. Another cast of it stands in the Statuary Hall of the US Capitol in Washington, DC. A different statue of the priest stands near the church he built on Moloka'i's Kalaupapa Peninsula.

At the corner of Beretania and River Streets, beside the bridge, stands a bronze statue of **Sun Yat-sen**, leader of the Chinese revolution that overthrew the Manchu Ch'ing Dynasty in 1911, and founder of the Republic of China. Dr. Sun lived and studied in Hawai'i during his youth and while leader-in-exile of the Kuomintang. The statue was given to Honolulu by people of the Republic of China (Taiwan) in 1976. Flanking the same bridge on the opposite side of the stream is a statue of Philippine revolutionary leader **Jose Rizal**, erected by the Filipina Society of Hawai'i. Many Filipino immigrants first settled in this area of Honolulu.

PARKS AND GARDENS

The triangle formed by King and Beretania Streets and Nu'uanu Stream is filled with the green haven of 'A'ala Park.

Here sprawling banyan and monkeypod trees shade the old residents of the area who come to play cards and 'talk story', and the more active local young-

Heliconia leaves.

sters who frequent the skateboard arena. The park is often the site of ethnic festivals staged by Hawai'i's many immigrant communities, and boasts a *dohyo* (ring) where amateur sumo wrestlers come to grips on

Sunday afternoons.

Foster Botanic Gardens, just *mauka* of downtown Honolulu, holds the nation's largest collection of tropical plants. Its twenty acres include labeled plantings of varieties of palm, heliconia, ginger and other fascinating plants; of special interest are the orchid garden and the grouping of prehistoric plants. Foster Gardens also encompasses forty-three of O'ahu's designated 'exceptional trees', which are protected by law. In addition to this garden, begun on a private estate in 1855, Foster Gardens administers the botanic gardens at Wahiawā, Koko Crater and Ho'omaluhia and Lili'uokalani Gardens. The Foster Botanic Gardens Gift Shop has packaged plants and seeds cleared for entry to the US mainland (see Fruit, Flowers & Foliage under SHOPPING) as well as plant-related clothing and crafts. Guided tours are available by reservation on Monday, Tuesday and Wednesday at 1pm. (daily 9am-4pm 180 N Vineyard Blvd 531-1939 admission)

The five-acre oasis of **Lili'uokalani Gardens** is a sheltered glade on the bank of Nu'uanu Stream, just *mauka* of the Lunalilo Freeway, near Foster Botanic Gardens. The small, natural park with its waterfall and swimming hole was a favorite recreation retreat for Queen Lili'uokalani and was left to the public by her. Nestled in a quiet, shady neighborhood of the style of 'Polynesian modern' homes typical in the South Seas, the park is reached via a narrow lane—called Waikahalulu, after the falls—off School Street.

Thomas Square, named for British Admiral Richard Thomas, is a soothing sward of green bounded by King, Beretania, Ward and Victoria, between the Honolulu Academy of Arts and the Blaisdell Concert Hall. Its central feature is a fountain flanked by four large

Soccer games regularly take place in Kapi'olani Park.

banyan trees. Admiral Thomas was thus honored for his role in restoring Hawai'i's independence in 1843, a few months after an overly zealous junior officer had unofficially placed the islands under the protection of England to thwart what he saw as the too-powerful American commercial interests. The park is regularly the site of local craft fairs (see LOCAL FESTIVALS/ CALENDAR OF EVENTS).

Seldom crowded and offering splendid, sweeping views of the city below and the mountains in the distance, **Pu'u 'Ualaka'a State Wayside** on the hill known as Round Top provides a great picnic setting, and is at one end of a pleasant, easy hiking trail. (park hours: May through September 7am-7:45pm; October through April 7am-6:30pm 3 miles up Round Top Drive from Makiki)

The well-watered upper reaches of the Mānoa Valley offer ideal conditions for the University of Hawai'i's **Lyon Arboretum**, a botanical research facility in a delightful tropical rainforest setting. Visitors are welcome to tour portions of the 124-acre site, viewing striking flowers, fascinating food plants and both useful and ornamental trees. Guided group tours are available by arrangement. (M-F 9am-3pm 3860 Mānoa Road 988-3177)

Wa'ahila Ridge State Recreation Area, atop the spur of the Ko'olau Mountains that separates the Mānoa and Pālolo Valleys, is an excellent picnic spot and affords splendid views of the coastal plains around Diamond Head and the sea beyond as well as being the starting point for a delightful hike into the mountains through glades of guava,

Lush ferns cover the mountains in 'Aiea.

Norfolk Island pines and native koa. (May through September 7am-7:45pm; October through April 7am-6:30pm end of Ruth Place, via Peter Street from St Louis Drive off Wai'alae Avenue)

The green expanse of **Kapi'olani Park**—on the edge of Waikīkī and bounded by Monsarrat and Pākī Avenues, Poni Mō'ī Road and the Pacific Ocean—was initiated as a public recreation area by a group of influential citizens, and opened on Kamehameha Day, June 11, 1877. The 170-acre park, named for the queen-consort of King Kalākaua, was landscaped by Archibald Cleghorn, father of Princess Ka'iulani, and originally included a racetrack and, later, a polo field.

Island, stood approximately in the place now occupied by the Honolulu Zoo. Kapi'olani Park is a popular center for jogging, kite flying, ball games, picnicking, concerts and many other family and community activities and is the site of both the Waikīkī Shell and the Kapi'olani Bandstand.

Ho'omaluhia is a gem missed by most visitors to our fair shores. Tucked away in a valley beneath the towering cliffs of Windward O'ahu, this combination nature reserve and botanic garden is a hiker's and picnicker's delight, and provides information and education in the bargain. Its four hundred acres are divided into sections devoted to different types of tropical plants.

Guided hikes, slide presentations and other educational programs deal with such diverse subjects as local bird life, lei making, traditional food and medicinal plants, cloud watching and ethnobotany. Swimming is not allowed in its thirty-two-acre lake. Everyone entering Ho'omaluhia should stop at the Visitor Center for pertinent information and permits. (daily 9am-4pm turn onto Luluku Road off

Red-footed boobies, Kane'ohe.

The lands it occupies were formerly known as Kaneloa and Kapua, and the Waikīkī end of the park once was covered with picturesque waterways—ponds and canals with arched bridges and little islands—which disappeared when the land was drained by the Ala Wai Canal. The largest of these islets, Makee

Kamehameha Hwy, between Kailua and Kāne'ohe [near Likelike Hwy] 235-6636)

The beautifully kept grassy expanse of **He'eia State Park** occupies a knoll that juts into Kāne'ohe Bay, providing excellent views of the surrounding sea and

the surrounding sea and the towering windward cliffs of the Ko'olau Range (also see Scenic Areas above and BEACHES). Adjacent to it is the ancient He'eia fishpond. (park hours: May through September 7am-7:45pm; October through April 7am-6:30pm)

was once a thriving agricultural community of 'ohana—people related by blood, marriage and hānai—which sustained itself by wetland agriculture and fishing in the nearby sea.

Valley residents, together with State Parks officials, have developed

Fiery sunset from Hawai'i Loa Ridge.

There is no charge to wander around the six acres of **Haiku Gardens,** a private estate featuring lawns, lily ponds and exotic bowers, but you might want to stop for refreshment and a lingering look from the *lānai* at the restaurant on the hill overlooking this tranquil setting. (Tu-Su 8:30am-7pm [or dark] 46-336 Ha'ikū Road 247-6671)

Kahana Valley State Park, off Kamehameha Highway on O'ahu's Windward side, has been desig-nated a 'living park' by the State Legislature. The beautiful valley

a program for visitors which includes a visitor center where about 150 residents and others demonstrate their skills within the context of traditional life in the Kahana Valley. The 5260-acre 'living park' includes hunting and hiking areas, for which permission must be obtained (see Permits and Licenses under GETTING HERE, and Hiking and Hunting under SPORTS & RECREATION). The park is open to visitors during daylight hours only.

Sacred Falls State Park, located off Kamehameha Highway a mile

Windward coast, encompasses the lower reaches of Kaluanui Stream, at the head of which is the eighty-foot cascade of Sacred Falls, known to Hawaiians of old as Kaliuwa'a.

The area was, indeed, sacred to the ancients, being the birthplace of the pig-god Kamapua'a, and many local visitors still leave ti-wrapped stones along the way in acknowledgement of the spirit of the place; there are many legends associated with the area. A hiking trail leads upstream to the falls, crossing the streambed twice (see Hiking under SPORTS & RECREATION). Cane fields and lush tropical vegetation make the Kaluanui Valley a beautiful natural setting.

Waimea Falls Park is described under Popular Attractions below.

At the junction of Highways 99 and 80, on the Leilehua Plateau of central O'ahu, the **Del Monte**

Pineapple Variety Garden displays living specimens of some thirty species of the South American bromeliad family, of which the pineapple plant is a member. Several varieties of the succulent fruit here keep company with their less productive cousins, and labels explain the life cycle of these plants and their cultivation. Pineapple plants grow from two to four feet high, and the fruit may weigh as much as four or five pounds, taking between eighteen and twenty months to reach maturity.

In the Moanalua Valley, only a few miles 'Ewa of Honolulu, **Moanalua Gardens**, part of the Damon Estate (a missionary-descended family), is a twenty-six-acre private park open to the public. Magnificent monkeypod trees shade the vast lawns, and two streams and a natural pool are bordered by ferns, vines, morning glories and garde-

Giant lily pads in the lily pond at Waimea Falls Park.

nias. White hibiscus trees soar three stories high. A cottage on the grounds, built in the 1850s to provide a card-playing haven for King Kamehameha V and his friends, was moved from a nearby site, as was the Chinese Pavilion. The gardens also include a taro patch, a carp pond and a group of ancient petroglyphs.

Each year in July, the Prince Lot Hula Festival is staged in the park (see LOCAL FESTIVALS/CALEN-DAR OF EVENTS). Groups of 25 or more require advance registration; guided tours of the gardens for such groups can be arranged through the Moanalua Valley Gardens Foundation for a nominal fee. To reach the Gardens take the Tripler exit off the Moanalua Freeway; they are located next to the highway on the *mauka* side. (daily 7am-6pm Gardens: 1350 Pineapple Place 833-1944, Foundation 839-5334)

FACTORIES

Towering above the factories and workshops along Nimitz Highway is the enormous pineapple-shaped water tank of the **Dole Cannery Square**. Don't be taken in by the myth told to tourists that it contains pineapple juice. Visitors to the cannery can watch a film about the pineapple industry, drink canned pineapple juice dispensed from a fountain and, on weekdays, watch the action in the cannery itself. Tours are available and a variety of Island-style retail shops greet visitors daily. (daily hours vary 650 Iwilei Street 536-3411 admission children under 12 free)

Hilo Hattie's Fashion Center is a popular stop included in many tour packages, and is often combined with stops at the Kodak Hula Show and the Dole Cannery Square. Here visitors can see aloha wear in the making and can purchase Island fashions at discount prices—for men, women and children. The free tour takes twenty minutes, and free buses to and from Waikīkī leave every half hour. (daily 8:30am-5pm 700 N Nimitz Hwy 537-2926)

Hawai'i's own **Lion Coffee** is roasted and packaged in Honolulu's historic Kaka'ako district, and visitors are welcome to tour the coffee roasting facility and taste free coffee samples. Packaged and bulk coffee—custom blends of the finest beans from the Big Island's Kona district and the rest of the world's best coffee-producing areas—can also be purchased here much cheaper than in stores, and mailing of vacuum-packed coffees can be arranged. Tours take about twenty minutes, and appointments are preferred, around 10:30am being the best time. (M-F 7:30am-5pm tours by request 831 Queen Street 521-3479)

The last remaining ukulele factory in Hawai'i, **Kamaka, Inc.**, a family enterprise, began operation in 1916. Free tours showing the instrument makers at work take about half an hour; morning is the best time. These beautiful instruments are crafted of koa wood and come in six sizes, with four, six or eight strings; and they can be purchased from the factory. (M-F 8am-3pm by appointment only 550 South Street 531-3165)

67

POPULAR ATTRACTIONS

The **Kodak Hula Show** is a Waikīkī institution. Started in 1937 when flash photography was not widespread or sophisticated, the show gave Honolulu visitors the opportunity to expose their Kodak film as well as themselves to performances of Hawaiian dance in an outdoor setting. Originally staged near the Natatorium (see Memorials above), the show now takes place on the grounds of the Waikīkī Shell in Kapi'olani Park. Performers include young and old, and they willingly pose for photographs and answer questions after the hour-long performance. They also offer brief instruction to those who care to try their hand— or hip—at the hula. (T-Th 10am Waikīkī Shell 833-1661 admission)

The forty-two-acre **Honolulu Zoo**, which has grown from an animal collection begun in 1915 by the City and County parks committee, is now home to about a thousand animals of three hundred species, including 175 kinds of birds, sixty-one of mammals and sixty-four of reptiles and amphibians. On Wednesday evenings in summer, the Zoo stages free local entertainment with 'The Wildest Show in Town'. (daily 8:30 am-4 pm Kapahulu at Monsarrat Avenue, opposite Kūhiō Beach 971-1717 admission)

The **Waikīkī Aquarium**, located along the seaward edge of Kapi'olani Park, was opened in 1904 as an end-of-the-line attraction for Honolulu Rapid Transit Company's new electric trams. Now associated with the University of Hawai'i and internationally recognized as a scientific research institution, the Waikiki Aquarium features fifty-three display tanks housing an enormous variety of tropical Pacific marine life, includ-

The Kodak Hula Show is a fifty-year-old tradition in Waikiki.

ing the endangered Hawaiian monk seal, rare corals, chambered nautilus, cuttlefish, giant clams, and more than 300 fish of 250 species, including the little one with the big name—Hawai'i's State Fish, the famous *humuhumunukunukuapua'a*. A museum display, 'Hawaiians and the Sea', explains the vital relationship between ancient Hawaiians and the marine environment; another, 'Edge of the Reef', recreates rocky shoreline and reef environments for a close-up look at that habitat. An exhibition garden features Hawai'i's coastal vegetation. Guided tours and audio guides are available. The Aquarium also hosts occasional guided day and evening walks along shore and reef areas. (daily 9am-5pm 2777 Kalākaua Avenue 923-9741 donation requested)

Located in the lush upper reaches of the Mānoa Valley, **Paradise Park**'s fifteen acres offer such enticements as a stroll along a boardwalk through a hau tree 'jungle', a walk through a bamboo forest, a Chinese garden, a Japanese garden, a flamingo lagoon, a trained bird show, an aviary and a 'dancing water' show. The park was closed for renovation and has even more attractions worth checking out now. (3737 Manoa Road 988-6686 admission)

O'ahu's **Sea Life Park** is an outstanding example of this type of educational entertainment center, and its coastal setting provides a backdrop not excelled anywhere. Its 300,000-gallon glass tank is eighteen feet deep, has seventeen viewing windows along a spiral ramp, and holds more than two thousand species

of marine life. Its Turtle Lagoon is a breeding facility for the endangered green sea turtle; its Seabird Sanctuary accommodates a nesting colony of boobies and is also home to other free-flying seabirds including albatrosses and frigate birds; and its Kaupō Falls area nurtures a variety of indigenous plants and island waterfowl. The Rocky Shores exhibit recreates the intertidal zone. Not only that, the Park offers three different shows throughout the day: one a pageant featuring dolphins and whales that draws upon Hawai'i's whaling days, another a behavioral display featuring the antics of

A show at Sea Life Park.

dolphins, sea lions and penguins, and still another featuring a diver hand-feeding residents of the enormous Reef Tank. Evening entertainment includes a Hawaiian revue in addition to everything shown during the day. (M-T-W & Sa 9am-5pm Th-F & Su 9:30am-10pm Kalaniana'ole Highway just past Makapu'u Point 259-7933 admission)

The most popular paid attraction on the Hawaiian visitor's destination list is the **Polynesian Cultural Center** at Lā'ie on O'ahu's Windward Coast. This forty-two-acre park features architecturally authentic village settings from ancient Hawai'i, Sāmoa, the Marquesas, Tahiti, Fiji, Tonga and New Zealand, usually peopled with natives from those islands, some demonstrating their indigenous crafts. In the afternoons, the waterborne 'Pageant of the Long Canoes' snakes its way along the canal that runs from village to village and, in the evenings, a Polynesian stage spectacular featuring traditional and modernized dance forms from all the island groups represented is offered at extra cost.

Traditional crafts of high quality and authenticity are for sale at the Center's gift shop. The admission fee is expensive, but well worth the price unless you prefer to visit southern Polynesia personally. Allow ample time as a thorough viewing of all that's available here easily takes all afternoon and, if you wish to see the Polynesian show, the evening as well. (M-Sa 12:30pm-9pm Kamehameha Hwy, Lā'ie; further details: 293-3333, 923-1861 admission)

Waimea Falls Park occupies eighteen-hundred privately owned acres of the picturesque valley above Waimea Bay. Waimea Valley was for centuries inhabited by a large population of Hawaiians who tilled its fertile soil and fished the nearby waters. There are some six thousand plant species in the park, including plantings from other tropical regions, and an especially interesting hibiscus garden that explains the evolution and eloquent hybridization at the hand of man of Hawai'i's State Flower.

Numerous types of ground birds including ducks, geese and peacocks wander freely; an aviary displays a variety of colorful and interesting non-native birds such as South American macaws; and lots of free-flying local birds hang around hoping for a handout. Open trams provide transportation around the park, with narration by very well-informed drivers, and short guided tours of particularly interesting areas are offered at frequent intervals throughout the day. There are also hiking trails through the lush forest that you may follow on your own. At less-frequent intervals are demonstrations of diving from the cliff beside the falls—which are pretty but not spectacular—and of a very *hele wiki* version of ancient hula. The hula is followed by a short demonstration of ancient Hawaiian games. (daily 10am-5:30pm off Kamehameha Hwy 638-8511)

The **Dole Pineapple Pavilion** on the Leilehua Plateau in central O'ahu's pineapple country is a refreshing stop on this long, cross-island drive. Sip juice, munch chunks of the fresh fruit and take a stroll over to the edge of the nearest field for a close-up view of the plants that produce this delightful delicacy. During the summer months, it is often possible to purchase whole pineapples here much cheaper than at the stores. (daily 9am-5:30pm 64-1550 Kamehameha Hwy 621-8408)

Immediately adjacent is the haven of **Helemano Plantation**, where residents and day workers raise flowers, fruit, and vegetables, operate a bakery and a country store, and serve up fine meals of their fresh foods in their own cafeteria. Classes and demonstrations in various traditional crafts are also held, and gift items handmade here are sold, along with other local merchandise, at the small shop.

Helemano Plantation is run as a self-help center for Hawai'i's mentally handicapped, and they are very proud of their success. They love visitors and here you will be greeted with real *aloha*. This special place is worth a look-in, even if your visit is fleeting. (daily 8:30am-5pm 64-1510 Kamehameha Hwy 622-3929)

Hawai'i's most visited tourist destination, the **National Memorial Cemetery of the Pacific** in Punchbowl crater, and the second-most-visited site, the **Arizona Memorial** at the site of the sunken USS *Arizona* in Pearl Harbor, are described under Cemeteries and Memorials above.

Fire knife dancer, Polynesian Cultural Center.

O'ahu Beaches

Twilight finds Sandy Beach deserted.

Walking on water, so to speak, during low tide at Hanauma Bay.

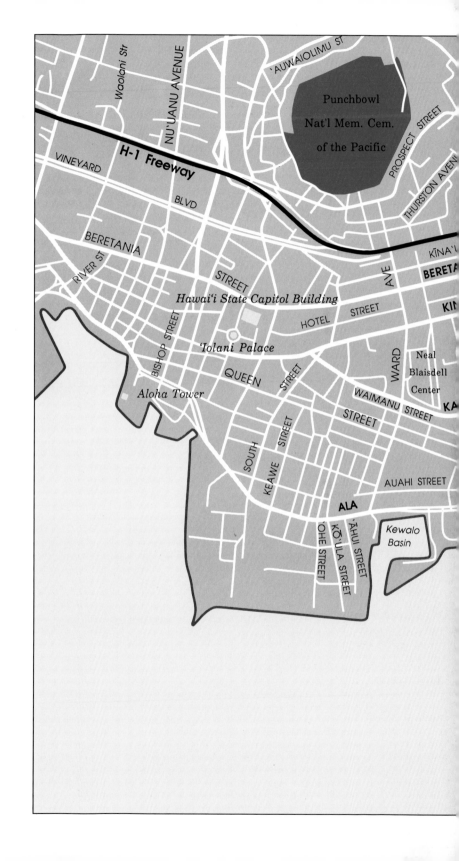

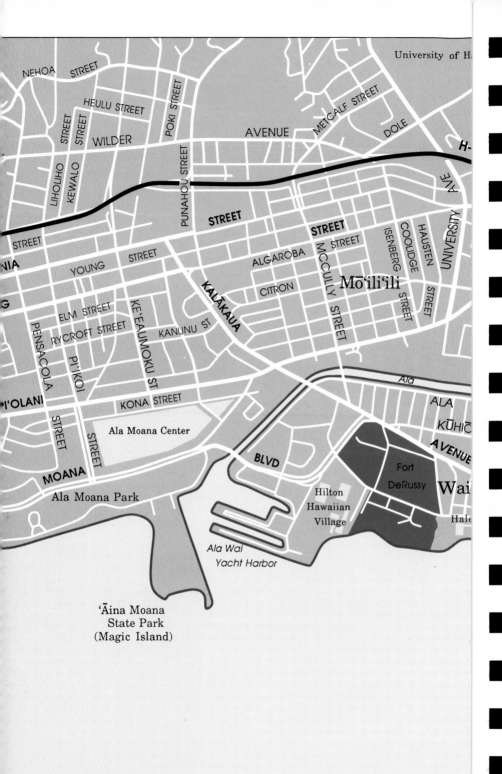

Taking a keiki for a walk on Waimanalo Beach.

BEACHES

O'ahu is wrapped in an almost unbroken ribbon of beaches. Ocean recreation was an important facet of life for the ancient Hawaiians, and remains a major feature of island life, for visitors as well as residents. Many island visitors come from inland areas and are unfamiliar with the awesome power of the sea and with the vagaries of its personality. For all its beauty, it must be approached with respect and caution, and then it provides a great deal of pleasure. This section contains information relevant to beach activity—including warnings—followed by descriptions and ratings of O'ahu's beaches.

BEACHBOYS

The professional beachboy is unique to Waikīkī. This phenomenon began after the opening of the Moana Hotel—the first large tourist establishment in Waikīkī—in 1901. As tourism grew, locals along the beach offered visitors various services.

Experienced and able watermen, they gave outrigger canoe rides and swimming and surfing lessons; they entertained their guests with songs and stories of old Hawai'i, and acted as unofficial ambassadors for their homeland. They were colorful cultural characters that enriched the experience of Hawai'i for those who passed this way. Long-lasting friendships often developed between tourists and their beachboy hosts; they were confidants and, occasionally, lovers. The romantic reputation of early beachboys is not entirely mythical.

What began simply as a gesture of friendship and welcome gradually developed into a business of sorts. Tourists of that era when sea travel provided the only access to Hawai'i were necessarily wealthy and usually were generous to the beachboys who befriended them.

The golden era of beachboys was probably in the 1930s when the Royal Hawaiian joined the Moana

on the beachfront and movies began to be made here, throwing the national spotlight on the island—and particularly on Waikīkī.

After the second World War, the advent of air travel brought an influx of tourists, and the beach scene became much livelier than in the preceding era. The profession of 'beachboy' also evolved.

Beachboys today must be licensed and hold lifesaving certificates; they still provide surfing lessons, canoe rides and camaraderie. Most can provide information about parasailing, jetskiing and canoe and catamaran rides, and all rent various types of surfboards and give lessons in this most Hawaiian of sports (see SPORTS & RECREATION).

Waikiki Beach Services (922-4422, 924-4941), has desks in front of the Reef Hotel and the Sheraton-Waikiki. **Outrigger Beachboy Service** (923-0711) at the Outrigger Main Hotel has lessons for slightly less than the going rate, and they also rent surfboards, body boards, mats and umbrellas. Oldest of the oldtimers, **Aloha Beach Service** (922-3111), fronts the beach of the Surfrider Hotel, and **Fort DeRussy Beach Service** (949-3469) is located at Fort DeRussy Beach Park.

Sandsliding's 'twisting flip' maneuver is a popular sight at Sandy Beach.

LIFEGUARDS

These highly trained and responsible individuals are stationed on the beach primarily to rescue people who get themselves into trouble. They are also an invaluable source of information and advice about ocean-related activities; but remember that their first duty is to be watchful of those in the water. Heed all warning signs posted at beaches. A little caution and awareness of local conditions can diminish these hazards and make all your memories of your Hawaiian holiday a pleasure to recall.

SUN

Many visitors spoil their vacations by spending too much time in the sun in the first day or two. The sun in Hawai'i is much harsher than in more northerly (or quite southerly) climes. Because of the islands' tropical location, the sun at noon is directly overhead twice a year and is never at an angle lower than forty-five degrees; and because of the clarity of the atmosphere over Hawai'i, nearly three quarters of the solar radiation penetrates, on a clear day, to sea level. This calls for sunblock for all but the most acclimatized and dark-skinned individuals. Even very dark-skinned people who are not used to such exposure can get serious sunburn. Fair-skinned people should exercise extreme caution at all times.

If you haven't brought sunblock with you, buy some. It is sold at stands along Waikīkī Beach, as well as in most stores. If you are unsure what level of protection is appropriate for your skin type, ask the beach attendants or store personnel. It's better to have too much than too little. It's also wise to limit your time in the sun to an hour or so the first day—depending on the fairness of your skin. You can increase this by ten or twenty minutes a day as you gradually develop a tan.

WAVE ACTION

One of the gravest potential dangers of the deep is the caprice of waves.

People with a knowledge of the sea can observe the cycles of the waves and form a fairly accurate judgement of what the surface action will be. There are, however, freak waves that surprise even the experts. 'Typical' wave action varies with the local shoreline and the season.

High surf

On O'ahu's North Shore in winter, the sheer size of the surf is dangerous, with waves cresting up to thirty feet. These are generated by seasonal storms in the North Pacific and travel unobstructed until they break on Hawai'i's shores. The Leeward (West) Shore surf is also high in winter, running as high as twenty feet. In summer, high seasonal surf of ten to fifteen feet can occur off the South Shore—still potentially dangerous.

Other wave and current action, too, can endanger life and limb, especially in areas where incoming waves are unobstructed by reefs. The South and Windward (East) Shores are mostly protected by long fringing reefs.

Shorebreaks

Where incoming ocean swells cross abruptly from a deep to a shallow bottom, the height of waves increases suddenly and dramatically, and the swells break with enormous downward force. Places where such waves break directly on or near the shore are known as shorebreaks and can be very dangerous, particularly for swimmers. These beaches are, nonetheless, popular as they provide excellent conditions for body surfing, and many people enjoy being tossed about by large waves. It is well, though, to know how to deal with them. Neck and back injuries can be sustained, even by experienced swimmers. Turning your back on or trying to jump over or through a large incoming wave invites trouble. The force of the wave can pound you against the bottom, knock your breath away and cause you to lose your sense of direction. The trick is to take a deep breath and dive *under* the wave.

Backwash

Another potential danger at such beaches is the backwash. Water which has been washed onto the shore must run back again to the sea. On steep beaches, or after the arrival of particularly voluminous waves, the force of this water can be almost as powerful as the incoming wave and can sweep a person off his or her feet and out to deeper water.

Rip currents

This water rushing back to the sea sometimes gets trapped by other incoming waves and can build to a considerable volume. When this happens, the only way it can move is sideward, creating a rip current that runs along the beach until it finds a deeper bottom. If you find yourself caught in a rip, the best course of action is to flow along with it until its force diminishes. Don't exhaust yourself trying to swim against it. It's easier and safer to walk back along the beach to the place where you started than to fight the water.

Some rip currents flow straight out to sea through channels in the reef. If you are caught in one of these, swim to the side of it to get out. This type of rip is far more dangerous.

Undertow

Sometimes this backed-up water cannot find an outlet and must flow back out *under* the incoming wave. This creates the condition known as undertow.

An undertow is a brief phenomenon, lasting only until the wave has passed. For a person pulled down in an undertow, a few seconds under water can seem much longer. Remain calm and come up for air on the other side of the wave.

Rock ledges

Another potentially dangerous wave action is the collision of deep ocean swells with rock ledges. It is never safe to venture out to the edge of rocks where surf is breaking. Freak waves can wash over the rocks without warning and many unsuspecting people have been swept away by such waves.

Underwater ledges, too, can present some danger from the surprise of a sudden dropping away of the bottom. Very shallow water can become very deep without notice, so non-swimmers should always keep away from such areas. Slippery rocks are also hazardous and should be approached with caution.

Tsunami

Seismic waves, known as tsunami, are sometimes referred to as 'tidal waves'. This uncommon phenomenon is mentioned in the section on Climate and Weather in the INTRODUCTION.

EXPLORING/Beaches

Pipeline in winter, home of international surfing championships.

BEACH RATINGS

We have rated the beaches according to our interpretation of the following criteria: water safety (marine hazards, presence of lifeguards), bottom configuration (sand, rock, coral), water quality, cleanliness/maintenance of beach area, and type and quality of facilities (toilets, showers, picnic tables, barbecue pits, parking). This is naturally arbitrary as not everyone feels the same about what's most important in a beach. There are no ugly beaches on the island.

Symbols denote beaches that are especially good for board surfing ●, body surfing ● (includes body boarding), windsurfing ●, snorkeling ●, and swimming ●. Scuba diving spots are not necessarily at beaches and are detailed in SPORTS & RECREATION. Seasonal variances are also noted. These are *VERY* important as they relate primarily to safety. If you are unsure of the safety of current water conditions, check with the lifeguard on duty.

The ratings and descriptions of beaches are arranged, after the discussion of those in the central tourist area, in geographical order around the island in a counterclockwise direction.

Pure paradise ★★★★★

Superb ★★★★

Excellent ★★★

Good ★★

Fair ★

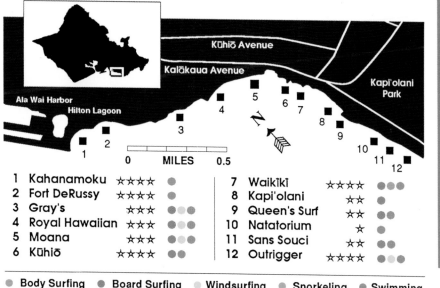

1	Kahanamoku	★★★★	●
2	Fort DeRussy	★★★★	●
3	Gray's	★★★	●●●
4	Royal Hawaiian	★★★	●●●
5	Moana	★★★	●●●
6	Kūhiō	★★★★	●●
7	Waikīkī	★★★★	●●●
8	Kapi'olani	★★	●
9	Queen's Surf	★★	●●
10	Natatorium	★	●
11	Sans Souci	★★	●●
12	Outrigger	★★★★	●●●

● Body Surfing   ● Board Surfing   ● Windsurfing   ● Snorkeling   ● Swimming

Waikīkī Beach

Perhaps the most famous swatch of coastline in the world, Waikīkī Beach is actually an almost unbroken two-mile string of a dozen beaches, stretching from the Ala Wai yacht basin to Diamond Head. Much of this shoreline fronts hotels, apartments, condominiums and private facilities, and only a small portion open parkland.

Some parts of the long stretch are better for swimming than others, some are better for surfing, all are good for people watching and basking in the super-strength Hawaiian sun.

Rentals of surfboards, windsurfers and other equipment as well as sailboat and outrigger canoe rides are also available at several locations along the beach.

It's impossible to rate this beach as a single unit. There are too many variances. Generally, the facilities of each section are meant only for guests of the nearest hotel, though there are some public facilities and

the beaches are all open to public access.

It is interesting to note that the Waikīkī shoreline has been changed significantly over the years through various developments, and that the beachfront was formerly cut by three streams, which were diverted by the Ala Wai Canal.

The individually named beaches along the Waikīkī shore are: **Kahanamoku Beach and Lagoon**, fronting the Hilton Hawaiian Village (and named for Hawai'i's famous surfer and Olympic swimmer Duke Kahanamoku); **Fort DeRussy Beach**, fronting Fort DeRussy and the Halekoa (military) Hotel; **Gray's Beach**, fronting the Halekulani (and named for a former beach hotel called Gray's-by-the-Sea); **Royal Hawaiian and Moana Beaches**, fronting those hotels; **Waikīkī Beach Center**, fronting the section of Kalākaua Avenue opposite the Hyatt Regency and Hawaiian Regent Hotels; **Kūhiō**

Beach Park, across Kalākaua Avenue from the entrance to the Honolulu Zoo (and named for Prince Jonah Kūhiō Kalaniana'ole, whose house once stood here); **Queen's Surf Beach Park**, at the 'Ewa end of Kapi'olani Beach Park (and named for the former Queen's Surf Hotel which once stood on the site); **Kapi'olani Park Beach Center**, opposite Kapi'olani Park (and part of that park); the **War Memorial Natatorium**, not a beach, but a saltwater swimming pool at the seaside (see Memorials under SIGHTSEEING); **Sans Souci Beach**, adjacent to the New Otani Kaimana Beach Hotel (and named for a hotel that formerly stood there); and the **Outrigger Canoe Club Beach**, fronting that exclusive private club.

1 Magic Island Lagoon and Ala Moana ★★★★ ●●

Across the Ala Wai Yacht Harbor from Waikīkī's Kahanamoku Beach are Magic Island Lagoon and Ala Moana Beach Park, both man-made on reclaimed land. Once the Honolulu garbage dump, this area is now the most popular urban beach park for local residents. Though the quality of the beach sand is coarser and, in patches, rockier than that at Waikīkī, this is offset by the large and well-kept park adjacent to it, and the availability of free parking, an amenity almost non-existent in Waikīkī.

84

2 Diamond Head ★★ ●●

There are four beach areas around the curve of Diamond Head; most afford poor swimming because of shallow inshore flats and coral. During periods of high surf, there are also dangerous currents, and there are no lifeguards. These beaches are most popular for basking and watching surfers, and as access points to well-known surfing breaks. Good swimming is available near the Black Point end at **Ka'alāwai** (better known locally as Duke's or Cromwell's) but the only parking near that beach is along nearby residential streets.

3 Kāhala and Wailupe ★★ ● (summer)

This beautiful strip of coastline fronts exclusive residences and the equally highbrow Kahala Hilton. The calm waters protected by fringing reefs are very shallow except in front of the Hilton where dredging has produced an excellent swimming spot. There are also occasional deeper holes on the flats. At low tide, you can continue walking past the Hilton to Wailupe Beach Park. The hotel provides lifeguards along its section of the beach; otherwise, there are none.

4 'Āina Haina to Portlock ★ ● (summer)

The small beach parks in this area are suited primarily to picnicking, the shoreline being mostly rock and mud and the bottom shallow. None of them have lifeguards. The turbulent water off Kawaihoa Point (commonly known as Portlock Point) can be extremely treacherous. Nonetheless, it is popular with advanced surfers. Wave surges across the rock terraces below the park pose danger, even for spectators. Wave watching from above is exciting, especially during high surf. The deep waters offshore are often a dark purple color.

1 Ala Moana
2 Diamond Head
3 Kāhala
4 Portlock
5 Hanauma Bay
6 Hālona Blowhole
7 Waimānalo Bay

● Body Surfing ● Board Surfing ● Windsurfing ● Snorkeling ● Swimming

5 Hanauma Bay ★★★★★ ●●

Hanauma Bay is a very special place. Nestled in a breached crater, this almost circular bay, its inner curve lined with a long, narrow, palm-fringed beach, has always been one of the favored scenic and recreation spots on Oʻahu, for Hawaiians and visitors alike.

Now an underwater park and conservation district, it serves as a haven for the many varieties of marine life that dwell in Hawaiian waters. The large, diverse, and now quite tame fish population, along with the rich coral reef in the bay, make this the favorite spot on Oʻahu for snorkelers and divers. There are large holes in the reef near the beach which afford good swimming. On either side of the bay, near the entrance, are peculiar natural features known as 'Witches Brew' (for the swirling, gurgling water) and 'the Toilet Bowl' (for the way in which this bowl-shaped natural formation empties and refills). Lifeguards are on duty every day of the year.

6 Hālona Blowhole to Makapuʻu ★★

Water conditions at the pretty beaches around this easternmost tip of Oʻahu are dangerous. Otherwise they'd get a higher rating. The little **Hālona Beach** below the blowhole lookout has no lifeguard, nor do those at **Wāwāmalu Beach Park** and **Kaloko Beach.** The daily, year-round lifeguards at **Sandy Beach** ●● and **Makapuʻu Beach** ●● (summer) make more rescues than occur anywhere else in Hawaiʻi. Despite the hazards, wave conditions at these two beaches are unequalled for experienced bodysurfers, thus attracting throngs of local youth as well as tourists seeking the thrill of turbulent waters. Board surfing is prohibited at Makapuʻu because of the density of bodysurfers in the water. Makapuʻu's water is calm enough for reasonably safe swimming in summer, and the shore-breaks are not as good for body surfing.

7 Waimānalo Bay ★★★★★

This beautiful sweep of white sandy beach is the longest on the island at about four miles, and encompasses five beach parks. Most of **Kaupō Beach Park's** ●● shore is fronted by reef and rock barriers; offshore areas provide good swimming and surfing. **Kaiona Beach Park** ●● is shallower and also protected from strong currents by the outer reef. **Waimānalo Beach Park** ●●● can develop a small shorebreak in rough weather but is typically calm and gentle. **Waimānalo State Recreation Area** ●●● , also known as Sherwood Forest, has a gently sloping sandy bottom, and is sometimes washed by strong currents along the shore. It generally has the strongest shorebreak in the bay (park hours: 7am-8pm May through September, 7am-6:30pm October through April). With one exception there are no lifeguards, but these beaches are generally very safe.

Lifeguards are stationed at **Bellows Field Beach Park** ●●● on weekends and national holidays, the only time there is public access to this beach, which is on a military reserve. Hours are from noon Friday to midnight Sunday and from dawn to midnight on holidays. The beach area north of Waimānalo Stream is restricted to military personnel. This and the neighboring Kailua Bay are the best spots on the island for windsurfing due to the almost constant presence of northeast tradewinds.

8 Kailua Bay ★★★★★

Almost contiguous with the beaches of Waimānalo Bay is the equally lovely Kailua Bay with its beautiful two-mile stretch of white sand beach gently sloping outward to deeper water. At the southern end is **Lanikai Beach** ●●● (occasional) ● , which is well-protected from strong wave action by outer fringing reefs. The adjacent **Kailua Beach Park** ●●● is cut by a canal which forms a *muliwai* [estuarine pond]; the beach is protected from strong wave action by the outer reef. This is the favorite spot for windsurfing due to the prevalence of onshore tradewinds, and has been the site of several local, national and international competitions in this sport.

Kalama Beach ●●● and **Oneawa Beach** ● (novice) are the unofficial names of the next two sections of **Kailua Beach**. Kalama has the biggest shorebreaks in this bay. The only lifeguards along the bay are at Kailua Beach Park.

9 Mōkapu Point and Kāne'ohe Bay ★

Mōkapu Peninsula is occupied by a Marine Corps Air Station and access to its beaches is for military personnel only. The entire shoreline of Kāne'ohe Bay is muddy with shallow flats fronted by rock and coral. There are four parks—**Kāne'ohe, He'eia, Laenani, Waiāhole**—none of which have beaches; they are, however, scenically lovely and ideal for picnicking and sunbathing. He'eia has park hours: 7am-8pm May through September, and 7am-6:30pm October through April.

10 Kualoa to Ka'a'awa ★★

The beaches and parks along this stretch of coastline all have shallow inshore waters and most have rocky bottoms. **Kualoa Regional Park** ●● is listed in the National Register of Historic Places. Traditionally one of the most sacred areas of O'ahu, it was very important in the life of the Hawaiian people. For this reason, it was chosen as the launching site for the original journey of the Polynesian voyaging canoe, *Hōkūle'a*, in 1972, and as the site for the canoe's triumphal

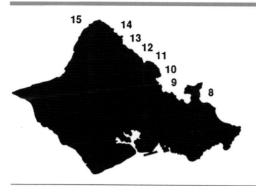

8   Kailua Bay
9   Kāne'ohe Bay
10 Kualoa to Ka'a'awa
11 Swanzy and Makaua
12 Kahana to Kaluanui
13 Mākao to Kaipapa'u
14 Kokololio
15 Kahuku to Waiale'e

● **Body Surfing**   ● **Board Surfing**   ● Windsurfing   ● **Snorkeling**   ● **Swimming**

return in 1987 from its two-and-a-half-year voyage throughout the South Pacific without navigational instruments (see Hawai'i Maritime Center under SIGHTSEEING). In honor of this monumental achievement by Hawaiians of many races—one which provoked a powerful emotional and spiritual response among Polynesian people everywhere—the beach at this park is now called **Hōkūle'a Beach.** A very large grassy park adjoins the long, fairly narrow sand beach, and it is open only from 7am to 7pm. Lifeguard service is provided daily June through August and on weekends throughout the year. **Kualoa Sugar Mill Beach ●** , **Kanenelu Beach ●●** , and **Kalae'ō'io Beach Park ●●** have no lifeguards. **Ka'a'awa Beach Park ●** has daily lifeguard service June through August.

11 Swanzy and Makaua Beach Parks ☆ ●

The unguarded beaches at these two popular parks disappear completely at high tide. Makaua Beach is overlooked by the rock formation resembling a crouching lion, and its waters are shallow and consist of coral reefs as does the neighboring Swanzy Beach area.

12 Kahana Bay to Kaluanui ☆☆☆

Good swimming is a primary attraction along this stretch of shore. The beaches are relatively narrow, but the inshore waters are calm and the bottom is sandy. Lifeguards are stationed at **Kahana Bay Beach Park ●●** (novice) ● from June through August. **Punalu'u Beach Park ●●** and **Kaluanui Beach Park ●●** are unguarded.

13 Mākao to Kaipapa'u ☆ ●

The beach areas here are mostly fronted by shallow water with rock and coral shelves extending right out to the reef, and much of the beach sand is covered at high tide. The tiny **'Aukai Beach Park ●** borders a small bay with a sandy bottom; **Hau'ula Beach Park ●●** (occasional) has a deep sand-bottomed channel at the northern end, but the strong currents there pose a hazard. Hau'ula has lifeguard service from June through August. **Kaipapa'u ●** is a rocky shoreline with a shallow, rocky bottom, no beach, and no convenient public access.

14 Kokololio to Malaekahana ★★★

There are lovely, long stretches of reasonably wide sandy beach along this coast. The only public access to **Kokololio Beach**● (summer) ● (occasional) is via a trail over the point separating it from neighboring **Pounders Beach** ●● (summer), one of O'ahu's most popular bodysurfing beaches. Both these are subject to shorebreaks and strong currents during the high winter surf from October to April. The mile-long sandy beach at **Laniloa** ● is fronted by shallow water over shelves of raised coral, except for two sandy pockets, but the inshore waters are protected and safe year-round. **Lā'ie Beach** ●●● has a protecting reef fronting the eastern end, and a small shorebreak at the western end, which can also have dangerous currents from October through April. **Moku'auia Beach** (summer)●● is on the leeward coast of Moku'auia (more commonly known as Goat Island); its waters are occasionally swept by strong currents between October and April. Access is by walking (appropriately shod) across the shallows separating it from Kalanai Point. The easiest and safest time to do this is in calm weather at low tide.

Walking around Kalanai Point provides the only public access to the long sandy curve of **Mālaekahana Beach**●● which fronts private homes. Its calm inshore waters are safe all year, and cover a gradually sloping sandy bottom with rock and coral patches. None of these beaches have lifeguards.

15 Kahuku to Waiale'e ★★

Little of the coast in this scenic rural area provides good conditions for water activities, and only the beach area at the Turtle Bay Hilton has lifeguard service. **Kahuku Golf Course Beach** ●, **Hanaka'īlio Beach**, **Kaihalulu Beach**, **Turtle Bay** ●, and **Waiale'e Beach Park** are subject to strong currents from April to October, and though waters are calmer in summer, they are poor for swimming because of the presence of rock and coral along most of the beachfront. The Hilton's little beach at **Kuilima Cove**●● is one of the nicest and safest in the area, and public access is allowed. The only access to nearby **Kawela Bay** ●●● another lovely, sheltered area, is by sea; its outer bay also has hazardous currents during heavy surf.

16 Sunset Beach to Hale'iwa ★★★

This strip constitutes O'ahu's 'North Shore', famous for the dramatic and dangerous surf that pounds the coast each winter. Spectacularly beautiful, and thrilling even to watch, its deadly potential is such that these beaches are rated lower than they would be for their summer conditions, which sometimes approach placid. Almost continuous sand for several miles, interrupted occasionally by rocky outcrops, this coast is almost entirely unprotected by reefs, and huge waves often crash directly on the shore. Winter erosion is also severe, and the ocean may remove as much as forty feet of the foreshore in a season. *Wave conditions that affect this area are described at the beginning of this section under Warnings.*

With the upsurge of interest in surfing during the past couple of decades, various areas of Sunset and Kawailoa have become popularly known by the names of the offshore surfing breaks that expert surfers from around the world

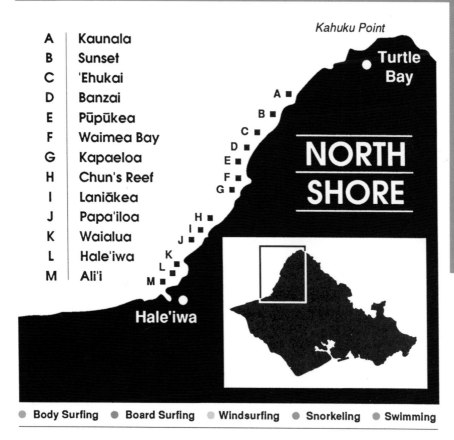

A	Kaunala
B	Sunset
C	'Ehukai
D	Banzai
E	Pūpūkea
F	Waimea Bay
G	Kapaeloa
H	Chun's Reef
I	Laniākea
J	Papaʻiloa
K	Waialua
L	Hale'iwa
M	Ali'i

Kahuku Point

Turtle Bay

NORTH SHORE

Hale'iwa

● Body Surfing   ● Board Surfing   ● Windsurfing   ● Snorkeling   ● Swimming

come here to ride. Watching them perch precariously on the huge cresting swells is awesome, but even such experts sometimes come to grief in these waters. *Any surfing here is recommended for experts only.* Civil Defense authorities often close these beaches in winter.

The first in this line of famous surfing breaks is Velzyland, off **Kaunala Beach** ● which is fronted by beach rock and reef, and has no lifeguards. **Sunset Beach Park** ●● (expert) ● (summer) is safe in summer, and in winter has some of the most spectacular waves on the island. It has lifeguards on weekends all year, but on weekdays only from June through August. **'Ehukai Beach Park** ●● (expert) ● (spring/summer) is small and not even visible from Kamehameha Highway, but it is one of the best places to watch surfers in the renowned Pūpūkea and Pipeline surfing breaks which lie to the east and west, respectively. It is manned by lifeguards daily throughout the year. The Pipeline is sometimes also referred to as the Banzai Pipeline, a name consequently applied to the nearby shore area known as **Banzai Beach** ● (expert) ● (summer), which has some dangerous shore currents even in calm seasons.

The large area of **Pūpūkea Beach Park** (summer) ●● is fronted almost entirely by reefs, but the area known as Shark's Cove provides excellent swimming and snorkeling in summer; in winter the water is too dangerous to go near, to say nothing of into.

The biggest rideable waves in the world roll into Waimea Bay in winter (see

Ka'ena Point). Besides the towering, murderous breaks outside the point, the shorebreak often runs as high as fifteen feet. In summer the bay looks like a lake, making **Waimea Bay Beach Park** ●● (expert) ● and ● (summer) a haven for casual and peaceful water recreation. The park has daily year-round lifeguard service. The unguarded areas known as **Kapaeloa Beach** ●, **Chun's Reef Beach** ●● (summer), **Laniākea Beach** ●● (summer), and **Papa'iloa Beach** ● (summer) are fronted by rocks and broken reefs or are subject to strong currents even in calm seasons, making them ill-suited for swimming at any time.

The point outside Waialua Bay and the breaks opposite **Waialua Beach** ● offer the last of the great North Shore surf. The protected cove of **Hale'iwa Beach Park** ●●● (off the point) with its shallow sandy bottom, offers safe swimming all year. The park has lifeguard service daily June through August; **Ali'i Beach Park** on the opposite side of the bay (part of Waialua Beach) has lifeguards daily in summer and on weekends and holidays throughout the year.

17 Mokulē'ia Shoreline ☆

The protected waters of **Kaiaka Bay** ● are usually muddy and the bottom drops away abruptly, but swimming there is safe year-round (there are no lifeguards) The park area is open 7am to 8pm from May through September and 7am to 6:30pm from October through April. The beach areas between here and Ka'ena Point—the westernmost tip of the island—have little or no public access [only **Mokulē'ia Beach Park** ● (summer) and **Keālia Beach** ● (summer)] and offer poor shore conditions for swimming; in winter the inshore currents are dangerous and can be strong even in summer.

18 Ka'ena Point

Though there are no beaches near Ka'ena Point, on either side, this coast is worthy of note for the raw beauty of its rugged lava and reef-bounded shoreline and its turbulent waters. Even on calm days, the nearshore currents are powerful, and when the high winter surf is running, the height of the waves here *averages* thirty to forty feet, with freak waves even higher, making it the biggest surf in Hawai'i. No one has ever even attempted to ride these waves, though there is persistent speculation on the subject amongst the expert surfing fraternity. In the right season, there is no better place to pay homage to the might and majesty of the sea.

19 Yokohama Bay to Mākaha ☆☆

O'ahu's other world-famous surfing area is this far end of the Leeward (West) coast. Though the winter waves on this side do not reach the monumental heights of those on the North Shore, they are still spectacular—*and dangerous*. Surfing in these waters is best left to the experts. The only lifeguards in the area are at Mākaha Beach Park. The first beach area south of Ka'ena Point is **Yokohama Bay** ●●● and ● (summer). It also marks the end of the paved road. The beach is narrow in winter and wide in summer. **Makua Beach** ●●● and ● (summer) has similar, only slightly less dangerous, conditions. **'Ōhikilolo Beach** ● (in cove) is accessible only by a trail from Kāneana Cave and its rocky shoreline fronts deep and dangerous water, but there is a small

EXPLORING/Beaches

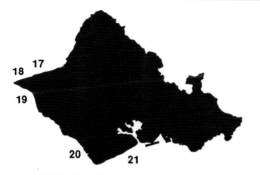

17 Mokulē'ia
18 Ka'ena Point
19 Yokohama to Mākaha
20 Wai'anae to Nānākuli
21 Barber's Point to Sand Island

● Body Surfing   ● Board Surfing   ● Windsurfing   ● Snorkeling   ● Swimming

secluded cove where a shallow inshore pond provides safe swimming. Most of the long stretch of **Kea'au Beach Park** ●● (summer) is fronted by coral and sharp lava rock that preclude swimming.

Mākaha Beach Park ●●● and ● (summer), site of the annual Makaha International Surfing Contest since 1952, has some of Hawai'i's best surfing waves between October and April. Swimmers during this season must beware not only of dangerous wave action but also of loose surfboards. The beach is narrow in winter with a steep foreshore; the sand returns in summer and the beach is wide with a gentler slope. A tiny cove in the long rocky shoreline shelters a small beach called **Laukīnui**, and **Papaoneone Beach** ●● (summer) lies in the crook of the point below Mauna Lahilahi [thin montain]. Both these have inconvenient public access. **Mauna Lahilahi Beach Park** ●● has fairly safe inshore waters even when the surf is up, but the water is often murky from runoff. The shoreline is mostly rock with a stretch of sandy beach that is seasonally wide or narrow where a lifeguard tower is manned daily during summer.

20 Wai'anae to Nanakuli ★ / ★★

Wai'anae Regional Park ★ is fronted by a low sea cliff that drops sharply to deep water, but across the bay at **Pōka'ī Bay Beach Park** ★★ ●● (winter) is a lovely sheltered beach fronted by a sandy, gently sloping bottom providing good, safe swimming all year. Lifeguard service is provided at this park daily from June through August and on weekends all year. On the point at the edge of the park lie the ruins of a *heiau* known as Kū'ilioloa. The long strip of almost contiguous beach parks called **Lualualei** ★ ● (winter) ● (summer), **Mā'ili** ★ ● (winter) ● and ● (summer), and **Ulehawa** ★ ● (winter) ● (summer) ● (in lagoon) have sandy beaches that are largely washed away in winter and are fronted with reef and rock, making swimming virtually impossible anytime except in sandy pockets along the shore: in front of the lifeguard stands at Mā'ili and Ulehawa (manned daily in summer and on weekends all year) and at the western end of Ulehawa where an enclosed lagoon provides safe swimming even when the surf is high.

Nānākuli Beach Park ★★ ●● (summer), almost divided in half by a tract of homes, has areas of sandy beach at each end which are subject to heavy shorebreaks and rip currents in winter, and are lifeguarded daily from June through August. **Manner's Beach** ★ ●● and **Hawaiian Electric Beach Park** ★ ●●● and ● (winter) have generally safe water conditions all year, though there are sometimes strong currents when the surf is high. **Kahe Point Beach Park** ● (winter) ● and ● (summer) has water access only at a small cove on the eastern edge where water conditions are unsafe from October through April.

21 Barber's Point to Sand Island

This is the only section of O'ahu's accessible coastline that generally rates no stars. Most of the beach areas along this oceanfront are limited to military personnel, and those with public access afford poor shore conditions for water recreation. **'Ewa Beach Park** ★ ●● (summer) is locally famous as the best place to collect several varieties of edible seaweed and attracts aficionados from all over the island. There are rideable waves in summer and swimming is okay if you don't mind the seaweed.

The waters of Pearl Harbor, Ke'ehi Lagoon and Honolulu Harbor are too polluted for swimming, though there is a public park on the shore of each. Outrigger canoe races are held at **Ke'ehi Lagoon** every summer and can be watched from the stony shore of the park there. **Sand Island State Beach Park** ★ ● (summer) occasionally has small rideable waves offshore and is a delightful place for picnics (park hours: 7am-8pm May through September, 7am-6:30pm October through April).

EXPLORING/Beaches

SPORTS

Scuba diving
Windsurfing
Golf
Hiking

SPORTS & RECREATION

H awaiians have always been enthusiastic sportsmen and had developed a variety of sports and games prior to the arrival of Europeans. Traditional sports and games are too numerous to detail here. The ones still popular today are surfing—which has spread to many parts of the world—and outrigger canoe racing, though they have been substantially altered from the way they were done in ancient times. Hawaiians also took readily to many of the sports introduced by various immigrants to these islands, and today the people of Hawai'i participate in a wide cross-section of recreations and competitive events (see LOCAL FESTIVALS/CALENDAR OF EVENTS).

PARTICIPANT SPORTS

A large portion of O'ahu's visitors choose to take advantage of our near-perfect climate and involve themselves in outdoor recreations.

For those who've had too hefty a dose of our super-strength sunshine, or who simply prefer the shade, there are also numerous indoor recreations.

Addresses of rental and charter companies are listed at the back of this book in the APPENDIX Section.

Swimming

The most obvious outdoor activity available on a tropical island is swimming. Swimming was so much a part of the daily lives of ancient Hawaiians that it wasn't really classed as a sport. It was just something that everyone did every day (except during periods of *kapu*) as a matter of course. They did, though, greatly enjoy cavorting in the water, and were excellent swimmers.

Most of O'ahu's beaches accommodate swimmers, though some are fringed with shelves of rock and coral or have hazardous wave conditions. The island's beaches are described in the BEACHES section, with notations about conditions for swimming and other water activities. Many hotels also have swimming pools.

Snorkeling

For swimmers curious about submarine scenery, snorkeling provides excellent and easy access to the underwater world. Snorkels, masks and fins are available from all Waikīkī beachboy services (see Beachboys under BEACHES), from **Seaction** (946-6133) at the Hilton Hawaiian Village, and from **Naish Hawaii** (261-6067) in Kailua on the Windward side, as well as from any dive shop, listed below under Scuba Diving. **Captain Bob's** (926-5077) **Aloha Funway Rentals** (942-9696) in Waikīkī also rents snorkeling equipment (in addition to their unusual run of wheeled conveyances).

There are many excellent inshore snorkeling areas around O'ahu. The best is the undisturbed and protected reef community at Hanauma Bay, a

fishing and collecting coral is prohibited, and the inhabitants know it. They thrive in these waters and encourage the throng of visitors to their home to hand feed them—by their eager acceptance of such offerings. Other good snorkel- ing areas are denoted by the symbol ● in the BEACHES section of this book. Boat excursions to good snorkeling spots are described under Sailing below and under Water Tours in GETTING AROUND.

Scuba diving

For an even deeper look at O'ahu's undersea environment, take a tank dive. Certified divers may rent equipment and go out on their own, or may arrange a chartered excursion. Those unfamiliar with local conditions are encouraged to take an escort. Introductory classes are readily available for those seeking certification. Dives take place wherever conditions are best at the time; this generally means the North Shore in summer and the South Shore in winter, as this is the prevailing pattern of calm waters.

Depths range from ten to seventy feet with most areas falling into the middle of that spectrum.

In addition to the haven of **Hanauma Bay**, which is calm most of the time and is accessible from the shore as well as by boat, there are ten major dive spots around O'ahu. Off the North Shore, **Shark's Cove** affords the best and most popular cavern dives on the island, and the nearby **Three Tables** area offers caverns, ledges and large rocky formations; both these are accessible only from the shore and

Lemon butterfly fish contrast the deep blue Pacific Ocean.

diveable only during summer. Lava formations including caverns and arches are also the principal attraction at Leeward O'ahu's **Mākaha Caves,** accessible from either boat or shore, though the frequent presence in the area of large green sea turtles also draws many underwater wildlife enthusiasts. A sunken minesweeper named **Mahi** off Mā'ili Point, also on the Leeward coast, offers an interesting dive and lots of colorful marine life; it is accessible only by boat. A good site for beginners is **Rainbow Reef,** accessible by boat or from shore, off Ala Moana Park where lovely tropical sea creatures are fond of being hand-fed. Lava formations, small caverns, underwater canyons, a sunken barge and an abundance of beautiful fish, eels, turtles and crustaceans give the stretch of offshore waters from Diamond Head across Maunalua Bay the best concentration of fascinating diving on the island. Popularly known as **Hundred Foot Hole, Fantasy Reef,**

Kahala Barge, Big Eel Reef and **Turtle Canyon,** these dive spots are accessible only by boat. Dive rates usually include transportation to and from hotels in Waikīkī; the cost of equipment depends on what's required. **South Sea Aquatics** (538-3854) is the oldest dive shop in the State, and has one of the largest chartered dive boat on the island; they also run night dives a couple of nights a week. **Aloha Dive Shop** (395-5922) in Hawai'i Kai has also been around a long time, and is slightly less expensive. They also rent thirty-five millimeter underwater cameras. **Aaron's Dive Shop** on the Windward side (261-1211/235-3877) is well established and has a good reputation for finding the best diving conditions. **Steve's Diving Adventures** (947-8900) are experienced and inexpensive. Located on the North Shore, **Hale'iwa Surf 'n' Sea** (637-9887) runs scuba charters and offers a wide range of other water activities.

Making an appearance for a curious visitor.

'Scuba halo'.

Surfing

It is not surprising that Polynesians invented the sport of surfing, since these island-based people lived constantly within reach of the sea and its changing waves. While many other Polynesian groups enjoyed riding surf in their outrigger canoes, Hawaiians alone developed the art of riding boards specifically designed for play atop the rolling waves. In modern times, this ancient sport has been refined and extended beyond anything its inventors ever imagined and its popularity has spread around the globe, professional surfers demonstrating their skill and daring while vying for six-figure purses. The manufacture of surfing equipment and accessories has become a major industry. Several types of board surfing have also developed as well as, in recent years, the new variant: surf sailing or windsurfing. The areas of O'ahu best suited to these various types of surfing are noted in the BEACHES section.

Board surfing

Board surfing is the original. No one knows how long ago it developed, but Hawaiian petroglyphs dated to about the eighth or ninth century show people board surfing, and as early as the fifteenth century, Hawaiians had so refined the sport that contests between champions were held—for what even we would consider to be high stakes. Ancient Hawaiians gambled with unbridled enthusiasm at every possible opportunity, wagering their property, their wives, even their lives on the outcome of a single contest. Many famous surfing exploits were passed down through the voluminous oral history of these people. Their name

for what we call surfing was *he'enalu*, which can be loosely translated as 'wave sliding' but which, like everything else in the Hawaiian language, is rich with a range of subtlety and poetic nuance that says much more. The best surfing breaks were reserved for use by the ruling chiefs, and violators of this *kapu* could be punished by death.

Surfing, like all things Hawaiian, declined dramatically during the first century or so of European immigration to the Islands, but surfing—both on boards and in canoes—began to be promoted again in Hawai'i early this century with the establishment of the Outrigger Canoe Club and Hui Nalu, both of which are now focused on canoe paddling rather than surfing. Surfing's international fame began to spread with the demonstrations in Atlantic City and Australia that were given by surfing champion and Olympic gold medal swimmer Duke Kahanamoku.

The original boards were eighteen-foot, hundred and fifty pound monoliths, often made of koa. This began to change in the mid-1940s with the development of hollow boards and ones built of such lightweight materials as balsa and redwood, then fiberglass and synthetic foam. The evolution of surfboards has also seen a wide variety of lengths, widths and thicknesses, and these variations on the theme have been found to excel in varying conditions so that, today, top surfers keep collections of several boards from which to choose.

O'ahu has the most murderous and spectacular surfing conditions on Earth (see BEACHES), but it also has gentler waves for the novice.

(see Beachboys under BEACHES) rents surfboards and gives lessons, and these highly trained and experienced watermen can teach nearly anyone to surf—from tots to *tutus*. **Seaction** (946-6133) at the Hilton Hawaiian Village beach, also rents and gives lessons on surfboards as well as offering the same service for many types of water sports. **Local Motion** (955-7373) rents surfboards by the day, as does **Downing Hawaii** (737-9696), the latter charging substantially less. On the North Shore, **Hale'iwa Surf 'n' Sea** (637-9887) gives surfing lessons and rents all kinds of water sports equipment.

Paipo boarding

A paipo board is a 'bellyboard', and the term is a post-World War II corruption of the Hawaiian *paepo'o* (see Body Surfing below).

This type of wave-riding board is short and thin—three or four feet long and only a quarter to half-an-inch thick—either flat or with a slightly concave surface to fit the body. They are mostly homemade and mostly used by Hawaiians. Their use requires skill and they have been largely superseded in popularity by the now well-known 'Boogie® board'.

Gotcha Pro Surfing Competition, Sandy Beach.

Body surfing

Body surfing stems from the same principle as board riding except that the body replaces the board as the vehicle—a cross between surfing and swimming. The ancient Hawaiians called this activity *kaha nalu* or *pae* or *paepo'o*.

There are two basic techniques for accomplishing this feat: keeping the body straight with the arms pinned against the sides while riding the shoulder of the wave just ahead of the breaking water, and the alternative of keeping one or both arms straight out in front for greater maneuverability. The former technique seems to work

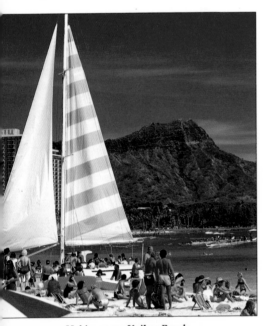

Hobies cover Kailua Beach.

best in offshore breaks such as those at Makapu'u Beach, while the latter seems best in the large, shallow shorebreaks of beaches such as Sandy. Most expert bodysurfers use both, sometimes while riding the

same wave.

Though purists decry it, virtually all body surfers also use fins to increase propulsion and enhance their ability to catch a wave.

Body boarding

Developed from the paipo board described above, the body board (commonly known by the original brand name, Boogie® board) was invented in Hawai'i in the early 1970s by Tom Morey, and is made of flexible foam. The 'boards' are a couple of feet wide, about four feet long and around three inches thick and, like their parent paipo, are ridden prone. The latest development along this line is a high performance body board—now termed 'turbo' board—that was invented by Russ Brown in 1983. Considered the Porsche of body boards, it is stiffer and faster than the standard model. These inexpensive water toys have become ubiquitous in Hawai'i.

Every Waikīkī beachboy service rents them, as do **Seaction** (946-6133) at the Hilton Hawaiian Village, **Naish Hawaii** (261-6067) in Kailua and **Haleiwa Surf 'n' Sea** (637-9887) on the North Shore.

Sand slidiing

This, too, is an ancient pastime that has been given a modern tool. The original idea was to throw oneself onto the sand at the precise moment when a receding wave had left just a thin sheet of water on which the body would then slide.

Precise timing was—and is—essential as too early a leap results in a mere sinking to the sand and

SPORTS & RECREATION

too late a leap in an abrupt, abrasive halt. Bare-body sand sliding is seldom seen anymore, but paipo boards and the more recent body boards are also used in this fashion. Nowadays the hot trend is the 'skimboard', a short foam 'board' about three quarters of an inch thick that is thrown onto the receding wave then jumped upon. Skilled standing riders have developed some fancy skateboard-like maneuvers on this type of board, and contests have been held at Sandy Beach and Waimea Bay. It can also be ridden as a 'bellyboard' in waves.

Windsurfing

The most innovative modern variation of the ancient sport of surfing was its hybridization with sailing, conceived in 1970 by Californian Hoyle Schweitzer and executed by his friend Jim Drake. The popularity of this new sport spread like wildfire, and a circuit of amateur and professional contests is already well established. Windsurfing championships held for years on O'ahu have recently been canceled due to the Pro World Tour that has lured away all the big-money prize winners. Waikīkī is not really a good place to windsurf—though a lot of people do it there for convenience—because of the prevailing offshore winds and choppy water conditions. If you're expert, Diamond Head and the North Shore afford the most challenging wave jumping. Otherwise Kailua Bay, on the Windward coast, is O'ahu's best windsurfing spot because its waters are protected by a fringing reef, and the prevailing northeast trade winds blow fairly steadily onshore (see BEACHES). These conditions also make it one of the easiest places to

Windsurfing at Mokulē'ia on the North Shore.

sailboards also give lessons.

Topping the list for having been around the longest, Kailua's **Windsurfing Hawaii** (261-3539) runs a professional operation. Rates for standard equipment are quite modest and custom equipment costs only slightly more; instruction is reasonably priced. Another established company, **Kailua Sailboard Company** (262-2555) offers beginner lessons as classes—one on land and two at sea—and as private instruction. **Aloha**

Windsurfing (926-1185) in Waikīkī has also been around awhile and their beginner lessons, held at Kailua, cost slightly more. They also charge per maneuver for coaching experienced windsurfers. **Naish Hawaii** (261-6067) also rents custom and stock boards at reasonable rates and gives lessons as classes or as private instruction. **Haleiwa Surf 'n' Sea** (637-9887) rents sailboards and gives lessons.

Canoe surfing

Waikīkī is, at present, the only place in the world where visitors can take an outrigger canoe ride. Locals engage in canoe paddling races elsewhere, but canoe surfing is different and Waikīkī is an ideal place to do it. Most beachboy services offer outrigger canoe rides (see Beachboys under BEACHES),

and those that don't can steer you in the right direction. This is an exhilarating experience that no one should miss. Prices vary greatly, so shop around. A number of fun races in the Waikīkī surf—usually fundraisers—are held throughout the year by various canoe clubs and other organizations.

Kayaking

This ancient Eskimo pastime translates well to the tropics and has become very popular in

Hawai'i. In addition to the waters around Waikīkī, two of O'ahu's most scenic bays, Kailua and

Kayaking through rough waters near Koko Head.

Kāne'ohe, are frequented by the regulars.

Seaction (946-6133), on the beach at the Hilton Hawaiian Village, rents kayaks and provides instruction for beginners. **Adventure Kayaking International** (924-8898) runs two-hour adventures off Diamond Head and Waikīkī, including sunset and moonlight trips by arrangement, and two different daily Kahana Bay trips—one from Ka'a'awa to Kahana Bay and the other from Kahana Bay to Punalu'u—both traveling up Kahana Stream, which is gorgeous. These moderately priced trips are each four hours long and include lunch. Adventure also runs trips on a charter basis along the North Shore in summer and the South Shore in winter, as well as overnight expeditions to the outer islands. They use West German Metzeler Riverstar kayaks, 'the Cadillac of inflatable kayaks'. **Bob Twogood Kayaks Hawaii** (262-5656) rents tri-ski kayaks for a day or a half day, and gives free introductory lessons in Kāne'ohe Bay that last an hour. They also conduct weekly clinics. **Tropical Kayaking Hawaii** (293-5339) and **Adventure Kayaking International** (924-8898) also rent kayaks.

Wave skis/surf skis

A modern cross between a surfboard and a kayak, the wave ski has indentations for derriere and heels and is both powered and steered by the rider wielding a double-bladed paddle.

Wave skis can be rented from **Seaction** (946-6133) at the Hilton Hawaiian Village beach. **Naish Hawaii** (261-6067) in Kailua also rents wave skis. Surf skis are similar but longer and less stable, and they are steered by foot pedals connected to a rudder; they too are driven with a hand-held, double-bladed paddle. Both surf skis and wave skis can be rented from **Downing Hawaii** (737-9696).

Sailing

Hawaiian waters offer exquisite sailing, on whichever scale you choose—from fourteen-foot catamarans to sixty-foot yachts. Small boats, such as Hobies, are available for anywhere from half an hour to all day. A good place for this service, and for lessons if you're new to the sport, is **Seaction** (946-6133), conveniently located on the beach in front of the Hilton Hawaiian Village. **Aloha Windsurfing** (926-1185) in Waikīkī also rents catamarans. All of the Beachboy services in Waikīkī offer catamaran rides (see BEACHES). **Kailua Sailboard Company** (262-2555) on the Windward side also rents catamarans. **Aikane Catamaran Cruises** (522-1533) offers a three-hour midday snorkeling excursion (Tu-W-Th) off Waikīkī aboard their hundred-foot, double-hulled vessels, which includes either live or recorded music and lunch as well as snorkeling equipment, and leaves from Kewalo Basin at 11:30am. **Paradise Cruises'** (536-3641) inexpensive two-and-three-quarter-hour 'Sailing Hawaii' tour departs twice daily from Ke'ehi Lagoon and includes transportation from

SPORTS & RECREATION

104

Waikīkī, heavy snacks, open bar, and snorkeling and swimming off Waikīkī, equipment provided.

Twice daily, **Tradewinds Sailing Charters** (533-0220 or 533-7734) offers half-day sailing/snorkeling excursions, leaving from Ke'ehi Lagoon and sailing to Diamond Head, stopping on the way back for frolicking with the friendly fish off Magic Island and Ala Moana; snacks, beverages and equipment are included in the moderate price. The friendly and helpful Tradewinds crews encourage hands-on participation by passengers in the sailing of the vessel as well as in snorkeling. They also offer a three-hour sunset sail from Ke'ehi at 5pm daily, limited to six passenger/crew and including ample *pupus* and champagne. This excellent estab-

lishment also offers numerous other hands-on sailing excursions by arrangement; for details see Charters under GETTING AROUND.

To participate in a four-hour sail on a forty-three- or fifty-four-foot yacht from Ke'ehi Lagoon, contact **Honolulu Sailing Company** (235-8264). Their excursions are un-crowded, include full snorkeling equipment and, for a small additional charge, lunch, with an open bar; transportation from Waikīkī is included in the moderate cost.

If you prefer to be pampered while afloat—even chauffered to your yacht in a Rolls Royce—see Water Tours under GETTING AROUND.

Kenwood Cup Yacht Race, summertime.

Waterskiing

The most popular areas around the island for waterskiing are Ke'ehi Lagoon, Maunalua Bay and Kāne'ohe Bay. **Jet Ski Hawaii** (943-8938) rents water ski equipment and conducts waterski outings.

Water cycles

These large, colorful, pedal-driven craft come in a couple of styles: the flat-bottomed, paddle-wheel-driven pedalboats, and the fantastic aqua-cycle which looks like an overgrown tricycle or a tractor gone wrong and is propelled by fins on its huge, brightly colored tires catching the water as they turn.

Both are popular with Waikīkī beach goers. They can be rented by the half hour or hour from **Seaction** (946-6133) at the Hilton Hawaiian Village beach; pedalboats are also available to hotel guests from the beach service concession at the Kahala Hilton.

Jetskis

Aloha Ocean Sports (396-4899) and **Tradewinds** (973-0311) rent jetskiis–mostly in Maunalua Bay.

At Waikīkī, every beachboy service can rent or provide information on renting jet skis.

Parasailing

All Waikīkī beachboy services offer parasailing or can lead interested persons to parasailing trips. **Sea Breeze Parasailing** (396-0100) provides free Waikiki pick up and return, as does **Aloha Parasail** (521-2446).

All offer comparable rates for this not inexpensive joy ride.

Hang gliding

The thousand-foot cliffs above Makapu'u Beach are a prime takeoff point for expert hang gliders, who come from all over the world for a Hawaiian high, sometimes reaching a two thousand-foot cloud base. Championship winner Mike Benson of **Tradewinds Hang Gliding** (396-8557) has been instructing daredevils for over ten years and, for a substantial fee, will take you for a one hour flight on his tandem hang glider. The photo opportunities are unbeatable. Tradewinds stresses this as a full instructional lesson; they are very professional and very careful.

This sport is highly dependent on the tradewinds, the gustiest of which are present in the spring.

SPORTS & RECREATION

106

Gliding

The only glider-plane rides are available at **Dillingham Field** (677-3404) in Mokulē'ia, which operates a regular flight schedule: 10am to 5pm daily. The short flights are a little expensive, but sensational. Customers are taken up on a first come, first served basis.

Tennis

Tennis has long been a staple sport in Honolulu and continues to gain popularity, especially amongst the Japanese community. Convenient public courts can be found at **Ala Moana Park** (10), **Diamond Head Tennis Center** (9), including one paddle tennis court, **Kapi'olani Park** (4) and, a little farther away, **Koko Head** (6). Reservations are not available at these courts; players simply wait their turn. **Honolulu Tennis Club** (4) (944-9696), on top of Pay & Save, has reasonable rates that include transportation from Waikīkī, and can provide equipment to people who haven't brought their own. Hotels in Waikiki that have courts and allow non-guests for a modest fee are **Hawaiian Regent** (1) (922-6611), **Ilikai at Waikiki Beach** (6) (949-3811) and **Pacific Beach Hotel** (2) (922-1233). On the North Shore, the **Turtle Bay Hilton** (10) (293-8811) offers similar rates for non-guest use of their courts.

Racquetball

Racquetball is available for out-of-town enthusiasts at the **Gold's Gym** (973-4653) and at the **Hono**– **lulu Tennis Club** (944-9696). Each charge by the court/hour.

Volleyball

A great seaside pastime is beach volleyball. There is a net at **Fort DeRussy Beach** where anyone with a volleyball can play here. One major professional tournament takes place there during the summer drawing all the hot Southern California players.

Bowling

Going rates at Honolulu bowling alleys are fairly inexpensive. **Stadium Bowl-O-Drome** (949-6668) in Mō'ili'ili near Waikīkī is a nostalgic setting and a good place to go for a change of pace. **Waialae** **Bowl** (734-0293) in the suburbs *mauka* of Diamond Head and **Kapiolani Bowl** (536-7741), opposite the Neal Blaisdell Arena, are heavily used by local leagues.

Skating

Ice skating is a good way to cool off after a day in the hot tropical sun. **Ice Palace** (487-9921), near Aloha Stadium and Castle Park, is open during the day as well as in the evening. Hours vary slightly on different days (daily 9am-9:30pm); classes are held in the late afternoons on some days. A disc jockey spins records while you skate, and a few fun competitions are held during the evening. There are, at present, no roller skating rinks on O'ahu.

Skateboarding is extremely popular, and if you have your own board, you can enjoy the arena at 'A'ala Park (see Parks and Gardens under SIGHTSEEING).

Golf

O'ahu has more than two dozen golf courses and, as golf is a favored sport among the locals, most are crowded. **Ala Wai Golf Course** (296-4653), an easy course near Waikīkī, is especially crowded due to its popularity with both locals and tourists, who often come down and wait hours to get on the course. Tee times are booked a week in advance and the very low rates are slightly higher on weekends and holidays. **Hawaii Kai Golf Course** (395-2358) has two eighteen-hole courses that are often windy and difficult and their rates, which include a golf cart, are much higher. **Olomana Golf**

Links (259-7926) in Waimānalo costs slightly less. At the **Pali Golf Course** (261-7254) between Kailua and Kāne'ohe on O'ahu's Windward side, they strongly urge players to 'get a starting time', thus avoiding the standard wait of about three hours; their rates are very low. **Bay View Golf Center** (247-0451) has closed in order to enlarge the course, but will reopen in 1992. **Kahuku Golf Course** (293-5842), on the North Shore, is very low key, open Monday through Friday, and has the cheapest rates in town for nine holes, which is all they have; you must bring your own equip-

107

Hang gliding above Makapu'u.

ment. The **Turtle Bay Country Club** (293-8811), at the Turtle Bay Hilton on the North Shore, is a tough course with moderately high rates. **Mililani Golf Club** (623-2254) in central O'ahu, has the same rates. **Hawaii Country Club** (621-5654), near 'Ewa, is a short course with inexpensive rates. **Sheraton Makaha** (695-9511), on O'ahu's Leeward side is a long, tough and expensive course. The adjacent course at **Makaha Valley Country Club** (695-7111) is shorter and easier

and costs about a third as much. The **Ted Makalena Golf Course** (296-7888), in the Pearl City area, is inexpensive. **Pearl Country Club** (487-3802) in 'Aiea is a hard, hilly course, with moderately high fees. **Moanalua Golf Club** (839-2411) in the Moanalua Valley above Pearl Harbor, with nine holes, has moderate green fees during the week that nearly double on weekends. There is a driving range at **Kapi'olani Park**.

Hunting

O'ahu has a lot of wilderness land where hunting is permitted, the most common quarry being feral pigs and goats, which are prolific and are open game year-round. Pheasants, doves and francolin can be hunted on weekends and state holidays only from November through the third week in January.

Maps of public hunting areas are available from the Division of

Forestry and Wildlife (548-8850). All hunting requires a valid State of Hawai'i Hunting License; non-resident hunting licenses cost fifteen dollars and may be purchased from license agents at sporting goods stores or from the Division of Conservation and Resources Enforcement (548-8766). For more information, contact one of these two state agencies.

Fishing

Licenses are required for fresh-water fishing but not for recreational ocean fishing. Non-resident licenses are seven dollars and fifty cents and may be obtained at any major sporting goods store or the Division of Conservation and Resources Enforcement office (548-8766). The season is open year-round for most fish.

There are only two locations on O'ahu for public freshwater fish-ing—Wahiawā and Nu'uanu. Catches could include channel and Chinese catfish and tilapia.

Shore fishing is popular at Ala Moana, Waikīkī, Sandy Beach, Waimānalo Beach, Kāne'ohe Bay,

Waimea Bay, 'Ewa Beach and Pōka'ī Bay.

Deep sea fishing lures a lot of enthusiasts to Hawaiian waters to catch *mahi mahi* [dolphinfish], *ono* [wahoo], *'ahi* and *aku* [yellowfin and skipjack tuna] and, if lucky, *a'u* [marlin]. Most sport fishing trollers moor at Kewalo Basin, opposite Ward Warehouse. **Kono Charters, Ltd.** (329-3600) charges high prices for use of their gyro-stabilized boat, *Kono*, but prices for their other boats are competitive. **Coreene-C Sport Fishing Charters** (536-7472) has had many celebrity passengers including Michael Landon and Sylvester Stallone. Their rates compare with everybody else's. **Island Charters** (536-1555) have also been reeling them in for a long time. **Tradewinds Sailing Charters** (533-0220, 533-7734) are manned by an experienced and able deep sea fishing crew, and offer half-, three-quarter- and full-day excursions daily from Kewalo Basin aboard their thirty-five-foot *Bertram*, taking out no more than six fishermen at a time. Other well-known boats worth looking into are *Maggie Joe* (533-3330), *Kamome* (536-5931) and *Lynell* (521-8494). Reservations should be made in advance for these excursions; most trips are eight hours. Aficionados know this is not an inexpensive pastime. Most operators let you keep at least some of the fish caught, and it's customary to tip the skipper and mate, especially if the catch is good.

Hiking

O'ahu is a hiker's delight. Despite this island's 'most populous' status, and despite the millions of visitors who throng here annually, much of the landscape remains in a natural state and far from the madding crowd. While the Wai'anae Range of mountains is mostly cordoned off by the military and thus inaccessible, much of the Ko'olau Range can be explored on foot, offering unparalleled views, many types of tropical vegetation, streams, waterfalls and swimming holes and, above all, exquisite isolation.

There are long trails and short trails, easy trails and difficult—something to suit almost anyone—and many of the best are on the fringe of our most urban areas.

There are several publications devoted to or including specific details about hiking trails (see RECOMMENDED READING) and a number of local organizations that regularly schedule group hiking activities. These groups welcome visitors to join their excursions, and are happy to

Diamond Head Crater Trail.

provide tips for enhancing both the pleasure and the safety of individual hiking adventures. You may write in advance or telephone after arrival in O'ahu.

The **Sierra Club, Hawai'i Chapter** (538-6616) will, for three dollars, send an information packet

SPORTS & RECREATION

110

describing state trails and trip planning information. The **Hawaii Trail and Mountain Club** is also helpful in providing information for hikers. The **Hawaii Geographic Society** offers books, maps and other publications and requests written inquiries from Hawai'i-bound hikers as their information center (538-3952) does not have regular hours; you may also leave messages on their answering machine. They conduct archaeological tours in Nu'uanu Valley, Mākaha Valley and the North Shore. Their urban 'sociological' tours are listed under GETTING AROUND. The Hawai'i State Department of Land and Natural Resources, Division of Forestry (548-8850) has free trail maps of O'ahu.

O'ahu's most accessible trails include the following. The (.7-mile) trail to the top of **Diamond Head Crater**, undoubtedly the best-known landmark on the island, starts from inside the crater where there is a convenient parking lot (open 6am-6pm). This easy hike is mostly a stroll, taking 30-45 minutes. There are some steep steps to climb, and a couple of dark tunnels; use of a flashlight is recommended. The route leads to a spectacular panorama. Telephone State Parks at 548-7456 for further information.

A little farther from Waikīkī is **Koko Head**; the short hike (1 mile) from Kalaniana'ole Highway to the summit leads to fabulous views of Hanauma Bay and across the Kaiwi Channel to the islands of Lāna'i and Moloka'i. The road directly opposite, on the *mauka* side of Kalaniana'ole Highway, leads to **Koko Crater**, offering a (1 mile) hardy climb to the thousand-foot-

high rim for a great 360° panorama.

Above the Windward coast towns of Kailua and Kāne'ohe, the large nature reserve and botanic garden at Ho'omaluhia offer a number of fascinating hikes of varying lengths, with or without guides (see Parks and Gardens under SIGHTSEEING).

Hiking the trails (4.5 miles) in the beautiful **Kahana Valley** (see Parks and Gardens under SIGHTSEEING), farther up the Windward coast, requires permission from the Division of State Parks (548-7455). This valley has provided important archaeologcal information about the lives of ancient Hawaiians, and their descendants still living in this valley practice much of the same agriculture as did their ancestors. Above Kahana Valley, the steep and difficult (.8-mile) climb to the summit of **Pu'u Piei** rewards the intrepid with magnificent views of Kahana Bay and the coast.

Nearby **Kaluanui Valley**, important in legend as the birthplace of the pig-god Kamapua'a, is now better known as the location of **Sacred Falls**, called Kaliuwa'a by the ancients (see Parks and Gardens under SIGHTSEEING). The hardy (2.2-mile) hike up this valley runs alongside the stream and is subject to falling rocks and to dangerous flash flooding when heavy rains fall in the mountains above. Lives have been lost here, so check on the *mauka* weather, even if it's a sunny day at the shore. Despite its hazards this is one of the island's most popular hiking trails.

Just *mauka* of the beach at **Hau'ula** are three trails popular with locals, though few tourists visit the area. One trail goes (3 miles) up Ma'akua Gulch and, for part of the way is *in* Kaipapa'u Stream, so

Dusk falls upon the Mokulua Islands, Lanikai Beach.

trekkers here must get wet. The (2.5-mile) trail to the south of this requires clambering over and through some *hau*-tree tangles as it explores adjacent Papali Gulch and Stream; the (2.5-mile) trail to the north climbs a ridge and leads to a sweeping view toward the Ko'olau Mountains over Kaipapa'u Valley, and the Hau'ula coastline.

Behind the Mormon Temple and the Polynesian Cultural Center at Lā'ie is a tough (2-mile) trail through **Kahawainui Gulch and Stream** that climbs to an elevation of well over two thousand feet and leads to extraordinary panoramic views over O'ahu's North Shore. Permission for this hike is required from Zions Securities (293-9201).

There are excellent hiking trails in the **Waimea Valley**, a private park which charges admission (see Parks and Gardens under SIGHT-SEEING).

The highest peak on O'ahu, **Mt Ka'ala** (4020 feet), is in the Wai'anae Mountain Range and the (4-mile) hike to it, traversing Kaupakuhale Ridge, is the most difficult and dangerous on the island. This trek requires a sure foot and a stout heart, and permission to undertake it requires both a hiking permit from the Division of Forestry (548-2861) and a liability waiver from the Waialua Sugar Company (637-4436), whose land must be crossed to reach the Dupont Trail. The summit is capped by the white dome of satellite radar installations.

Ka'ena Point, the westernmost tip of O'ahu, can be reached only by hiking, and is accessible from either side. From the North Shore, drive as far as you dare past Mokulē'ia then proceed on foot. To approach from the Leeward side, drive to the end of the road, just past Yokohama Bay, and walk from there. The (2-mile) trail is hot and dusty, and well worth the effort (see BEACHES and Historic Sites and Buildings under SIGHTSEEING).

For a rough, wet hike (3 miles) into the lovely **Poamoho Valley** (there is no trail) following the streambed, permits are required from both the Division of Forestry (548-2861) and the US Army (Range Control Schofield Barracks 655-0033). From this valley, you can ascend to the trail along **Poamoho Ridge**. Access is from Whitmore Avenue, just north of Wahiawā, on the island's central Leilehua Plateau.

To reach the crest of the Ko'olaus above Kahana Valley for a fabulous vista eastward, you can take a strenuous (4-mile) trek along a trail that begins off California Avenue, just south of Wahiawā; again, permits must be obtained from both the Division of Forestry and the Army (see Poamoho above). The trail follows the ridge between the north and south forks of **Kaukonahua** Stream through lush stands of native plants, and a side trail on the north leads via a steep descent to good swimming holes.

The long (7.1 miles) and difficult hike up the Ridge above Waimano Stream begins at the end of Waimano Home Road, above Pearl City, and leads past exceedingly beautiful views of the Waimano Valley to the north and the Waiau Valley to the south and terminates at the summit (2200 feet) overlooking the Waihe'e Valley to the east. The native flora in this area is superb, and the trail offers, at several points, access to refreshing swimming holes.

The hardy (4.8 miles) hike that begins above Keaīwa Heiau (see Sacred Sites under SIGHTSEEING) at the end of 'Aiea Heights Drive follows the **'Aiea Loop Trail**, climbing a ridge for good views of the adjacent Hālawa Valley then descending to and crossing 'Aiea Stream. This trail also passes the 1943 crash site of a C-47 cargo plane.

A delightful little (.5-mile) stroll into the past can be had by walking down the segment of **Old Pali Road** that leads off to the right from the Nu'uanu Pali Lookout (see Historic Sites and Buildings under SIGHT-SEEING). Construction of the new road destroyed part of the old road, so you must retrace your steps uphill.

The short (1.3-mile) loop hike across Nu'uanu Stream and around the delightful **Jackass Ginger Pool**, is reached from Nu'uanu Pali Drive, just above Honolulu. Stop just before the bridge marked '1931'. Those so inclined can indulge in the ancient Hawaiian sport of mudsliding here—a favorite pastime of the *ali'i*—either by using the traditional ti-leaf toboggan or by bringing along a plastic sheet.

Behind and above Punchbowl crater is the knoll called **Round Top**, and above that, the summit called **Tantalus**. There are a dozen trails all over these hillsides—many of them interconnecting—affording pleasurable hiking conditions to suit almost any preference. Several of these trails can be trod in sequence to create an excursion tailor-made for your requirements, including the option of taking the (1.4-mile) **'Aihualama Trail** to Mānoa Falls in the valley below.

An easy and pleasant hike is the (.8-mile) trail from the end of Mānoa Road, just past Lyon Arboretum (see Parks and Gardens under SIGHTSEEING) up **Mānoa Stream** to **Mānoa Falls**. This trail traverses lush rainforest, and the stream offers several natural pools where swimming is permitted. A popular excursion begins here and ascends

Mount Ka'ala in the Wai'anae Mountain Range rises 4020 feet above sea level.

'Aihualama Trail to Pauoa Flats on Tantalus then down several trails to the end of Makiki Heights Drive in **Makiki Valley.**

Overlooking Mānoa Valley from the other side is the lookout from **Wa'ahila Ridge** (see Parks and Gardens under SIGHTSEEING), reached from the end of Ruth Place atop St Louis Heights. The trail affords a hardy (2-mile) hike with splendid views, but it is illegal to hike from here to the crest of the Ko'olaus as the trail traverses the Honolulu Forest Watershed; you can descend here into the Mānoa Valley via a steep trail that emerges at the end of Alani Drive.

Access to the crest is legal from the next ridge over, **Mau'umae Ridge**, on the opposite side of Pālolo Valley and reached from the summit of Maunalani Heights (atop Wilhelmina Rise). This trail skirts Ka'au Crater, which lies at the foot of the Ko'olaus, and leads to a summit called **Pu'u Lanipō** (2621 feet) that affords breathtaking views over Kailua and Waimānalo. This trek (3 miles) is strenuous and, in places, steep, muddy and wet, requiring some agility from the hiker.

The parallel hike (3 miles) along **Wiliwilinui Ridge,** flanked by Wai'alae Nui Gulch and Kapakahi Gulch is less arduous for most of the way but also less appealing as it follows an old vehicular track; the last half-mile of the trail is often wet and muddy. This leads to the other side of **Pu'u Lanipo** and affords a stunning view of eastern O'ahu from Kualoa to Waimānalo.

In the interest of safety, hikers are urged to seek further information on trails that appeal to them from one of the organizations listed above or from more specific hiking books (see RECOMMENDED READING). O'ahu's hiking areas are beautiful and unspoiled; most of them are pristine. If you carried it in, carry it out.

Physical Fitness

Physical fitness is a trend that has become, for large numbers of people, a way of life. Honolulu residents have ample opportunity to keep fit, and visitors are welcome to join in the many health-promoting activities popular here, both indoors and out. Jogging and running, yoga, aerobics and fully equipped gyms are everywhere to be found, and Honolulu hosts a number of regular competitive and fund-raising events such as triathlons, biathlons, marathons, walkathons, fun runs and more (see LOCAL FESTIVALS/CALENDAR OF EVENTS).

Gyms and aerobics

Most Honolulu gyms offer special arrangements and rates for out-of-town guests. **Gold's Gym** (973-4653) on Kapi'olani Blvd. charges a guest fee & offers the most complete fitness facility available to visitors. In Waikiki, the **World Gym Waikiki** (942-8171) has many facilities, charges a moderate drop-in fee, and is open twenty-four hours a day. **Clark Hatch Physical Fitness Center** (536-7205), downtown, charges even less. **Marina Athletic** (395-4244) charges about the same as the downtown gym, and **Spa Health & Fitness Center** (949-0026) charges the same guest fee as International. All are fully equipped and all except World offer aerobics classes. Except for locker rooms, facilities are shared by men and women. **The Honolulu Club** (543-3900) is not *just* a fitness center, but a private club with amenities that include, among other things, racquetball and squash courts, therapeutic massage and fine dining. Their non-resident memberships, for the frequent or long-term visitor to O'ahu, afford these benefits and more.

Jogging and running

This is a very popular regimen—almost a pastime—amongst Honolulu's many fitness-minded residents, an almost unending procession of whom can be seen hurrying along such byways as Kapi'olani Park, Ala Moana Park and the Ala Wai Canal, especially in the early morning and late afternoon 'rush hours'. If you feel inclined to join them, just fall in step.

If you're indefatigable, try the ten-kilometer run around Diamond Head—just follow the road.

For the competitive of spirit, there are about a hundred running events in Honolulu every year, including the well-known Honolulu Marathon (see LOCAL FESTIVALS/ CALENDAR OF EVENTS). These are listed in a calendar of events published by the City and County Department of Parks and Recreation's Advisory Board for Jogging and Long Distance Running (650 South King Street Honolulu 96813 486-3310).

The calendar also lists sponsors and contacts for further information and entry forms.

The Great Aloha Run takes place in February.

Yoga

Whether you're new to yoga and just feel like doing something unusual for yourself during an extended holiday, or are an ardent practitioner of the art, you are welcome to join the classes at the **Silent Dance Center** (941-8461) in Mō'ili'ili.

All the Center's instructors are trained in the Iyengar method of teaching Hatha Yoga, and some hold senior teaching certificates from the Iyengar Institute in India. Classes are available for beginners and for experienced students. Telephone for details and class times.

Kite flying

Kite flying was a sport popular with the ancient Hawaiians. Their kites were made of tapa or finely woven sail matting, and were six or seven feet wide and up to fifteen feet long. Sandy Beach Park, Kapi'olani Park and the long, open beaches on the Windward coast are terrific and popular places for flying kites. If you didn't bring yours and want to join the fun, stop into a kite shop such as **Kite Fantasy**, conveniently located near Waikīkī, at the New Otani Kaimana Beach Hotel, opposite Kapi'olani Park. You won't find an ancient Hawaiian model, but there are some fabulous modern creations around, mostly in brightly colored nylon. The shapes are amazing and these things really fly. Free lessons are available, even pre-purchase test flights.

This is also very pleasant as a spectator sport. Your friendly neighborhood kite merchant can tell you where and when demonstrations and contests are being held, in case you want to lie back on a beach mat and gaze at the sky while other people do the legwork.

SPECTATOR SPORTS

There's always some sporting event during the various seasons of the year. Hawaiian outrigger canoe races take place primarily during spring, summer and early autumn, though there are a few special events outside the normal racing season. Summer sailing races occur annually and semi-annually. Hobie cat races take place throughout the year. There are many types of ball games in various seasons including the Hula Bowl and Pro Bowl football games at Aloha Stadium, the Aloha Basketball Classic at Blaisdell Arena as well as a full schedule of collegiate events. Tournaments are plentiful from tennis to golf—for example, the Hawaiian Open. Polo season runs throughout the summer at Mokulē'ia on O'ahu's North Shore. Some of the world's top surfing contests are held on various parts of O'ahu's coastline at different seasons, the most spectacular being those braving the mountainous North Shore winter waves (see BEACHES).

For details of sporting and other events, see LOCAL FESTIVALS/ CALENDAR OF EVENTS.

ENTERTAINMENT

O'ahu's nightlife
Lu'au
Local musicians
Calendar of events

ENTERTAINMENT and NIGHTLIFE

Entertainment and nightlife are, for an overwhelming majority of visitors, as much a part of a holiday on O'ahu as are the ocean, the beaches and the palm-shaded sun worshippers. A Polynesian show or a *lu'au* is on almost every first-time visitor's agenda, and most seek out Hawaiian music, knowing they're not likely to find it anywhere else. But there's also plenty of international fare, sometimes with a local flair.

The biggest stars in the entertainment business like to come here, too, and they often append their Hawaiian holidays to concert engagements. Local entertainers are adept at the wide variety of musical styles popular in the world today, and there are plenty of venues affording them opportunities to display their talents. Music, dance and comedy abound.

Nor are the classics forgotten; theatre, opera, ballet, symphony and chamber music are offered in regular seasons by local repertory compa-

nies, and visiting classical artists come to Honolulu on tour. There are also frequent performances of various ethnic music and dance from the traditions of Hawai'i's many immigrant groups.

There are sedate dinners, elegant lounges, rowdy crowds, club-dancing and just plain drinking. O'ahu has it all and Waikīkī is the entertainment center of the island.

This section outlines the entertainment scene generally. Specifics change often, and details are available from free tourist publications (many listing only advertisers) and from local newspapers, magazines and radio stations. Reliable sources include the calendar of events in the Entertainment Section of the *Honolulu Advertiser*, the *Honolulu Star-Bulletin*'s Weekend Pass, the Club Guide in 98 Rock's *The Beat* magazine, *Honolulu* magazine's Calendar of Events section, and radio station KRTR's Island Life Report (96.3 FM).

POLYNESIAN SHOWS

The 'Polynesian Show' has become virtually *de rigueur* tourist entertainment on nearly every island in the Pacific Ocean, Polynesian or not. These shows stage performances based on the traditional music, dance and costumes of Hawai'i, Tahiti, Sāmoa, New Zealand and, occasionally, Tonga and the Cook Islands; sometimes, primarily Melanesian Fiji is also included. They are glitzy, show-biz interpretations, and the Tahitian *tamure* invariably highlights the evening with its fast-paced hip-

swiveling, grass skirts, tall head-dresses and wildly beating drums. Another show-stopper is the Samoan fire dance or its close kin, the knife dance. Hawaiian *hula* is usually the *'auana*, or modern, variety, though some shows include a traditional *'ōlapa* or *kahiko* hula as well. The Maori (New Zealand) contributions are always a *poi* dance (*poi* in Maori are the white balls on string that the women manipulate so expertly in some of their dances), and the fierce *haka* where men challenge each other (and their audience) with spears and protruding tongues.

The biggest and best known of these shows is the dazzling extravaganza at the **Polynesian Cultural Center** in Lā'ie (see Popular Attractions under SIGHTSEEING). **Kalo's South Seas Revue** at the Ala Moana Americana Hotel's Hula Hut and **Tihati's** at the Ainahau showroom

The Polynesian Cultural Center's spectacular evening revue.

ENTERTAINMENT

120

showroom at the Princess Kaiulani Hotel present a similar program on a smaller scale, twice nightly.

An all-Hawaiian show is included in the entertainment three nights a week at **Sea Life Park** (see Popular Attractions under SIGHT-SEEING). Most dinner shows include a variety of Polynesian dance numbers as part of a more diverse program (see Dinner Shows below).

LU'AU

The most famous feast on your entertainment menu is undoubtedly the lu'au. This Polynesian custom resembles the American Thanksgiving feast, except that the lu'au can be given at any time, for any reason. One good, traditional reason for a lu'au is to honor and entertain visitors, so your attendance at one is entirely appropriate. The feast is named after the taro tops [*lu'au*] that are always served at one. Usually cooked with coconut cream, they are delectably delicious and unreservedly recommended. Other traditional fare on such occasions includes dishes like *laulau*, small packages of fish, pork, chicken or beef, often with taro tops, wrapped in ti or banana leaves and baked; *poi*, a thick, purplish paste made from the cooked and pounded base of the taro plant (the staple starch food of the Hawaiians); *kālua* pig, traditionally cooked in an underground oven [*imu*]; and *haupia*, thick, creamy coconut pudding. The introduction of European and Asian foods to Hawai'i has added great variety to the culinary concoctions that are now traditional at a lu'au. There is so much to choose from that the lu'au can please the palate of almost everyone.

Though the focus of this feast is food, lu'aus include a host of entertainments to feast the eye and ear as well. Music, dance, and usually a bit of comedy enhance the festive atmosphere and add to the fun. They are staged on a grand scale.

Chuck Machado's Luaus (836-0249), held on Friday, Sunday and Tuesday evenings beside the pool at the Outrigger Hotel, are the least expensive, and include an open bar, the full feast and a Polynesian show, the whole lasting about two hours. In the event of heavy rain, the lu'au may be canceled. The **Royal Hawaiian Luau** (923-7311), on Mondays only and at twice the price, is a longer and more elaborate affair, lasting around three and a half hours. Starting with a mai-tai reception and get-together on the ocean lawn, enlivened by Samoan fire and knife dances, it moves inside to a sit-down dinner in the Monarch Room where an unlimited feast of traditional foods is followed by a Polynesian show, starring local celebrities Marlene Sai and Brickwood Galuteria. Mostly Hawaiian with a bit of Tahiti and New Zealand, the show is, at the time of this writing, the slickest and best of its type in town.

Midway between these pricewise is the **Paradise Cove Luau** (945-3539), which offers far more than either, but is much farther away. Buses transport visitors from Waikīkī to the beachfront Campbell Estate, past 'Ewa—about a thirty-five minute drive. On arrival, guests are treated to demonstrations of ancient Hawaiian games and sports, and are invited to try their hand. Crafts are also demonstrated, and such ancient skills as coconut-tree-climbing, which guests are discouraged from attempting. The fun and games are followed by a *hukilau* [seine net fishing party], which guests may watch or join, then the full feast. A Polynesian show is presented on a triple stage, positioned so that everyone has excellent views of the dancers. This excursion lasts five and a half to six hours, including the drive. The lu'au is held every night, and vast tents are available in case of rain.

Germaine's Luaus (941-3338) are held every night on the beach at the nearby Campbell Industrial Park, for about the same price, and include bus transportation, unlimited food and drink, and a Polynesian show, all lasting around four hours; in the event of rain, this lu'au is canceled. Chuck Machado's is the most intimate, usually serving around two hundred guests at a time; the Royal Hawaiian serves four to five hundred, Germaine's several hundred, and Paradise Cove sometimes a thousand or more.

Reservations at least a day in advance are preferred for most lu'au.

DINNER SHOWS

Not all dinner shows are 'Polynesian shows', though all have some Polynesian content and a distinctive 'Island' touch. All have a late, after-dinner 'cocktail' seating, which is significantly less expensive, and a few have a second show.

A number of Hawaiian 'stars' headline their own shows and have been long-time fare on the visitor nightlife calendar. They include **Al Harrington**, known as 'The **South Pacific Man**' (923-9861), the inveterate 'Tiny Bubbles' **Don Ho**, appearing Sunday through Friday at the Hilton Hawaiian Village Dome (949-4321), **Danny Kaleikini** at the Kahala Hilton's Hala Terrace (734-2211) Monday through Saturday; the spirited **Society of Seven** at the Outrigger Hotel (923-0711) Monday through Saturday; and the dynamic duo the **Brothers Cazimero** at the Royal Hawaiian Hotel's Monarch Room (923-7311).

The Hilton Hawaiian Village also features magician **John Hirokawa** in his 'Magic of Polynesia' show nightly at the Dome (973-5828), as well as the multi-talented **Charo!** nightly in the Village's Tropic Surf Club (942-7873). The Hula Hut Theatre Restaurant (955-8444) presents **Flashback**, a Las Vegas-style revue featuring entertainers impersonating stars of the 50's and 60's, and the Sheraton Waikiki presents a Polynesian revue (922-5811). The Royal Hawaiian Luau really qualifies as a dinner show as well (see Lu'au above).

ENTERTAINMENT

DINNER CRUISES

A number of operators offer dinner offshore, complete with live entertainment; prices are comparable and all these cruises last about two hours. The one with the best reputation for quality is aboard the seventy-two-foot *Hilton Rainbow I*, run by the Hilton Hawaiian Village (949-4321), leaving nightly at 5:30pm from the Hilton's private pier and including an open bar and live Hawaiian/contemporary entertainment.

Aikane Catamaran Cruises (522-1533) has two dinner cruises nightly aboard their hundred-foot-long double-hulled vessels, both leaving from Kewalo Basin opposite Ward Warehouse. The sunset cruise leaves at 5:15pm and the moonlight cruise at 7:45pm; local musicians play Hawaiian and contemporary music during both, and both offer an open bar. The moonlight cruise is slightly less expensive than the sunset one. **Ali'i Kai** (522-7822) offers similar sunset and moonlight dinner cruises,

complete with stage show, leaving from Honolulu Harbor at 5:15pm and 8:30pm. **Hawaiian Cruises** (947-9971) has a nightly two-hour dinner cruise leaving Kewalo Basin at 5:30pm and including a mini-Polynesian revue and a live band. The **Royal Prince** (944-3260), a 65-foot newly refurbished yacht offers dinner sails nightly except Sunday. An elegant sit down dinner and cocktails are served; entertainment and dancing throughout. Leaves Pier 8 at 5:30pm.

Some also offer daytime excursions that provide passengers with opportunities for offshore swimming and snorkeling; these are described under Sailing in the SPORTS & RECREATION section and under Charters in GETTING AROUND (private charter); water-borne sightseeing excursions are listed as Water Tours under GETTING AROUND.

DANCE

In addition to the shows described above, there are other dance performances to watch and enjoy—and there's the dancing to join in, to either live or recorded music.

Hula

The hula is the heartbeat of Hawai'i. An integral part of the ritual life of the ancients, the old hula never died. New dances derived from it became popular entertainment for visiting sailors, who paid well to witness these

alterations, but Hawaiians didn't fundamentally connect this new and lucrative enterprise with their sacred dance. There are two distinct classes of hula, the ancient and the modern.

Hula 'olapa, more recently known

as *hula kahiko*, the old style, is performed to the accompaniment of chanting and percussion *only*. Traditionally, the dance was done to accompany the chant, which was of primary importance, and it was performed on most occasions by men. Though most hula groups today have a preponderance of women, the men's hula is every bit as beautiful, and is energetic with a virile grace that seems absent from the aggressive men's dances of other Polynesian cultures. Chanting, too, is an art that is experiencing a revival, along with the upsurge of interest in the language itself. The chants are always in Hawaiian. The women's hula is softer than the men's, but still has strength and precision. Precision is a vital element of this hula style, and while there is ample scope for the enactment of modern tales in the ancient mode, the rules are strict and strictly followed.

It is interesting to note that the most famous symbol of the hula, indeed of Hawai'i—the grass skirt—is not Hawaiian at all. The grass skirt was introduced from Micronesia by laborers from the Gilbert Islands in the early nineteenth century. Hawaiians subsequently used native materials, such as ti leaves, in a similar fashion but they were always fresh and green out of respect for the gods. This innovation is strictly Hawaiian. Prior to European visitations, their garments had been of barkcloth [*kapa*]. *Hula ku'i*, a transitional form that combines traditional hula movements with those of nineteenth-century European ballroom dance, arose at this time. Prior to this innovation, men and women seldom danced together; in most ancient hulas performed today, they still do not.

Hula 'auana, the modern style, is much more flexible than its ancient forebear, just as modern ballet can be interpreted more freely than classical. Its costuming is limited only by the imagination and is keyed to the story being told. Modern hula is usually accompanied by both melody and lyrics as well as ukuleles, guitars and other instruments, and the songs may be in any language, though English and Hawaiian are most common. This hula is pure entertainment, and a delightful one it is.

Amongst the most appealing sights you'll see is a well-trained hula troupe of children [*keiki*]. The free **Young People's Hula Show** on Sunday mornings (9:30am) at Ala Moana Center's Center Stage is a good place to start. For the adult version, there's the **Kodak Hula Show** at Kapi'olani Park (see Popular Attractions under SIGHT-

123

Hula kahiko.

SEEING). There are many *halau* [hula schools], but their performances are not regularly scheduled.

It's well worth scanning the local papers for events (see LOCAL FESTIVALS/CALENDAR OF EVENTS) that feature hula, because what you'll see is significantly different from what you'll see in a Polynesian show, especially if you can catch a good *kahiko*. **Ka Pā Hula Hawai'i** is a superb group, dancing primarily to chants from the Kalākaua period, in both *'olapa* and *ku'i* styles; their women are divine, and their men are especially exquisite.

Hālau Hula o Kukunaokala dances more than one style of *kahiko* and specializes in chants from the island of Moloka'i. **Nā Pualei o Likolehua** and **Pua Ali'i 'Ilima** dance a variety of *kahiko* and *'auana*. **Hālau Hula o Maīki** dances mostly *'auana*, as does **Nā Kamalei**; the subjects of their hulas vary widely. Notable *keiki* groups are **Hālau Hula Olana Ai** and **Hula Hui o Kapunahala**.

Other ethnic

Hawai'i's ethnic diversity brings with it a wealth of customs from many cultures, including a splendid variety of traditional dance from many nations. **Onoe Kikunobu** presents both classical and folk dances of Japan; the **Pamana Dancers** perform Filipino folk dances; the **Omega Dancers** specialize in Russian dances; and **Los Danceros** dance the dances of Mexico and Spain. These troupes perform at irregular intervals throughout the year. This local talent is augmented by visiting groups, especially from Asian countries, often sponsored by the East-West Center and performing in their Kennedy Theatre. If you have the opportunity to see one of these, take it. Check the entertainment listings in local publications for performances current during your visit.

Contemporary and rock

Music played at Honolulu's dance clubs can be divided into two groups, contemporary and rock. Contemporary signifies the pop music on the charts of Billboard's Top-40 hits.

Although some overlap exists between this and rock music, the clubs listed under Rock fall into post-punk and progressive music categories, if they can be categorized at all, with a lot of European imports comprising the playlists. Clubs listed here rely on recorded music.

Similar clubs hosting local bands—also good places to go dancing—are listed below under Live Music.

Most clubs have kept up with such innovative trends as video-enhanced music, and most levy a small cover charge. All stay open till between 2 and 4am on weekends, some closing earlier during the week. Although the drinking age is twenty-one, some allow eighteen-year-olds, at a much higher cover charge, to dance and drink soda.

Contemporary clubs

Heading the list is **Spats** (Hyatt Regency Waikiki 923-1234), where the decor is classy and a crowd is guaranteed. That club, **Annabelle's** (Ilikai Hotel 949-3811) and **The Point After** (Hawaiian Regent Hotel 922-6611) have long been favorites of our visiting nightowls. Others prefer **Scruples** (2310 Kūhiō Avenue 923-9530). Two other fun places, just out of Waikīkī, are **Bobby McGee's Conglomeration** (2885 Kalākaua Avenue 922-1282), where they consistently respond to requests, and **Rumours** (Ramada Rennaisance Ala Moana Hotel 955-4811); their 'Big Chill' promotion on Friday nights is popular amongst fans of late sixties and early seventies music.

Rock clubs

Also listed under Live Music, but dependable for alternative dance music between live sets is **Wave Waikiki** (1877 Kalākaua Avenue 941-0424); look for the 'Fish Lady' mural.

Around the corner and across the street, **Pink Cadillac** (478 'Ena Road 942-5282) stands as the newest and most progressive of Honolulu's modern dance hangouts. Recorded music at **Studebaker's** in Restaurant Row (526-9888) spans the ages—but is mostly 50's type bop.

Hula's Bar and Lei Stand (2103 Kūhiō Avenue 923-0669), an enclave of the gay community, has eccentric disc jockeys and a dance floor with mirrors all around. It's free to walk in, as is the high energy **Blue Water Cafe** (2350 Kūhiō Avenue 926-2191).

Ballet

The **Hawai'i Ballet Theatre**, the state's oldest and largest ballet company, stages a few major productions each year including such works as *The Nutcracker* and *Firebird*. A youthful company of ten- to thirteen-year-old aspirants, the **Hawai'i State Ballet** performs irregularly. Modern ballet is presented by local troupes like **Dance Works** and **Dances We Dance**. Honolulu is also on the circuit for touring ballet companies from the US and other countries, and has hosted such international luminaries as Mikhail Baryshnikov, Alexander Godunov and dancers from the New York City Ballet.

Ballroom dancing

Nostalgia buffs can sway and swoon to the tunes of a bygone era on Monday evenings in the **Monarch Room** at the Royal Hawaiian Hotel (923-7311) where Del Courtney and his fourteen-piece orchestra turn back the clock with big band classics. The **Maile Lounge** at the Kahala Hilton (734-2211) features Kit Sampson, a band with a contemporary Latin sound, every night except Sunday; and Sea Breeze at the Sheraton-Waikiki Hotel's **Hanohano Room** (922-4422) rolls out tunes from the forties and fifties, Tuesday through Saturday.

LIVE MUSIC

There's nothing quite like being there, seeing the music in the making, watching the fingers pluck the strings or caress the keys, making eye contact with the singer of your favorite song.

Honolulu is home to a wealth of talented musicians, expressing themselves in many styles, and is host to many more.

Hawaiian

Hawaiians—indeed, all Polynesians—demonstrated a remarkable natural affinity with and talent for both melody and harmony, neither of which had existed in their traditions prior to European contact. They also adopted enthusiastically the stringed instruments these visitors introduced, and each Polynesian group has developed a distinctive musical style during the past century or two.

Though the guitar is probably the instrument most commonly used by Hawaiian musicians today, its baby brother, the 'ukulele, is most strongly identified with Hawai'i. *'Ukulele* is, in fact, a Hawaiian word. It means 'leaping flea' and was first applied as a nickname to Edward Purvis, a popular nineteenth-century player of the instrument who jumped around while he · strummed. Brought to Hawai'i by Portuguese laborers in 1879, the diminutive instrument was known to them as *braquinho*. The other stringed instrument immutably linked with Hawai'i is the steel guitar, played horizontally with a metal slide. Last but certainly not least is the 'slack key' guitar, a tuning effect achieved by loosening the strings, which is much favored by Hawaiians and for which they have developed a distinctively Hawaiian style of playing.

Today's Island music has continued to evolve and is now less stereotypical and more grounded in true expression of the feelings of Island life. Within it, naturally, are varieties—and insertions from the contemporary idiom—but the unique island flavor is discernible throughout.

In addition to the Dinner Shows described above, a number of Waikīkī venues are noted for their regular presentation of Hawaiian music. The Halekulani's **House Without a Key** (923-2311) features a Hawaiian band, usually accompanied by a hula dancer, on the terrace at sunset. The **Aloha Bar** (924-8824) at the Reef Towers Hotel always has live Hawaiian music, as does the Pacific Beach Hotel's **Polynesian Pub of the Surf** (923-3638). Many places play a mix of Hawaiian and contemporary music. Most of the lounges at the Hilton Hawaiian Village (949-4321) do so; the most popular is the **Shell Bar**. The **Chart House** at the Ilikai (947-2490) features mostly Hawaiian music on weekends. The Ramada Rennaisance Ala Moana Hotel **Garden Lanai** (955-4811) has been the showcase of Hawaiian/contemporary singer Melveen Leed for many years. The **Spindrifter** always has a good mix of lounge acts, as does **Stuart Anderson's** in Ward Warehouse (523-9692). Strolling minstrels playing traditional Hawaiian music can be enjoyed at the **Mai Tai Bar** of the Surf Room in

ENTERTAINMENT

the Royal Hawaiian Hotel (923-7311) in the early evening, and at **The Willows** (901 Hausten Street 946-4808) on Fridays at lunchtime. A nice drive in the country on a Sunday can take you to good Hawaiian music at **Kemoo Farm** (621-8481) on the island's central Leilehua Plateau—near all those pineapple fields. Radio station **KCCN** (1420 AM) plays Hawaiian music all day, every day (except on Sunday mornings when they broadcast several hours of Christian religious services).

Local musicians

The musicians who provide this delightful diversity display a range of talents and styles of presentation. Many are multi-talented and hard to categorize. Our most notable and popular entertainers are listed here in alphabetical order. With a few exceptions, noted below, they rarely play the same venue for long; free tourist newspapers such as the *Waikiki Beach Press* are good sources of information on who's playing where. Almost all are recording artists, so you may take their voices home with you (see Records, Tapes & Discs under SHOPPING).

The **Ali'is** are a popular male vocal group. Singer/guitarist **Haunani Apoliona** is with the group **Olomana**. **Kapono Beamer**, part of a famous musical family, plays guitar and sings. His uncle, **Mahi Beamer**, is a popular lounge pianist. **Jimmy Borges** is a jazz singer.

The **Brothers Cazimero** (Robert and Roland) are one of the islands' most popular singing duos. **Tony Conjugacion** is an outstanding and popular falsetto singer. **Nohelani Cypriano** is a popular female vocalist.

Brickwood Galuteria is a well-known and very popular singer and radio/television personality. **Loyal Garner** belts out the hits, and she plays the piano. **Al Harrington**, an all-around showman, presents a varied show for visitors.

Singer **Myrtle K. Hilo** isn't always in town, but when she is, don't miss her if you fancy hearing a little Hawaiian grandmother sounding like Liza Minnelli. **Don Ho** is Hawai'i's most famous entertainer. **Azure McCall** is a popular jazz singer/entertainer. **Carole Kai** has an upbeat style to the contemporary songs she sings. **Kalapana** is a contemporary Island rock group. Singer **Danny Kaleikini** is a long-standing local star.

Kaleo o Kalani is a popular female vocal group. **Sonny Kamahele** sings and plays steel guitar. **Henry Kapono** is a noted male vocalist, and **Kapena** is a male vocal trio. **Moe Keale** is a highly regarded male vocalist. Female vocalist **Genoa Keawe** is a master of the high falsetto warble so typical of Hawaiian music. **Karen Keawehawai'i** is a grand singer and comedienne with a high profile in Hawai'i.

Audy Kimura sings with a soft touch and plays guitar. The **Kipapa Rush Band** is a popular local group. The **Kuhina Serenaders** are a female singing duo specializing in Hawaiian originals.

Nolan Hao and the Ho'aikanes are a young, grassroots instrumental group. **Melveen Leed** has a country and western style of singing contemporary and Hawaiian songs. **Jay Larrin** is a lounge pianist, singer and composer who also plays the old Hawaiian favorites. The **Makaha Sons of Ni'ihau**, a down-to-earth Hawaiian group, are extremely popular with local audiences. The **Makapu'u Sand Band** is a male vocal group playing in the old Hawaiian style. **Peter Moon** , with his popular band, plays modern Hawaiian tunes.

Alan and Clayton Naluai are a local duo singing traditional and contemporary Hawaiian songs with lovely harmony. **Brother Noland** (Conjugacion) is a locally recognized male vocalist who leads the group **Pacific Bad Boys**. **Herb Ohta,** an ukulele man, plays regularly in Waikīkī. **Nalani Olds** is a popular female vocalist, and **Noly Pa'a** is a piano-playing male vocalist. **Dennis Pavao** is a great falsetto singer.

Regal singer **Marlene Sai** is very big on the Hawaiian music scene. **Owana Salazar** is a lyrical female singer. **Jerry Santos** sings and plays guitar with his group, **Olomana**. The **Society of Seven** is a very popular and successful male vocal entertainment group. The **Sons of Hawai'i** with **Eddie Kamae**, an ukelele master, perform Hawaiian songs. The popular duo **Steve and Teresa** (Mai'i and Bright) sing original and traditional Hawaiian songs. **Sugar Sugar** is a popular duo. **Betty Loo Taylor** is a jazz singer. **Three Scoops of Aloha** is an accomplished male vocal group.

Palani Vaughan is a well-known male vocalist. **Joy Woode** sings jazz. **Mokulani Young** sings Hawaiian songs like Nat King Cole.

The Royal Hawaiian Band

Hawai'i's first European-style band was The King's Band, established rather informally around 1836. William Merseburgh, who came to the Islands from Weimar, East Germany in 1849 under contract to Kamehameha III, was the Band's first professional leader. Its successor, the **Royal Hawaiian Band**, was founded in 1870 by King Kamehameha V and, ably led after 1872 by German bandmeister Heinrich Berger, quickly became a local institution. Berger, who served as band leader until 1915, became known as the father of Hawaiian music, teaching and inspiring two generations of local musicians as well as composing music for some seventy-five original Hawaiian songs, arranging more than a thousand and conducting in excess of 32,000 concerts. The Royal Hawaiian Band (922-5331) is still going strong and performs regularly in free concerts at 'Iolani Palace, Kapi'olani Bandstand, the Fort Street Mall, and Ala Moana Center.

Contemporary

Many places present live contemporary music, which often gets louder as the hour gets later. Some of the softer sounds can be heard at **Lewers Lounge** (the Halekulani 923-2311), which features a pianist, and at **Trader Vic's** (International Market Place 923-1581) where a singer/guitarist plays. **Monterey**

Bay Canners (Outrigger Hotel 922-5761; Ward Centre 536-6197) has low-key acts at their Ward Centre location. **Buzz's** in Mō'ili'ili (2535 Coyne Street 944-9781) regularly spotlights contemporary music. Louder shows include the popular duo at **Nick's Fishmarket** (Waikiki Gateway Hotel 955-6333) and the

Captain's Table (Holiday Inn Waikiki 922-2511); the latter presents Karen Keawehawai'i on weekends. The Black Orchid Restaurant in Restaurant Row (521-3111) is a gathering spot for contemporary and jazz music fans; and singer Jan Brenner has been

headlining at Esprit (Sheraton-Waikiki 922-4422) for years. The band at Nicholas Nickolas (Ramada Rennaisance Ala Moana Hotel 955-4466) adds Top-40 and 'oldies' tunes to its contemporary repertoire.

Rock

The top rock spot is Wave Waikiki (1877 Kalākaua 941-0424), bringing in many Mainland bands, usually on the progressive side of the spectrum. The Waikiki Broiler (200 Lewers Street 923-8836) also serve regular rock and roll fare. The Jazz Cellar (205 Lewers Street 923-9952) is anything but what its name implies; it's a rowdy, hard rock club popular with military men. This crowd also favors the nearby Moose

McGillycuddy's (310 Lewers Street 923-0751). Moose's has another location in Mō'ili'ili which is popular with University students (1035 University Avenue 944-5525), and both venues usually have good rock and roll bands or recorded music. Also in Mō'ili'ili, Anna Banana's (2440 S Beretania Street 946-5190) features funky Island music and reggae groups.

Jazz

Jimmy Borges who tops the list of local jazz singers performs every Saturday evening at the Hilton Hawaiian Village's Paradise Lounge (949-4321) and on Sunday afternoon with the Del Courtney Orchestra at

the Royal Hawaiian (923-7311). The Captain's Room (956-1111) at the Hawaii Prince Hotel features jazz notables such as Gabe Baltazar, Azure McCall and Augie Rey.

Piano bars

This popular low-key entertainment is offered in places too numerous to mention, but a few Waikīkī establishments are especially noteworthy.

The Library (Hawaiian Regent Hotel 922-6611) is a favorite, as is The Shell Bar at the Hilton Hawaiian Village (949-4422). A mixture of Hawaiian and contemporary songs are the usual musical fare at Andrew's Restaurant (Ward Centre 523-8677) and the Great Wok of

China (Royal Hawaiian Shopping Center 922-5373), and Michel's at the Colony Surf presents mostly easy listening music. Pianists at South Seas Village (2112 Kalākaua Avenue 923-8484) and House of Hong (206A Lewers Street 923-0202) are adept at almost anything you request; and the Hanohano Room at the Sheraton Waikiki (922-4422) offers piano stylings before its dance sets.

A special category

The open-air atmosphere of the Halekulani's oceanside **Orchids** restaurant (923-2311) worthy of special note because of its quiet elegance and the music provided at Sunday brunch. Celestial strains evoked from the harp and flute by Susi Hussong and Susan Gillespie lift this always special meal to a higher plane. In the same way, White Eisenstein, a guitar/recorder duo, plays a variety of tunes, some haunting and some lively, nightly in the outdoor lounge area under the Banyan at the Sheraton Moana Surfrider.

Visiting artists

There is an almost continuous stream of visiting artists in concert in Honolulu. Superstars such as Lionel Richie, Kenny Loggins and U2 have played at Blaisdell Arena, but sometimes even that's too small. Santana, Billy Joel and the Beach Boys need Aloha Stadium. A special place to see a show is at the open-air Waikīkī Shell, where Jimmy Buffett has performed many times. Some entertainers like Tom Jones or Jim Nabors opt for the intimacy of a showroom at one of the Waikīkī hotels.

Tickets range widely in price and are virtually always available from Funway Ticket Outlets (949-6999), which has several Waikīkī locations.

Classical

Our thriving local music scene also encompasses a variety of classical presentations in the finest European tradition.

Some of these are offered in regular 'seasons', others are staged at irregular intervals throughout the year. Announcements of visiting classicists will be found in the local press.

Symphony

The **Honolulu Symphony Orchestra** (942-2200), led by Donald Johanos, is one of the oldest in the country. Based at the Blaisdell Concert Hall, the orchestra presents regular seasons of classics and a pops series of concerts from July to May.

If you're here in late summer, catch the pops series under the stars at the Waikīkī Shell.

The **Honolulu Youth Symphony** does a winter concert at Blaisdell Concert Hall (531-8071).

Chamber

The **Hawaii Chamber Orchestra Society** (734-0397) gives concerts at St. Peter's on Queen Emma Street in downtown Honolulu. Their regular season runs from October to May, and during July and August they present a weekly summer jazz and Broadway festival.

Chamber Music Hawaii (261-4290) is made up of three ensembles: Spring Wind Quartet, Honolulu Brass, and Galliard String Quartet, each comprised of Honolulu Symphony Orchestra musicians. They perform high quality chamber

ENTERTAINMENT

130

music in various concert series that run from October through May at places such as Lutheran Church of Honolulu (1730 Punahou Street) and Honolulu Academy of Arts (900 S Beretania Street).

Opera

The **Hawaii Opera Theatre** (521-6537) stages three full length operas in mid-winter at Blaisdell Concert Hall (see CALENDAR OF EVENTS).

COMEDY

The most popular local comedian is **Frank DeLima**, known for insulting every public figure and ethnic group in sight, including his own. His fast-paced presentation is so heavily swathed in pidgin, local references and innuendo that visitors may not get all the jokes, but the butts of some jokes are famous enough to entertain even foreign visitors. DeLima plays at various locales in Waikiki and is worth asking a hotel concierge where to find his show. There is also on-going stand-up comedy at **Honolulu Comedy Club** (946-9111) located at 1777 Ala Moana Boulevard.

CINEMA

All currently popular American films, as well as a healthy smattering of offbeat and avant garde ones, play the local cinemas. Standards are shown at **Waikiki Theatres 1 & 2** (333 Seaside Avenue 923-2394) and **3** (2284 Kalākaua Avenue 923-5353), **Kuhio Theatres 1 & 2** (2095 Kūhiō Avenue 841-4422), **Marina Theatres 1 & 2** (1765 Ala Moana Blvd 949-0018), **Varsity Theatres 1 & 2** (1106 University Avenue 946-4144) and the brand new **Kahala Theatres** complex (Kahala Mall 735-9744). To catch the offbeat films, check newspaper listings for **Hemenway Theatre** (UH Mānoa 2445 Campus Road 956-6468) and **Honolulu Academy of Arts Theatre** (900 S Beretania Street 538-1006).

An outstanding annual event is the Honolulu International Film Festival which hosts works from Asia, the US and Pacific nations (see LOCAL FESTIVALS/CALENDAR OF EVENTS). Sponsored by the East-West Center, this week-long presentation of free showings and discussions with the producers, directors and actors is intended to promote international understanding through film as well as to showcase artistic and documentary achievement from the region.

THEATRE

The history-rich and distinguished **Diamond Head Theatre** runs its season from October through August and includes large-scale musicals such as *A Chorus Line*, *Oklahoma!* and *Carousel* as well as dramatic productions such as *Plaza Suite*, *Death of a Salesman* and *The Man Who Came to Dinner*. The theatre, which hosts seven major productions every year, is located at Diamond Head (520 Makapu'u Avenue 734-0274). The **Hawaii Performing Arts Company** is the resident company in a smaller theatre, the Manoa Valley Theatre (2833 E Mānoa Road 521-3487). Internationally known for outstanding Asian productions, the East-West Center's **Kennedy Theatre** (UH Mānoa campus 948-7655) season runs from September through May.

The **Starving Artists Theater Co.** (942-1942), one of the newer dramatic groups, has garnered positive reviews for contemporary productions presented at the Mid-Pacific Institute. Many traveling Broadway shows come to Honolulu's Neal Blaisdell Concert Hall. These have included such renowned productions as *Annie*, *Cats*, *Hello Dolly* with Carol Channing and *Camelot* with Richard Harris. The Arts Council of Hawaii (524-7120) publishes a monthly guide to cultural events.

132

SOCIAL DRINKING

After a hectic day of sightseeing, sand-snoozing or whatever else has occupied the hours, many people just want to relax with a drink, with or without a companion.

We have broken down the social drinking scene into several subcategories, one of which is bound to suit your mood and circumstance. Because most popular watering holes also offer entertainment, there will be some overlap between this and the Live Music and Dance subsections above.

Quiet enough for conversation

A tranquil setting for a casual drink with soft background music is the **Sunset Lanai** at the Kaimana Beach Hotel (923-1555). Also oceanside and featuring a Hawaiian band at sunset is the Halekulani's **House Without a Key** (923-2311). The more sedate of mien enjoy **The Library** at the Hawaiian Regent (922-3111); **Hy's Steak House** (2440 Kūhiō Avenue 922-5555). Most of the bars at the Hilton Hawaiian Village have low-key, relaxing atmospheres. The **Chart House** at the Ilikai, with its Hawaiian music, overlooks the yacht harbor, and **Horatio's** at Ward Warehouse overlooks the wharf at Kewalo Basin. The Kahala Hilton's open-air **Plumeria Cafe** is a casual spot to sit and watch the often famous guests come and go.

Too loud to talk

Sometimes low-key, but louder at mealtimes, late hours and weekends, these establishments attract high intensity singles-type crowds.

Ryan's Parkplace Bar & Grill (Ward Centre 523-9132) and **Compadres Mexican Bar & Grill** (Ward Centre 523-1307; 2500 Kūhiō

Avenue 924-4007) are trendy California-style bar/restaurants. Another Mainland clone is **TGI Friday's** (950 Ward Avenue 523-5841), attracting a young and boisterous singles clientele. Honolulu's newly established **Hard Rock Café** (1837 Kapi'olani Blvd 955-7383) has been consistently drawing crowds since its opening. **Nick's Fishmarket** (Waikiki Gateway Hotel 955-6333) appeals to sophisticated singles; noise levels rise around mid-evening. Also extremely popular are the **Rose** and **Crown** (King's Village 923-5833), The **Black Orchid** lounge (521-3111), and the **Row Bar** at Restaurant Row.

The crowds get thicker and younger at **Moose McGilly-cuddy's** (both locations), **Hot Rod's** (955-1956) and **Blue Water** (see Rock under Live Music above).

Gay bars

Unofficial headquarters for Honolulu's gay community is the bar of **Hamburger Mary's Organic Grill** (2109 Kūhiō Avenue 922-6722). **Hula's Bar and Lei Stand** (2103 Kūhiō Avenue 923-0669), a dancing club next door, is the annex. Hula's is a lot noisier than Mary's.

The clientele at these venues can steer you to other appropriate places if you're so inclined.

Queen's Surf Beach is the daytime gathering place of choice (see BEACHES).

Korean bars

'Korean Bar' is the local term for 'hostess' clubs.

These often have strip shows and similar entertainment. They are easily recognized by their names— which usually start with 'club' or end with 'lounge'—and are concentrated in the area *mauka* of Ala Moana Center, downtown around Hotel Street and in Kalihi Kai.

Erotica

Yes, there is pornography in paradise, though it's not encouraged and is kept pretty low key so as not to offend the vast majority of our visitors. The 'Ewa end of Kalākaua is where most of the peep shows and blue movies are housed. Along Waikīkī's side streets, too, there are some Japanese language ones with signs that would scandalize many American passersby if we could read them. There are also a couple of clubs along this stretch of Kalākaua that feature topless dancing girls.

Other such establishments are found downtown on Hotel Street, established more than a century ago as Honolulu's center for commercial sex.

CALENDAR OF EVENTS

JANUARY

Annual Ala Wai Canoe Challenge—outrigger canoe competition on the Ala Wai canal. Waikiki 967-7676.

Queen Emma Museum Open House—free admission 595-6291

Hula Bowl—annual college all-star football classic. Aloha Stadium 486-9300

Chinese New Year—date and animal fluctuate for this colorful celebration.

January - March

Hawai'i Opera Theatre Season—for details call business office 521-6537 or ticket office 537-6191

Narcissus Festival—celebrates the Chinese New Year with queen pageant, coronation ball, Chinese cooking, lion dances, firecrackers, food booths and arts and crafts. 533-3181

January - April

Cherry Blossom Festival—colorful Japanese cultural celebration. Includes a fun run, song contest, culture show, music concert, queen pageant and coronation ball. 949-2255

FEBRUARY

NFL Pro Bowl—annual all-star football game involving the National and American Conferences of the National Football League. Aloha Stadium 486-9300

Annual Hawaiian Open International Golf Tournament—$500,000 PGA Golf Tournament featuring top professional golfers. Waialae Golf and Country Club 526-1232

Punahou School Carnival—rides, arts, crafts, ethnic foods, plant and white elephant sale. Punahou School 944-5752

Great Aloha Run/Walk—an eight-mile run from Aloha Tower to Aloha Stadium. Variety Club School 732-2835

Hawaii Mardi Gras—annual celebration week or more before beginning of Lent. Music, dancing, foods and costumes. Restaurant Row 538-1441.

Lei Queen Competition—McCoy Pavilion, Ala Moana Beach Park. Parks and Recreation 521-9815

Sandcastle Building Contest—University of Hawaii architectural students compete against professional architects for the most imaginative sand sculptures. Kailua Beach Park 948-7735

MARCH

Annual Oahu Kite Festival & Hawaii Challenge National Stunt Kit Festival—colorful, exciting competition including many unusual and gigantic kites flown by the pros. Kapi'olani Park 922-5483.

Buffalo's Annual Big Board Surfing Classic—two-day surfing event with Hawiian entertainment and food booths at Mākaha Beach. 696-3878

Saint Patrick's Day Parade—Fort DeRussy to Kapi'olani Park in Waikīkī. Open house party follows parade. 946-1010

Hawaiian Song Festival—Kapi'olani Park Bandstand. Parks and Recreation 521-9815

Kamehameha Schools Song Contest—Neal Blaisdell Center. Kamehameha Schools, Special Events 842-8211

Prince Kūhiō Day—state holiday honoring Hawai'i's Prince Kūhiō. Celebration at Prince Kūhiō Federal Building. 546-7573

135

APRIL

Punchbowl Easter Sunrise Service—National Memorial Cemetery of the Pacific (date fluctuates). Hawaii Council of Churches 531-4888

Bud Light Tin Man Biathlon—2.7-mile run, 800-meter swim at Ala Moana Beach Park. 926-5755

Buddha Day Celebration—flower festival pageant at island temples statewide to celebrate the birth of Buddha. Hawaiian Buddhist Council 536-7044

Aloha Basketball Classic—collegiate basketball tournament at Neal Blaisdell Arena. 537-1493

Annual Carole Kai Bed Race and Parade—charity fundraiser involving a zany race with beds at Kapi'olani Park, preceded by a parade through Waikīkī. Bed Race Office 735-6092

Carole Kai Concert—a variety of island celebrities perform in concert at the Waikīkī Shell in Kapi'olani Park as part of the Carole Kai Bed Race fundraiser. Bed Race Office 735-6092

International Fair—cultural performances, children's games, costume pageant, international food. East-West Center Public Affairs 944-7715

April, June

Annual Hawaiian Festival of Music—music groups from Hawai'i and the Mainland compete in a festival of stage, symphonic bands, concert choirs, madrigal, swing groups and marching bands. Also in June. Waikīkī Shell 637-6566

ENTERTAINMENT

MAY

Lei Day—annual celebration highlighting statewide lei competitions and exhibits. Kapi'olani Park 521-9815

Annual 'Ohana Festival—Arts, crafts, martial arts, ethnic dances and a variety of music by some of Hawai'i's favorite musicians. St Louis High School, Parent Teachers Guild 735-4819

Pacific Handcrafters Guild Spring Fair—arts and crafts from Hawai'i's artists; ethnic foods and entertainment. Ala Moana Park 538-7227

Memorial Day Special Military Services—National Memorial Cemetery of the Pacific (Punchbowl) 541-1430

May - June

Annual Festival of the Pacific—opening ceremonies: entertainment by the Honolulu Boy's Choir and a presentation of forty flags of the Pacific area. Full week of athletic tournaments, music, songs and dances of the multi-ethnic people of the Pacific. 732-4461

50th State Fair—held on consecutive weekends: commercial exhibits, produce, food booths, entertainment. Aloha Stadium Area Lot 536-5492 or 533-4112

JUNE

King Kamehameha Celebration—state holiday honoring Kamehameha the Great, Hawai'i's first monarch. Lei draping ceremony at King Kamehameha statue, opposite 'Iolani Palace. Celebration on all islands. King Kamehameha Celebration Commission 548-4512

Kamehameha Day Parade—beginning downtown with floral floats, pageantry, bands and an awards ceremony and *ho'olaule'a* (street party) in Kapi'olani Park.

Gotcha Pro Surfing Championship—top world-ranked surfers compete for big prize money. Ocean Promotion (Big Island) 326-1011

King Kamehameha Annual Hula and Chant Competition—Friday night ancient hula, Saturday night modern hula, Neal Blaisdell Center. State Council of Hawaiian Heritage 536-6540

June - July

Hawaii State Farm Fair—nurseries, produce, farm animals and rides. McKinley High School grounds 848-2074

Beachtown Hawaiian Pro Am Circuit Contest—surfing competition on Oahu's South shore. Hawai'i Surfing Association 671-6255

Mission Houses Museum Mid-nineteenth Century Celebration—quilt exhibit, living history program, craft demonstrations, entertainment and food. Mission Houses Museum 531-0481

ENTERTAINMENT

JULY

Blue Hawai'i State Amateur Surfing Championships—Sandy Beach, Diamond Head and Kūhiō Beach. Hawaii Surfing Association 671-6255

Walter McFarland Canoe Regatta—canoe surfing races at Kūhiō Beach Park in Waikīkī. Outrigger Canoe Club 689-6798

Kenwood Cup Yacht Race—One of the top international ocean racing events. Ends in August. Sponsored by Royal Hawaiian Ocean Racing Club 941-1273

Bud Light Tin Man Triathlon—about 1000 triathletes gather at Ala Moana Park to swim 800 meters, bike twenty-five miles and finish with a 6.2-mile run around Diamond Head to Kap'iolani Park. 926-5755

Annual Prince Lot Hula Festival—*halau* [hula schools] from all islands perform; concessions, T-shirts. Moanalua Garden Foundation 839-5334

Pacific Handcrafters Guild Summer Fair—quality arts and crafts from Hawai'i's finest artists. Craft demonstrations, ethnic foods and entertainment. Thomas Square 538-7227, art and entertainment in Foster Botanic Gardens 538-7227

July - August

Obon Festival—traditional Buddhist celebration to thank ancestors; service and bon dances. Haleiwa Jodo Mission 637-4382

AUGUST

State Championship Hobie Cat Races—14- and 18-foot Hobies compete at Kailua Beach. Sponsored by Coca-Cola and Michelob 261-3189

Na Hula O Hawai'i Festival—hula festival, Kapi'olani Park Bandstand. Parks and Recreation 521-9815

Floating lantern ceremony, Waikiki.

Queen Liliu'okalani Keiki Hula Competition—girls and boys ages six to twelve compete dancing modern and ancient hula. Kamehameha Schools, Kekuhaupi'o Gym 521-6905

Hawaiian Open State Tennis Championships—held at Ala Moana, Ke'ehi and Diamond Head tennis courts. Diamond Head Tennis Center 923-7927 or 521-7664

Admission Day—state holiday recognizing Hawai'i's statehood.

Duke Kahanamoku Canoe Races—from Magic Island to Kailua Beach Park, sponsored by Lanikai Canoe Club.

SEPTEMBER

Waikiki Rough Water Swim—two-mile swim from Sans Souci Beach to Duke Kahanamoku Beach (Hilton Hawaiian Village). All ages and categories. American Lung Association 988-7788

Aloha Week Festivals—major events, including Hawaiian pageantry, royal ball, canoe races, *ho'olaule'a* in Waikiki and Downtown; parades and entertainment. Aloha Week 944-8857

A Day at Queen Emma Summer Palace—Hawaiian arts and crafts fair including entertainment. Daughters of Hawai'i 595-6291

Na Wahine o Ke Kai—Women's Moloka'i-to-O'ahu Canoe Race. Women paddle across the rough Kaiwi (Moloka'i) Channel in Hawaiian outrigger canoes, finish at Fort DeRussy in Waikiki. 525-5413

OCTOBER

Pacific Handcrafters Guild Fall Fair—quality arts and crafts from Hawai'i's finest artists; craft demonstrations, ethnic foods and entertainment. Ala Moana Park 538-7227

World Invitational Rugby Tournament—Kapi'olani Park. Harlequins, Hawai'i Rugby Football Union 523-1305

Bank of Hawaii Molokai Hoe—Men's Moloka'i-to-O'ahu Canoe Race. Men paddle across the rough Kaiwi (Moloka'i) Channel in Hawaiian outrigger canoes, finish at Fort DeRussy in Waikiki. 842-5500

Discoverers' Day—Hawaiian equivalent of Columbus Day.

Annual Orchid Plant and Flower Show—Blaisdell Center Exhibition Hall, Blaisdell Center 527-5400

Annual Waimea Falls Makahiki Festival—celebrating the historic harvest time. Hawaiian games, crafts, music and foods. Waimea Falls Park 638-8511

ENTERTAINMENT

138

Bishop Museum Festival—all-day Hawaiian cultural festival with hula, contemporary and Hawaiian music, demonstrations of traditional folk art by contemporary artisans; some for sale. International and Pacific-Asian foods. Bishop Museum 847-3511

NOVEMBER

Annual Veteran's Day Turkey Swim—held at Ala Moana Beach Park. Nu'uanu YMCA 536-3556 ext. 217

Pearl Harbor Aloha Festival—food, games, entertainment. Richardson Field 477-0818

Veterans Day Parade—from Fort DeRussy to Kapi'olani Park.

Mission Houses Museum Annual Christmas Fair—Hawai'i's finest crafts people present their handicrafts, including Christmas items, in an open market. Mission Houses Museum 531-0481

November - December

Triple Crown Hawaiian Pro Surfing Championships—Hard Rock Café World Cup at Hale'iwa, Billabong Hawaiian Pro at Sunset, Marui Masters at Pipeline; held on four days within each ten-day period depending on surf conditions. 638-7266

Hawai'i International Film Festival—cross-cultural films by award-winning film makers from Asia, the Pacific and the United States. East-West Center, Office of Culture and Communication 944-7603

DECEMBER

Bodhi Day—Buddhist temples commemorate day of enlightenment of Buddha. Hawai'i Buddhist Council 536-7044

Pacific Handcrafters Guild Christmas Fair—a chance to but Christmas gifts from some of Hawai'i's finest craftsmen; held at Thomas Square. 538-7227

Honolulu Wheelchair Marathon—a part of Honolulu Marathon, same course and distance. Honolulu Marathon Association 734-7200

Annual Honolulu Marathon—starts at Aloha Tower and finishes at Kapi'olani Park. Honolulu Marathon Association 734-7200

Aloha Bowl—collegiate football championship held at Aloha Stadium. 488-7731

Annual Rainbow Classic—invitational tournament of collegiate basketball teams at Blaisdell Center Arena. Sports Information, University of Hawai'i 956-7523

Lei of Lights Festival—holiday celebration in Waikiki. 732-4461

Jingle Bell Run—five-mile run for individuals, friends, groups and families. Costumes, contests, singing and awards. 525-8000

SHOPPING

Centers
Clothing
Art
Handcrafts

SHOPPING

R are is the visitor who doesn't go shopping—for *something*—during a Hawaiian holiday; and Honolulu shops have just about anything you're likely to want, as well as lots of things you don't know you want until you see them. Waikīkī has the greatest concentration of shops and the widest variety of goods for sale, but there are shopping centers and boutiques elsewhere on the island that are also worthy of note.

This section details shops large and small, listing some of the more notable ones by type of merchandise. Addresses and telephone numbers of these are listed at the back of this book in the APPENDIX Section. Prices vary widely, as does quality.

CENTERS

The outstanding Waikīkī shopping centers are the Hyatt Regency's **Atrium shops,** located on the hotel's first three balcony levels; and the **Royal Hawaiian Shopping Center,** three interconnected four-story buildings around open courtyards, where free entertainment is staged several times each week. As well as catering to the upper end of the market, both these centers house a variety of casual clothing stores, eateries and souvenir shops.

Opposite the Royal Hawaiian Center is the **Waikiki Shopping Plaza,** a multi-level conglomeration of small shops carrying a wide variety of merchandise, centered around an almost unbelievable towering plastic water 'sculpture', *enhanced* with colored lights, which is most striking when viewed from the escalators.

The undisputed center for souvenir shopping is the famous **International Market Place**—scores of little kiosks in the open space under the banyans between Kalākaua and Kūhiō Avenues. A minor repetition of the same theme is the narrow pedestrian walkway nearby called **Duke's Lane,** also

between the two main thoroughfares. Opposite this on Kūhiō is another arcade called **Kuhio Mall** with the usual assortment of aloha wear, beachwear and souvenir shops. The **Waikiki Trade Center** at the corner of Kūhiō and Royal Hawaiian Avenues provides a dazzling, ultra-modern setting for the boutiques and bistros on its ground and mezzanine levels.

A little of the flavor of Disneyland can be found at **King's Village,** on Ka'iulani Avenue between Kalākaua and Kūhiō. Built on the same three-quarter scale as that famous theme park, the 'village' shops sell nice fabrics, clothing, jewelry and souvenirs as well as fast foods.

The Hilton Hawaiian Village's **Rainbow Bazaar** houses the whole range of shopping prices and types and also creates a little world of its own. Nearby **Eaton Square** on Hobron Lane is a small European-flavored shopping mall with quality art, antique and clothing shops as well as one of Honolulu's finest French restaurants, Chez Michel.

Located at the edge of Waikīkī, **Ala Moana Center,** the world's largest 'open air' shopping center,

SHOPPING

Ward Centre, one of Honolulu's newest shopping arcades.

offers an enormous variety of fashion, food and fun shopping. At last count there were more than 180 businesses offering everything from diamonds to dustclothes to dictionaries to dining. The center is also home to four large department stores: Sears, J.C. Penney, Shirokiya and Liberty House. The newly added **Palm Boulevard** section of the center boasts upscale fashion boutiques such as Chanel, Escada and Gucci among many other trendy high fashion shops. A stage in the center of the complex is used by various groups who provide free entertainment very often.

A little farther down Ala Moana Boulevard, the elegant **Ward Centre** offers quality shopping for clothing, art and unusual gift items as well as gourmet food and wine and the best European pastries in town. The Centre's upper level is devoted entirely to popular restaurants offering a variety of cuisines.

Almost next door, the **Ward Warehouse** occupies former warehouse buildings opposite the docks at Kewalo Basin, and its more casual atmosphere provides relaxed shopping for clothing, books, art, epicurean cookware, health foods and much more, as well as a variety of eating establishments, fast and slow.

From the other end of Waikīkī, follow Kapahulu Avenue almost to the *mauka* end to find **Kilohana Square,** a pleasant little assemblage of clothing, antique and gift shops.

On the other side of Diamond Head, the **Kahala Mall** includes such exclusive shops as Benetton, Bebe, and Carol & Mary's as well as moderately priced boutiques and shops and a Liberty House department store. A recent and popular addition to this center is a five-auditorium cinema complex.

Other big centers outside the city are **Windward Mall** in Kāne'ohe and **Pearlridge Center** (Phases I & II) in Pearl City.

SHOPPING

DEPARTMENT STORES

Hawai'i's home grown department stores are **McInerny's** and the much more ubiquitous **Liberty House,** and they carry the latest of everything in an atmosphere comparable to that of US mainland stores. **Sears** and **J.C. Penney** differ little from their Mainland branches except that they have aloha wear and Hawaiian souvenir departments. **Shirokiya** is much like any Tokyo department store, which is much like most American department stores in presentation, but the merchandise in some departments is distinctly Oriental.

CLOTHING

Apparel tops almost everyone's shopping list when visiting the Islands, and there are hundreds of stores dedicated to fulfilling your fantasies as well as meeting your needs. Honolulu offers the most elegant and sophisticated fashions, and the most casual attire—the most conservative styles and the most outrageous.

Aloha wear

*Mu'umu'u*s [long, loose dresses] and shirts in bright, flowery prints put visitors in the lighthearted 'aloha' spirit quicker than a mai-tai. People in Hawai'i really do wear these casual, comfortable clothes, although couples with matching outfits are found only at masquerade parties, on stage or in Waikīkī.

A large quantity of reasonably priced aloha wear is available at **Especially For You** shops on Ward Avenue and other locations, **Island MuuMuu Factory** in Dole Cannery Square, and the **Hilo Hattie's** **Fashion Center** on Nimitz Boulevard. Better tailored and more expensive aloha wear is stocked at **Liberty House** and **Carol & Mary's** and, for men, **Reyn's** and **Ross Sutherland**. **Mamo's** and **Blue Ginger** in Ward Warehouse offer designer island fashions. **Mamo** also has a shop in Dole Cannery Square. **Kula Bay** in the Hilton Hawaiian Village specializes in designer aloha shirts and tropical wear for men. Teens find great gear at **Local Motion**.

Women's boutiques

There are many fine women's boutiques on O'ahu, ranging from the most expensive designer styles at the high-fashions shops in **Ala Moana's Palm Boulevard** and The **McInerny Galleria** in Waikiki to interesting one-of-a kind creations from shops such as **Pomegranates in the Sun** in Ward Warehouse, which along with its neighbor, Ward Centre, has an array of interesting women's boutiques. Other quality designer fashions are available at **Cielo** and **Alion** in Kahala Mall. A special shop offering exclusive unique creations and custom-designed imports, often in Thai or antique Japanese silks, is **Mandalay** at the Halekulani. Classic styles are found at **Ethel's Dress Shoppe** and **Jeffrey Barr** of Kahala Mall.

Men's stores

Honolulu's outstanding men's fashion shops are **Reyn's**, noted for inside-out aloha shirts, and **Ross Sutherland** at Ward Center and Ala Moana. **Chapman's** is popular with older men. All carry fashionable aloha wear. **Altillo** in Waikiki and the Kahala Mall has fashions for the man with European flair.

T-shirts

Almost everybody wears T-shirts once in a while. Their popularity never seems to fade and their diversity has unfolded in almost miraculous permutations over the past few years. Fortunes have been made. The classic success story and the undisputed king of trendy tees in Hawai'i is **Crazy Shirts**. Their many shops carry a large selection of designs, but few styles. Their hallmark is the delightful device of depicting on the back of the shirt a rear view of whatever is on the front. A good selection of quality T-shirts decorated with Hawaiian floral designs can be found at the **Foster Botanic Gardens Gift Shop**. Other than that, T-shirts are everywhere to be found.

Swimwear

Splash! at Ala Moana Center and the New Otani Kaimana Beach Hotel is expensive but has the most up-to-date bikinis and one-piece swimsuits. **Splash! for Men** is located at the New Otani Kaimana Beach. Another good bet for the younger set is **Local Motion** on Kapi'olani Boulevard, just *mauka* of Ala Moana Center. Nearly next door is **Blue Jeans 'n' Bikinis**, a boutique specializing in those two items, but also carrying other sportswear.

The selection of swimwear in Hawaii is almost overwhelming and it is found everywhere. In Kailua on Windward Oahu **Tres Sea** offers one-and two-piece swim fashions directly from the factory.

FABRIC

Those who prefer to craft their own tropical fashions can find printed fabric in many Waikīkī shops and in the large department stores. The only honest-to-goodness drygoods store left in Waikīkī is the **Cherry Blossom** toward the 'Ewa end of Kalākaua has the largest selection of dry goods in town, and **Creative Fibres** on Ward Avenue specializes in exotic prints.

JEWELRY

Elegant, expensive jewels are showcased by **Hildgund** at **Dawkins Benny** downtown and at the Windward Mall, by **Bernard** **Hurtig's Orientwest** at the Kahala Hilton, by **Cartier** in Ala Moana, and **Tiffany** in Waikiki's Sheraton Moana Surfrider Hotel, by

Haimoff & Haimoff Creations in Gold at the Halekulani and Ward Centre, by **Carol & Mary's** at Ala Moana and by Mitsukoshi at the Hyatt's Atrium Shops.

For basic beauties in diamonds and gold, **Security Diamond** and **Conrad Jewelers** at Ala Moana, **Zales** and **Granat Bros** are good choices. Many shops offer Victorian 'heirloom' Hawaiian jewelry: heavy gold bracelets, rings and pendants bearing a name transliterated into Hawaiian and enameled in black, Victorian lettering. You may want to find out what the Hawaiian word that sounds like your name actually means. Check *Hawaiian Names* by Eileen Roof.

Pearls, coral and jade jewelry are all over the place in Waikīkī and elsewhere—for example, at **The Jade Tree** at King's Village, the **Coral Grotto** and the **Pearl Factory**.

For the unconventional, go to **Following Sea** at the Kahala Mall, where local artists, silversmiths and goldsmiths showcase their work. Unusual and very classy jewelry in shells, feathers, porcelain, silk and other materials are available from **Elephant Walk** at Ala Moana Center. **Past Era**, in the Mills Gallery downtown offers fine antique and estate jewelry.

Local jewelry stores also carry necklaces [*lei*] and bracelets [*kupe'e*] of Ni'ihau shells, the only shell classified as a gem and insurable. Difficult to see in their natural environment, these tiny, varicolored shells are found only on the tiny island of Ni'ihau and on the southwest coast of Kaua'i. Multiple strands fetch very high prices.

ART

Artists of every ilk flourish in the tranquil tropical environment of Hawai'i. Probably the most famous artist to live and work here was **Madge Tennent**, whose bold oil paintings of monumental Hawaiian women have become world-renowned and are represented in the National Gallery of art in Washington, DC, as well as in numerous private collections. Her works are now available only through private auction and have begun to fetch six-figure prices. A private collection of her paintings and drawings can be viewed at the Tennent Gallery, a museum, and a beautifully illustrated book, *The Art and Writing of Madge Tennent*, describes her life and her philosophy.

Another locally famous artist was **Jean Charlot**, a muralist well known for his works in Mexico and elsewhere before he moved to Hawai'i. The ceramic Hawaiian warrior on the lawn of the Ala Moana Americana Hotel is one of Charlot's works. The simplistic style of his paintings is much more engaging, evoking an essence of primeval power from his representational images. Expensive originals and prints of this and other quality artists are sold at the **Manoa Gallery**.

Today, in the tradition of capturing the beauty of big Hawaiian women, **Pegge Hopper's** large, colorful, Gauginesque canvases depict their strength and serenity, and her works (originals, limited edition prints and posters) are beautifully showcased and sold from her **Pegge Hopper Gallery** on Nu'uanu Avenue; poster prints are available from myriad frame and poster shops all over town, as are those of **Diana Hansen Young**, another local artist whose pretty women have become extremely popular. Well known and highly regarded for his seas and ships as well as his island women is Big Island artist **Herb Kawainui Kane**, whose works are also readily available as poster prints. **Robert Lyn Nelson** is famous for his undersea paintings with the landscape above.

Another painter well known for his Hawaiian subjects is French artist **Guy Buffet**, whose bright, happy style is reminiscent of Tennent, but with more sense of fun. Framed and unframed prints of his work are available from fine art shops around town.

Watercolorists popular on the Hawaiian art scene are **Susan** McGovney Hansen, Robert Wyland, James Taylor Roberts, George Sumner and **Richard Pettit**, whose work adorns the cover of the 1987 telephone directory's white pages. **Ramsay Galleries** feature primarily works by **Ramsay**, but also have showings of other artists' works, changing monthly. **The Art Loft**, a fine contemporary gallery, stages exhibits that change monthly and also has a small gift gallery.

The **Island Heritage Collection** (487-7299; neighbor islands, US mainland and Canada 1-800-468-2800) features signed, limited-edition lithographs of well-known local or part-time resident artists who specialize in Hawaiian subject matter. The list includes **Luigi Fumagalli**, whose Hawaiian and Japanese women are rendered with intense color; **Kristin Zambucka**, capturing the tranquil strength of Polynesian men and women in soft pastels; Big Island resident and realist **Mary Koski**;

Demonstrating the making of handcrafts at Waimea Falls Park.

Anthony Casay, a split-view land- and seascape artist; **Les Nitta,** whose hallmark is airbrush floral painting; and **Leslie B. De Mille,** an oil and pastel portraitist and two-month-a-year resident of Maui for the past twenty years.

For the less discerning consumer of original artworks, a fun place to shop is the **Weekend Art Mart,** on the Diamond Head side of the Honolulu Zoo fence, where amateur and a few professional artists hawk their wares on Saturdays and Sundays (10am-4pm). The quality may range from the sublime to the ridiculous, but if you like it you can get the best price here, where the artists are cutting out the middle-man. The better artists are usually toward the *mauka* end of the row; it is perfectly possible to get a treasure here for a song.

Away from the urban environ-ment, an earthy gallery worth visiting on weekends and Mondays is **Hart, Tagami & Powell and Gallery and Garden** in Kāne'ohe. This peaceful gallery/garden contains an aviary, Japanese teahouse and other rural wonders. The Gallery suggests making an appointment before making the trip.

ANTIQUES

In Waikīkī, **Robyn Buntin** at Eaton Square offers a good selec-tion of antiques and artifacts from the Far East. Also, **Antiques Pacifica** at the Royal Hawaiian Hotel has an impressive collection of netsuke. **Eurasian Antiques,** located on Nimitz Highway across from City Mill, carries a large selection of both antique and reproduction furniture as well as smaller antique items.

Downtown in the lovely old Dillingham Transportation Build-ing, the **Mills Gallery** presents a superb selection of European and Oriental antiques; within this shop, **Past Era** offers fine antique and estate jewelry.

Other favorite antique shops are situated in Kilohana Square: the **Carriage House** specializes in European and **Miko Oriental Art Gallery** specializes in old ceramics and cabinet pieces.

Out-of-print and rare volumes are the specialty of **Pacific Book House** in Kapahulu.

HANDCRAFTS

Leaves of *hala,* or pandanus, [*lauhala*] were traditionally woven and plaited by Hawaiians into all manner of useful items including floor mats and baskets; today the range has been expanded to include handbags, lamp shades, placemats and much more. Similar items are made in tapa [barkcloth], but this is not, alas, the traditional Hawaiian *kapa,* as the art of making the fine felt-like material the Hawaiians produced—the finest in all Polyne-sia—was lost generations ago. The tapa you buy here is, however, authentic; it is produced by hand using the ancient methods in Sāmoa, Tonga and Fiji.

Another traditional craft still very much alive and thriving is the making of permanent leis. These were and are made from feathers, seeds and shells. Ni'ihau shell leis now command hefty prices (see Jewelry above), but attractive strands of other local shells are quite reasonably priced. Feather leis are a bit more expensive, but require much more time and care in the making as well as more material. Feather neck and head leis were traditionally worn by the *ali'i*, as were *lei palaoa*, hook-shaped pendants, originally made of whale ivory.

Woodcarving, too, has expanded far beyond its traditional application in creating *akua ki'i*, images representing gods. Indigenous woods such as koa, milo and monkeypod are carved into decorative bowls and other utensils. You can also buy modern renditions of ancient gods, as well as more mundane figures such as fish and pineapples.

Most of these crafts can be found at the **International Market Place** and in many shops around Waikīkī, and the **Little Hawaiian Craft Shop** in the Royal Hawaiian Shopping Center has a quality selection. Fine Hawaiian woodcarving is sold at **Irene's Hawaiian Gifts** in Ala Moana Center, and **Blair Ltd** in Kaka'ako carries a selection of quality carved wooden articles from Hawai'i and the Philippines. **Pauahi Nuuanu Gallery** displays koa bowls and fine quality Hawaiian crafts. **Lanakila Crafts**, part of a rehabilitation center in Nu'uanu, has pieces crafted by handicapped workers. These can be bought from selected gift shops as well as at the Center. Fine furniture of local woods is crafted by local artisans in the workshops of such firms as **Martin & MacArthur**, examples of which are displayed in their

Dear prices are paid for traditional feathers leis.

downtown showroom; they also make custom pieces to order. Locally famous Emgee Ornaments are sold at Ala Moana's **Cathedral Gift Shop**. There are numerous good potters in town. **Tropical Clay** welcomes visits to their factory's showroom on Nimitz Highway, Diamondhead of Hilo Hattie's factory, as well as to the showroom on Ward Avenue near Ward

Warehouse. **William Waterfall Gallery** located on Nuuanu Avenue specializes in handcrafts from around the Pacific, as well as unique photographic art. For an overview of a wide variety of handcrafts, visit a Pacific Handcrafters Guild Fair, or some other local fair (see LOCAL FESTIVALS/CALENDAR OF EVENTS). There are lots of these at different times and places throughout the year.

SOUVENIRS

The number one stop for souvenir items is Waikīkī's **International Market Place**. The **ABC Stores,** found on almost every block in Waikīkī, also carry a range of souvenirs as do **Hawaiian Etc, A to Z** and **The Food Pantry**. Several shops in the **Royal Hawaiian**

Shopping Center are filled with them. Merchandise is available for all tastes and budgets. If you've had too much of the usual ticky-tacky, wander up to the second level of the Royal Hawaiian Center and find the little Oriental shop that sells Chinese tongue scrapers.

SHELLS

Many visitors like to take home shells from their tropical holidays, but there are few to be found on the Islands' accessible beaches. Numerous shops carry a wide variety of tropical shells large and small—in better condition than any you are likely to find on a beach, if you find any—as well as an incredible

potpourri of useful and decorative things made from shells. **Island Shells** at Ala Moana Center has an excellent selection, as do **Nautilus of the Pacific** on Kālia Road and at the Hawaiian Regent, and **Shellworld Hawaii**, with locations at Kahala Hilton and the Royal Hawaiian Shopping Center.

FRUIT, FLOWERS & FOLIAGE

Many people wish to ship fresh Hawaiian fruits to friends, or to themselves, or to take back with them flower leis, or cuttings and seeds of colorful tropical plants that they can grow at home as a living reminder of their colorful Hawaiian

holiday. This is easy to arrange; many vendors will ship purchases for you. Some fruits and flowers are subject to quarantine regulations imposed by the US Department of Agriculture and are prohibited from entry to Mainland states.

Pineapples are no problem, but professional packing is preferable to ensure they arrive undamaged. The only papayas allowed are those that are sold at the airport, having been treated and passed by agricultural inspectors. Only the frozen flesh of mangoes is allowed; the seeds are forbidden unless they are split open and inspected. Guavas and passion-fruit [*liliko'i*] are not allowed at all. Coconuts are fine and fun. Don't bother packing them; just buy them (or pick them up off the ground if you find yourself in an area where they don't trim the trees) still in the outer husk. This is excellent natural packing and has served to float coconuts for thousands of miles across open oceans to be dashed by waves, unharmed, upon foreign shores. Not only that, they survive the rough handling of the US Postal Service. Just write the address on the coconut itself— unwrapped—and paste on the postage stamps. The Post Office actually accepts these unorthodox parcels.

and leis containing them will be confiscated. The best place on the island to buy inexpensive leis is Maunakea Street, downtown.

Sterile cuttings and seeds of many tropical and semitropical plants are sold in sealed packages that have been passed and certified by the US Department of Agriculture, and these will pass inspection without difficulty. They are sold in many souvenir-type shops and in almost all plant and garden

Leis of fern, plumeria, orchid and pua kenikeni.

shops. An ideal shop for such purchases is the Foster Botanic Gardens Gift Shop.

For specific inquiries and further details you may telephone the O'ahu office of the State of Hawai'i Department of Agriculture at 548-7175 or 836-3827 and ask for Mainland export information.

RECORDS, TAPES & DISCS

The **House of Music** at Ala Moana Center has the best selection of Hawaiian music in town.

The less expensive **Gem** store opposite Ward Warehouse also has a good Hawaiian Music department.

Tower Records, just *mauka* of Ala Moana, has an extensive selection of Hawaiian music, as well as an astounding array of tapes and compact discs of nearly every genre. They are always open till midnight.

JR's Music Shops have an extensive selection of C.D.'s. and four locations throughout the islands.

If you're interested in old records and tapes, **Jelly's** specializes in second-hand books, has a good music department.

BOOKS

At the back of this guide, we have listed books we recommend for more detailed information on Hawai'i. Most of these are easy to find in our local bookstores, but may be not so easy to find back home. Books are the surest way to take a permanent remembrance of Hawai'i home with you.

The two biggest bookshops Honolulu has to offer are **Honolulu Bookshops** with five locations in Oahu; and branches of the giant Mainland chain, **Waldenbooks**, with nine locations in Oahu along. **Liberty House** also has a good book selection. There are some delightful little shops as well. The best place in town for art books is the The **Academy Shop** at the Honolulu Academy of Arts, and the Bishop Museum's **Shop Pacifica** carries the biggest selection of works on Hawaiian and other Polynesian cultures and natural history. A very good shop within its limited range of historical works is the **'Iolani Palace Shop**. Nearby in Merchant Street, downstairs under the Croissanterie, is a gem of a little bookshop that has an outstanding selection of Hawaiiana, ancient and modern, along with the more usual topics, and somehow or other seems to be able to offer even the latest releases cheaper than everybody else. Called **Book Cellar**, this quaint shop deals in both old and new books, hardcover and paperback. Another delightful downtown book nook is **Sandwich Island Books**, found up an alley between Queen and Merchant Streets just 'Ewa of Bishop Street—then down the stairs to a treasure trove of rare and out-of-print volumes, and a lot of just plain used books.

If you enjoy nighttime book browsing, you'll enjoy an evening stroll to **Froggies** or **Interlude Books**, both located at the corner of Kalākaua and King, where books, records, tapes, magazines and comics can be bought and sold. On Piikoi across from Ala Moana Shopping Center, **Jelly's** also has similar service.

SHOPPING

GROCERIES

Those visitors with kitchen facilities may not choose to eat out for every meal. Local supermarkets carry most of the standard items that you're used to, and a lot more, including large sections of Oriental staples and standards. Some visitors find a tour of the large grocery stores an amazing experience, especially in the produce department where you may see a number of things you don't recognize.

The large supermarket chains on O'ahu are **Foodland, Safeway, Times**, and **Star Market**, all with locations convenient to Waikīkī shoppers with private transportation. There are, too, some small grocery stores around Waikīkī, notably the **Food Pantry** and the

Waikiki A-1 Superette, right on Kalākaua at Royal Hawaiian Avenue. **Diamond Head Market**, on Monsarrat up the street from the Zoo, is a famous gourmet haven for both locals and frequent visitors, and it also sells ordinary grocery items. Favorite local snack foods found in most stores (and packable to take or send home) include Maui potato chips, taro chips, won-ton chips, Kauai Kookies, Hawaiian Sun fruit juices, Lion Coffee and an array of Yick Lung 'crack seed' (Oriental salted and dried or marinated fruit) as well as the famous and delectable macadamia nut, transplanted to Hawai'i from its native Australia and sold in countless presentations almost everywhere.

CONVENIENCE STORES

The most ubiquitous stores in Waikīkī (twenty-eight locations at last count) are the **ABC Discount Stores**, which carry a little of just about everything.

There are also several **7-Eleven Stores**, familiar to most Mainlan-

ders, but not carrying anything like the array of merchandise to be found at the ABC. The Mainland **Circle K** chain is now available on the island as well. If you're out driving around, you'll find convenience stores virtually everywhere.

SPECIALTY FOOD STORES

For fresh local fish and an array of Polynesian staples not found in most stores (such as cooking bananas and, in season, breadfruit), **Tamashiro Market** in Pālama can't be beat. Another good fish market with a slower pace is **Slow Poke'** (*poke* means 'to slice' in Hawaiian) in Wai'alae and Kāne'ohe. Prepared concoctions of sliced octopus—*tako poke*—and other fish are the drawing

card for **Fort Ruger Market**; locals come for miles for the popular local delicacy as offered by this otherwise quite ordinary local grocery shop. Green bananas, taro and, seasonally, breadfruit can also be found at **Tuli's**, a Samoan grocery shop and bakery at 951 North King Street. On Saturday and Sunday, the proprietor of this store offers freshly baked Samoan taro (not *poi*) and homemade *palusami*, a Samoan delicacy made from baked taro tops and coconut cream that is surely on the menu of the gods.

A variety of packaged and prepared gourmet delights is available from the above mentioned **Diamond Head Market.** For the epicure of European taste, the best gourmet shop in Honolulu is **R. Field Wine Company** at Ward Centre and Restaurant Row, offering far more than just wine, along with a divine selection of the vintner's art.

HEALTH FOOD STORES

Vim & Vigor is a well established health food chain with locations at Ala Moana, Kahala Mall and Pearlridge.

The title of Honolulu's best health food store is a contest between **Down to Earth** in Mō'ili'ili and **Huckleberry Farms** in lower Nu'uanu. The former gains an edge over its hottest competitor by sharing its premises with Healthy's, a popular vegetarian fast food outlet. Right in Waikīkī, on Kūhiō Avenue, is **Ruffage Natural Foods**, which offers both packaged products and a delicatessen.

DRUGSTORES

Conveniently located in the heart of Waikīkī are **Kuhio Pharmacy** on Kūhiō Avenue and **Outrigger Pharmacy** on Kalākaua Avenue. *The* local 'drugstore' is **Longs Drugs** with convenient locations at Ala Moana, Vineyard at Pali Highway, Kahala Mall, and elsewhere. It sells hardware, housewares, electrical and automotive supplies, pet supplies, camera equipment, film and processing, cosmetics, minor clothing, slippers, food, appliances, and potted plants—in addition to drugs and other pharmacy items—and is extremely popular among the natives.

MARKETS & FAIRS

Locals turn out in droves for markets and fairs, and visitors are encouraged to join the throng. Craft fairs are held with great regularity at **Ala Moana Park** and at **Thomas Square**, and schools, colleges and community organizations hold fairs and *ho'olaule'a* so often that there's one going on somewhere on the island almost every weekend—and sometimes in between. Annual favorites are the **Punahou Carnival** and the **50th State Fair** (see CALENDAR OF EVENTS). An all-time favorite for dedicated bargain hunters is the **Aloha Flea Market**, held at Aloha Stadium near Hālawa every Saturday and Sunday.

DINING

The 50 best restaurants
Fast foods
Bakeries
Shave ice

FINE and FUN DINING

E ating establishments on O'ahu offer a vast range of dining experience— in both foods and surroundings. From haute cuisine to ice cream, O'ahu has plenty to offer, and you can pick a venue to suit any mood.

THE 50th STATE'S BEST RESTAURANTS ON O'AHU

There are uncountable numbers of places to eat in Honolulu, plus a few notable eateries in other parts of O'ahu.

A selection of choice dining establishments is listed here, ranked in order of price and quality. A complete list, categorized by cuisine, is included as an appendix at the back of this book.

Fine dining

The following criteria were used in evaluating the quality of restaurants rated below:

indicated are per person and do not include drinks. Most restaurants accept major credit cards.

- texture and taste of food
- service
- price in relation to food
- melding of menu items
- china and napery
- decor and lighting
- physical property
- ambience
- an inherent essence of excellence

The following symbols will assist you in choosing a restaurant to suit your requirements, your taste and your budget. Price ranges

B	Breakfast
L	Lunch
D	Dinner
R	Reservations suggested
J	Jacket required
E	Entertainment/dancing
NW	No wheelchair access
$$$$$	very pricey
$$$$	$40 +
$$$	$30-$40
$$	$15-$30
$	$10-$15

DINING

156

Bali by the Sea $$$$ RE/D
Multi-level dining with views to the sea. Exquisite napery and crystal, superb wine list. Local favorites—veal sauteed with pepper sauce, fresh *'opakapaka* in light basil and lemon. Table cart chilled for sherbets. Hilton Hawaiian Village 2005 Kālia Road 949-4321

Bon Appetit $$$ R/D
Contemporary French country cuisine blends with Island provender. Fine wine bar. Four-course weekly gourmet dinner plus ala carte. Discovery Bay 1778 Ala Moana Blvd 942-3837

La Mer $$$$$ RJ/D
Made for sunset and moonlight dining, windows open wide to sounds of the surf and Hawaiian music. Menu is creative French with full use of Hawai'i's fresh produce. Lobster bisque starter, Strawberry Sunburst or cheese and port tray finis. The Halekulani 2199 Kālia Road 923-2311

Maile $$$$ RJE/D
Soft lighting, soft chairs, soft colors, dramatic flowers, unobtrusive service, international menu with an island touch. Baked *kumu* with fennel, roast Peking duckling, prawns with goose liver, truffles. Kahala Hilton 5000 Kāhala Avenue 734-2211

Michel's at the Colony Surf $$$$$ RJ (at dinner) / B L D
French restaurant, gold framed mirrors, velvet chairs, wide open to the breaking surf of Sans Souci Beach. Island touches—chicken in tarragon with papaya, local fish in cream wine sauce with Chinese pea pods. Particularly nice spot for Brunch. 3895 Kalākaua Avenue 923-6552

Roy's Restaurant $$$ R/LD
Nouvelle cuisine in a light and airy contemporary setting overlooking the water in Hawaii Kai. For good reason, award-winning Chef Roy Yamaguchi had a reputation for excellence before he opened this spot and the menu makes it well worth the extra drive. Sunday brunch offered. Hawaii Kai Corporate Plaza 6600 Kalanianaole Hwy. 396-7697

FOUR-STAR RESTAURANTS

Alfred's $$$ R/LD
Continental setting, hideaway chairs. Best of many cuisines—German, French, English, California, Hawaiian—complemented by well-chosen wines. Weiner schnitzel, *ulua* in lobster sauce, lamb Provencal, caramel Chantilly. Century Center 1750 Kalākaua Avenue 955-5353

DINING

157

☆☆☆☆

Bagwell's 2424 $$$$$ RE / D

Popular wine bar. Tall English-windows above Kūhiō Beach. Floor to ceiling glass fountain highlights bleached wood, beige velvet, tapestry upholstery. 'Opakapaka baked in filo, lobster and endive salad, tiny lamb chops broiled with carmelized garlic and sweet red peppers, double chocolate pate and zabaglione. Hyatt Regency Waikiki 2424 Kalākaua Avenue 922-9292

Chez Michel $$$ R / LD

No longer the original Michel, but still warm hospitality, cool ferns in pink and green setting for 'opakapaka saute Grenobloise, ris de veau in wine and cream, whole chilled artichokes with vinaigrette, Grand Marnier souffle, selective wine list. Eaton Square 444 Hobron Lane 955-7866

Golden Dragon $$$ RE / D

Chef Dai Hoy Chang moved beside the sea. Menu has fifty traditional Cantonese dishes, two masterpieces—Imperial Beggar's chicken and Imperial Peking duck. 'Tea Lady' brings twenty tea selections and Chinese Year fortunes. Special wines, beers. Hilton Hawaiian Village 2005 Kālia Road 949-4321

Il Fresco $$$ R / LD

Critics from all over the country have tossed kudos at this casual California-style restaurant that serves contemporary dishes from pastas to fine fish entres. A modern two-story restaurant, Il Fesco's piquant blackened ahi appetizers set the standard for this now-popular dish. The crab cakes are terrific and Il Fresco makes its own special ice creams for dessert. Ward Centre 523-5191

Matteo's $$$$ R / DE

Popular Italian restaurant in the classic style of fine Italian restaurants—Rococo decor, intimate tables, quiet. Honolulu magazine has called Matteo's the town's most popular restaurant. The food is excellent. Cocktails. Marine Surf Hotel 364 Seaside Ave. 922-5551

Nicholas Nickolas $$$ R / D

Continental with a touch of Chicago, an overlay of Greece, and Island-grown fare. Calamari steak in garlic butter, Greek chicken oregano, swordfish with spinach and feta cheese, baklava for dessert. Pastel decor, spectacular views, late supper and dancing. Ala Moana Americana Hotel 410 Atkinson Drive 955-4466

Restaurant Suntory $$$ R / LD

Elegant dining in orderly serenity. Nouveau bar in black, chrome; traditional noren-styled tepanyaki, shabu shabu and sushi dining. Pour soup from a teapot, braise fresh fish on hot stones, relish caviar and sea urchin sushi—fine wines, sake or beer. Royal Hawaiian Shopping Center 922-5511

The Secret $$$ R / D

With cocktails, nibble on fresh naan bread and duck pate. An open, high-ceiling room with colorful Camelot banners—and hideaway chairs. Offers medallions

DINING

158

****

of venison, seafood casserole in fennel sauce, bonbons in a mist, ten coffees, fifteen teas. Hawaiian Regent 2552 Kalākaua Avenue 921-5161

Sergio's $$$$ R / L D

From insalata to fettucine al burro, or antipasto marinara to tortellini in parmesan cream sauce, to veal piccata and real spumoni, this comfortable restaurant with dark polished woods and fine wines presents the best in Italian hospitality and satisfying dining. Ilima Hotel 445 Nohonani Street 926-3388

***

THREE-STAR RESTAURANTS

The Black Orchid $$$/$$$$ R / L D E

Locals residents consider the Black Orchid 'so L.A.' for good reason. TV star Tom Selleck originally created and opened it and it reflects the glamor of old Hollywood in its polished wood, brass, etched glass and autographed stars' pictures lining the walls. The food, classic fine restaurant fare with lots of French sauces, is usually good although it can be inconsistent. The restaurant with its jumping lounge is still Honolulu's hottest spot and worth a visit if only for the fun of it. Restaurant Row 500 Ala Moana Blvd. 521-3111

John Dominis $$$$$ R / D

Smashing view—boats under way, Waikīkī and Diamond Head gold at sunset, sparkling by night. Live lobster and crab navigate a brook around the dining room and central display of *ulua, onaga,* clams and oysters soon to be eaten at a dear price—also salads, steak, linguini and lamb. Kewalo Basin 43 'Āhui Street 523-0955

Keo's Thai Cuisine $$ R / D

Tropical ambience, white wicker furniture, hanging orchids. Gourmet Thai. Crispy noodles with chicken, sateh beef and hot peanut sauce, Evil Jungle Prince shrimp. Order entrees mild, spicy or hot; or order Singha beer. Celebrity hangout. 625 Kapahulu Avenue and at Ward Centre 737-9250

Musashi $$$ R / D

Small jewelbox Japanese restaurant. Imaginitive and traditional. Guests don hapi coats, and straw-wrapped keg of sake is wheeled in for first toast. Special Kaiseki—ten courses of seasonal delicacies noted for unique and beautiful preparation. Hyatt Regency Waikiki 2424 Kalākaua Avenue 922-9292

Nick's Fishmarket $$$$ R E / D

Fresh from early morning fish auctions—*'opakapaka, kumu, onaga, ulua, mahimahi,* all of Hawaii's great fish, and shellfish flown fresh from the Mainland. Salads and winelists chosen to complement the menu. Subtle decor and lighting. Waikiki Gateway Hotel 2070 Kalākaua Avenue 955-6333

DINING

TWO-STAR RESTAURANTS

Hanohano Room $$$$$ RE/BD

Tiered for a *hanohano* [glorious, magnificent] view up and down Waikīkī, morning or evening. Nightly entrees—abalone sauteed with dill sauce, rack of lamb roasted in herbs. Ride glass elevator for espresso at a bar with wonderful view. Sheraton Waikiki 2259 Kalākaua Avenue 922-4422

Orson's $$$ R/LD

A favorite local secret. Pleasing ambience and service, view over Kewalo Basin, and, maybe the best seafood in town—just steps from the fishing boats. Special- -deep-fried scallops or oysters, soft shell crab in season, chowder with sour- dough bread. Ward Warehouse, upper level 1050 Ala Moana Blvd 521-5681

160

Surf Room $$$ RE/BLD

Right where it should be: on the beach, in the center of everything. Big open terrace under turquoise and white awnings that bar the sun but don't spoil the view. Even first-time visitors get a sense of deja vu. This is Waikīkī. Breakfast is beautiful, the sand swept clean except for footprints of the first surfers. Goes with the clean taste of papaya and lime. The food is not as exciting. Royal Hawaiian Hotel 2259 Kalākaua Avenue 923-7311

The Willows $$$ RE/LD

Hospitable charm of old Hawai'i in a thatched roof cluster along a *koi* pond shaded by plumerias and willows. Kalua pork, *laulau*, *lomilomi* salmon, sweet potatoes, *poi* and *haupia*, served on china, royalty style. Also *haole* dishes. 901 Hausten Street 946-4808

ONE-STAR RESTAURANTS

Compadres Mexican Bar & Grill $$ BLD

The place to be for Margaritas at sundown—on the terrace or at the bar. Festive Mexican specialties all day, even breakfast with huevos rancheros and an omelette buffet. Big, open, sparkling. Ward Centre, upper level 1200 Ala Moana Blvd 523-1307

Dynasty II $$$ R/LD

Dine amidst marble floors, formal furniture, Chinese antiques and velvet Peking rugs on a variety of seafood and vegetable sizzling platters, spring rolls that almost fly away, or regal Peking duck. Ward Warehouse, upper level 1050 Ala Moana Blvd 531-0208

An eclectic blend of foods reflects Hawai'i's many ethnic groups.

Windows of Hawaii $$$ R/LD

Flying saucer revolving restaurant four hundred feet in the sky, 360° wall-to-wall scenic vistas that provide a circle trip of Honolulu in about an hour. New England-Hawai'i cuisine. Weekend champagne brunch, moonlight late suppers. atop Ala Moana Building 1441 Ala Moana Blvd 941-9138

Fun dining

In addition to world-class fine dining, O'ahu offers myriad eating experiences that provide taste treats and just plain fun.

Baci Ristorante $$ R/LD

Newly 'in' spot. Dine in simple elegance on enticing and innovative Italian cuisine, with maybe a wait for service. Waikiki Trade Center 2255 Kūhiō Avenue 924-2533

Buzz's Original Steak House $$

Casual, Windward oasis celebrating twenty-five years of delicious *kiawe* -broiled steak and lobster, fresh fish, teriyaki ribs, chops, prawns—salad bar famous for Buzz's dressings, fresh avocado, pineapple, Maui onions, local greens, potato salad and warm garlic bread. 413 Kawailoa Road, Lanikai 261-4661 (also in Mōili'ili 2535 Coyne Street 944-9781, Pearl City 98-751 Kuahao Pl. 487-6465)

Captain's Galley $$$ R/D

Dining inside and out, steaks broiled to perfection over *kiawe* wood, seafood, special salads. Dancing and entertainment. Moana Hotel 2365 Kalākaua Avenue 922-3111

The Cove Restaurant $$$ RE/D NW

Try chilled *sashimi*; Tahitian crab meat soup with coconut meat; 'ahi with lobster sauce; medallions of veal, Hawai'i avocado and green pepper sauce. Cove coffee with chocolate, orange and whipped cream is very special; so is the view over the lighted bay. Turtle Bay Hilton, Kahuku 293-8811

Guiltless Gourmet $ LD

'Lite Restaurant and Dessert Shoppe'—food is delicious, filling, low in calories. No added fats, no added sugar, no added starches or preservatives. Full menus available lunch through dinner. 593 Kamehameha Hwy, 456-2288

Hard Rock Café $$ LD

Handsome, brand new building, with a decor featuring genuine rock and roll artifacts and, for a local flavor, surfing memorabilia; maintains the chain's confirmed allegiance to American food. Burgers, fries, malts, shakes, barbeque beef and munch, munch more; house specialties are lime barbeque chicken and baby rock watermelon ribs; background music is recorded rock and roll hits from the '50s to the '80s. corner Kalakaua Ave and Kapi'olani Blvd 955-7383

DINING

162

Jameson's by the Sea $ R / L D

View over river and Waialua Bay. Fresh caught fish, chowders, stews, scallops, oysters, biscuits, Irish fried potatoes. Any number of libations. Hale'iwa (next to the old iron bridge, facing the bay) 637-4336

Kemoo Farm $$ R E / L D

Old plantation manor house with fare to match. View over Lake Wilson, charming service, sixty-six years in operation. Fresh trout, boneless roast duck with macadamia stuffing, steaks, seafood, good wine list. Brunch and dinner hangout for the polo crowd in season. 1718 Wilikina Drive, Wahiawā 621-8481

La Salsa $/$$ L / D

Great Yucatan style Mexican food spotlighting natural ingredients and a large variety of freshly made salsas—hot, sweet, spicy and mild. Tortillas are made right on the premises; no lard is used, and black beans are imported. Sakaritas are made from saki and the adjoining cantina is a popular watering spot for local office folks. Restaurant Row 500 Ala Moana Blvd. 536-4828

Maple Garden $/$$ R / L D

This small but cozy Chinese restaurant is one of the local favorites. Gourmet Szechwan cuisine. Menu features a varied selection of entrees, including vegetarian specials. Try shrimp & chicken Ala Maple Garden, smoked Szechwan duck, Chinaman's Hat. Only 10 minutes away from Waikiki. 909 Isenberg Street 941-6641

Pagoda Floating Restaurant $$ R / L D NW

Wonderful place to take children for lunch to watch the fish fed, hundred of prized, multi-colored koi. French and Japanese cuisine in large-windowed rooms looking out over the ponds and Pagoda Gardens. Pagoda Hotel 1525 Rycroft Street 941-6611

Peppers $ D

Great Margaritas, kiawe-smoked ribs, Texas-red chili, chicken or beef nachos, and gringo Cobb salads, sourdough tuna melt and cheese steak on a Hoagie. Outrigger East 150 Ka'iulani Avenue 926-4374

Plumeria Cafe $$ R E / L

Cafe delectables in a courtyard atmosphere with a view of the world passing by—also late supper. Pastries, pasta, steaks, salads, fruit sherbet. Kahala Hilton 5000 Kahala Avenue 734-2211

Rainbow Lanai $/$$ L / D

This is a gem of a find right in the Hilton Hawaiian Village—fronting the beach in the Rainbow Tower. The menu is light, healthy and lively featuring "cuisine of the Islands"—including Moloka'i vegetables wrapped in nori (seaweed), taro soup, Moloka'i venison sausage, Kona yearling beef, fresh sashimi dishes among many, many others. Hilton Hawaiian Village 949-4321

DINING

163

Fun dining

Rose City Diner $$ B L D

A real fifties-style diner with a soda fountain and all the lip-smacking delicacies it can produce, burgers, fries and onion rings (and more), roller skating waitresses and a jukebox. No credit cards—just like the old days. Restaurant Row 500 Ala Moana Blvd. 525-ROSE

Ruth's Chris Steak House $$$$ R / L D

A version of the famed New Orleans restaurant, this ultra-modern pristine atmosphere focuses on one feature: excellently prepared Prime Beef! If that's your pleasure, you'll be right at home here. Cocktails. Restaurant Row 599-3860

Seafood Emporium $$ R / L D

Scrubbed-wood restaurant, sunny by day, candlelight by night. Excellent seafood, soft shell crab in season, seafood linguini, *ono* (that's both a fish and 'delicious'). Royal Hawaiian Shopping Center 922-5547

Shogun Japanese Steak & Seafood Restaurant $$ R / B L D

Want a short visit to Kobe? Elegant Japanese cuisine and service befitting a shogun, plus waterfalls and mermaids. Teppan tables and sushi bar. Pacific Beach Hotel 2863 Kalakaua Avenue 922-1233

Shirokiya's $ B L D NW

Most exciting okazu-ya (Japanese deli) is the food fair and restaurant on the store's second floor. In an active, noisy, exotic atmosphere, chefs deftly cook and process many specialties to sample. Adjoining is the neat, sunny restaurant with more than fifty bento boxes, sushi packs, donburi and hot noodle dishes and light snacks, or *kalua* pork, beef curry, barbecue chicken, rice and *namasu*. Ala Moana Shopping Center, mall level 941-9111

Tripton's American Café $$ R / D NW

All American menu—baked or barbecued chicken, steak, lamb chops, pasta, salads, homemade soup, homemade lemon meringue pie, mocha custard. 449 Kapahulu Avenue (above Hee Hing) 737-3819

Wo Fat $ R / L D NW

This famous Chinatown chop suey restaurant has been a dining experience for over one hundred years. Special—ham and chicken soup in winter melon, steamed whole fish with Canton sauce, taro duck with thousand layer buns. 115 North Hotel Street 533-6393

Woodlands $ R / L D

A well-appointed but homey Chinese restaurant that has garnered a long list of fans from all over the country—restaurant critics included. The Woodlands Pot Stickers will change the way you've ever thought of pot stickers—vegetarian as well as meat and seafood. Other dishes are easily among the best Szechwan food in town. 1289 S. King St. 526-2239

FAST FOODS

At Ala Moana Center, facing Ala Moana Park and the ocean on the lower level, is a vast food hall called the **Makai Market**—uncountable tables and chairs in the center, ringed by almost every type of fast food outlet yet conceived. The king of home-grown eateries is **Zippy's**, with over fifteen locations and about the same number of ethnic food combinations on their list. They're known primarily for their 'plate lunch' combinations, pizza, chili and an apple pastry called 'napples' from their in-house Napoleon's Bakery.

Hawai'i also hosts most of the big US mainland franchises—**McDonald's, Burger King** and **Jack-in-the-Box**—but with some local flavor added to most menus with items such as saimin, rice and Portuguese sausage. A North Shore hamburger favorite is **Kua'Aina**. Chicken is a big hit among the locals, evidenced by numerous chicken chains: **Kentucky Fried Chicken, Church's** and **Popeye's. Healthy's** and **Vim & Vigor** have fast food vegetarian fare. Another popular local food haunt is **Grace's Inn,** with favorites like hamburger steak and chicken katsu. In the same class are **Bea's, Bob's Bar-B-Que,** and **Ted's Kal-Bi Ribs.** The KC **Drive-Inn**—locally famous for waffle dogs and ono ono shakes—is almost a landmark. **Kozo Sushi** ranks high for Japanese food, and for saimin, check out **Shiro's,** where they have fifty-nine different kinds of saimin, the most popular choice being 'Dondonpa' with its ten different garnishes. **Washington Saimin Stand** is another popular choice. Pizza lovers will find happiness at **Harpo's, Hippo's, Magoo's** and **Zorro's,** as well as at popular franchises like **Pizza Hut, Round Table, Pizzeria Uno** and **Domino's**; and Mexican fast food can be found at **Taco House, Taco Bell** and others.

COOKBOOKS

Those doing their own cooking might wish to try some local recipes, taking advantage of the ready availability of all the ingredients—which are hard to come by in some areas and climates. Many such cookbooks are sold at bookstores and souvenir shops. Island Heritage has published three collections of local recipes which we can recommend: *Favorite Recipes from Hawai'i, Tropical Drinks and Pupus from Hawai'i* and *Entertaining Island Style* .

BAKERIES

Locals love baked goods, and there are many vintage bakeries on the island as well as a number of newer European-style patisseries. Old-timers include **Bakery Kapi'olani, King's Bakery** (with adjacent restaurant serving Portuguese sweetbread french toast), **Leonard's Bakery** (known for their malasadas), and **Dee Lite Bakery** (with scrumptious doughnuts). **Napoleon's** bakeries are found in most Zippy's locations. **St. Germain**, in Shirokiya department store, has melt-in-your-mouth muffins. Other European-style kitchens include the **Old Vienna Bake Shoppe** (superb breads), **The Patisserie** (highly visible in Waikīkī) and **Croissan-terie**, both located downtown, and **Mary Catherine's** in Ward Centre, producing an exquisite selection of the best cakes and Continental pastries on O'ahu. The **Yum Yum Tree** at Ward Centre and Kahala Mall is justly famous for its pies.

ICE CREAM and YOGURT

Hawai'i's ice cream and frozen yogurt selection is outstanding, and notable for its inclusion of exotic Island flavors often not readily available elsewhere; coconut, macadamia nut, poha, kona coffee, pineapple and passionfruit are amongst the local delights.

The national trend of made-on-the-premises ice cream and cookie/candy toppings is followed at **Dave's**, **Bubbie's** and **White Mountain Creamery**. Kaua'i-based **Lappert's**, a popular local favorite for years, has begun exporting to the US mainland.

Mainland franchises well-represented on O'ahu include **Baskin-Robbins**, **Swensen's**, **Haagen Dazs**, and **Dairy Queen**. TCBY (The Country's Best Yogurt) has become a favorite along with **Yami Yogurt** and **Penguins**, all of which are available in various locations. Most ice cream and yogurt establishments keep late hours.

167

NUTS, COOKIES and CANDY

Hawai'i is famous for macadamia nuts, and the succulent kernels are available roasted and/or laced with an imaginative array of coatings—in addition to chocolate, coffee and honey—in practically every shop in Waikīkī as well as in many stores all over the island. Some of the more notable outlets are **Morrow's Nut House**, **Hawaiian Holiday** and Waikīkī's ubiquitous ABC stores; less expensive alternatives are **Long's Drugs** and ordinary supermarkets.

The best cookie shops are franchises like the international **Mrs. Field's**, nationally known **Famous Amos** and locally founded **The Cookie Corner**.

Super-sweet Japanese confections—mochi, manju, chi chi dango—can be found at **Chikara-mochi Store**, **Crackseed World** and at **Nisshodo**, manufacturers for more than seventy years. The **Honolulu Chocolate Company** has quickly become a staple in Hono-lulu, offering unique confections

DINING

including truffles, white chocolate in the shape of tropical fish, shells and other fun things. **The Chocolate Lady** has also carved out a sweet niche for herself, as has the **Fudge Works** in Hale'iwa on O'ahu's rural North Shore. You can watch the confectioner turning it with perfect timing to cool on its marble slabs, and can have your purchase shipped directly to yourself or to some other lucky person.

SHAVE ICE

A visit to Hawai'i would be incomplete without at least one sampling of the endemic treat that can't be packed and shipped home: shave ice. This finely shaved ice with flavored syrup poured over it closely resembles what is generally known on the Mainland as 'snow cones', but it *isn't* the same. The texture of shave ice is much finer—more like actual snow, and the rainbow version is a delight to behold as well as to consume. On a hot afternoon, this treat is ultra-refreshing, and in a tropical setting it beats any snow cone.

Shave ice can be purchased from several Waikīkī snack shops (the most conspicuous is **Island Snow**) as well as from numerous mobile vendors along highways near beaches. **Matsumoto's** in Hale'iwa has become famous for its shave ice with ice cream or sweet bean paste underneath, and has beautiful T-shirts to commemorate the taste experience.

Shave ice, not to be confused with the Mainland snow cone, is unique to Hawai'i.

ACCOMMODATION

The 50 best hotels and condominiums
Bed and breakfast
Vacation homes
Cabins and campsites

ACCOMMODATION

T he first order of business for visitors is, of course, a place to stay—a home away from home. Nearly ninety percent of the more than forty thousand short-term rental units on O'ahu are located in the Waikīkī district. Most accommodations are hotel rooms, but also included are condominium apartments and rental rooms in private homes—an increasingly popular option.

O'ahu's fifty best hotels are described and rated below, followed by notations of other types of lodging; all are listed in alphabetical order as an appendix at the back of this book. While most people think automatically of hotels and condominiums when seeking lodging for their vacations, there are, in fact, several alternatives—such as hostels, camping cabins, private bed-and-breakfast situations, and the wonderful old-world guest house.

THE 50th STATE'S BEST HOTELS & CONDOMINIUMS

The ratings below indicate the quality of selected hotels on O'ahu. The criteria for a *good* hotel are simple: comfort, courtesy and cleanliness. In a *great* hotel, different things make different properties outstanding; our evaluations are based on the following criteria:

- architecture, decor, grounds and view
- well-trained, responsible and caring staff
- personalized consideration from manager, *concierge* and *maitre d'*, prompt room service, attention to details
- amenities and niceties such as fluffy towels, extra pillows, newspaper and wake-up coffee, flowers, beauty salons and shops

- fine dining, all-day restaurant and food service, poolside grazing
- most importantly, a memorable, warm, pleasing ambience

Unless you're traveling during the busy winter months (January through April with February at peak), reserving a room in advance shouldn't be a problem.

Room rates are seasonal, with the winter months fetching higher prices. The price ranges of the hotels listed are categorized as follows:

$$$$	luxury class
$$$	$100-$200+
$$	$70-$100
$	$35-$70

NW   No wheelchair/access

FIVE-STAR HOTELS

The Halekulani $$$$

The Halekulani is the essence of a world-class luxury hotel, and it's right on Waikīkī Beach; 465 expertly appointed rooms. La Mer is five ☆ restaurant; fine beachside dining, orchid swimming pool, cocktails, entertainment, boutique shops and superb service. 2199 Kālia Road 923-2311 (800 367-2343)

Kahala Hilton $$$$

On curving beach surrounded by Waialae Golf Course, 369 plush rooms, fifteen minutes from Waikīkī. Tennis, pool, watersports, dolphins, all amenities, upscale shops, cocktails, dancing, Maile Restaurant is five ☆. 5000 Kāhala Avenue 734-2211 (800 367-2525)

FOUR-STAR HOTELS

Aston Waikiki Beach Tower $$$ NW

One hundred and forty regal apartments, superb view across Kūhiō Beach. Two-bedroom suites, large living room, state-of-the-art kitchens, spa, sauna, pool, breakfast room service, concierge, parking valet. 2470 Kalākaua Avenue 926-6400 (800 922-7866)

Colony Surf $$$

Waikīkī's first condominium hideaway, on the beach beside the Outrigger Canoe Club, across from Kapi'olani Park. Bright rooms, 'glass walls', one hundred suites, run as a small European hotel, secluded five ☆ Michel's at the Colony and funky Bobby McGee's. 2895 Kalākaua Avenue 923-5751 (800 252-7873)

Hawaii Prince Hotel $$$

Waikīkī's newest luxury hotel offers 521 oceanfront rooms along with a swimming pool, restaurant, lounge and shops—as well as a location slightly closer to the financial district than most. 100 Holomoana St. 956-1111 (800 321-6284)

Hilton Hawaiian Village $$$$

Eighty million dollar renovation of rooms and grounds. Self-contained 2612-room resort, endless variety of shops, five ☆ and four ☆ dining, four-acre lagoon, grand pool, catamaran on private beach. Lounges, Hilton Dome showroom, many restaurants, large meeting space. 2005 Kālia Road 949-4321 (800 445-8667)

Hyatt Regency Waikiki $$$$

Twin forty-story towers with 1230 rooms connected by open-air Great Hall. Regency Club—special service, keyed elevators to top four floors. Six showplace

ACCOMMODATION

★★★★

restaurants and bars, jazz and swing club, swimming pool, two blocks of shopping. 2424 Kalākaua Avenue 923-1234 (800 233-1234)

Royal Hawaiian Hotel $$$$

Heart of Waikīkī, has private beach, cool green garden. 526 old-fashioned elegance, big rooms. Hawaiian show, tea dancing, beachside restaurant, swimming pool, shops. From era of great hotels. 2259 Kalākaua Avenue 923-7311 (800 325-3535)

Sheraton Moana Surfrider Hotel $$$

This is a glorious update to Waikiki's very first stylish, courtly hotel, renovated to bring back all its 1901 glories. The patio lounge and dining will help younger guests appreciate what those who flocked to the Moana in its hey day loved about it. 793 rooms total (with a 430 room tower, formerly called the Surfrider). Luxury boutiques, swimming pool—and great charm. 2365 Kalakaua Ave. 922-3111 (800 325-3535)

Turtle Bay Hilton & Country Club $$$

Under major renovation, this hotel resides on a lovely point on Oahu's gorgeous North Shore. With five miles of beach, 486 ocean view rooms and 86 elegent studio style cabanas, complete resort including golf, tennis, pools, shops, dancing and fine dining, this is a special destination for those who prefer to be out of Waikīkī's hustle and bustle. Kahuku 293-8811 (800 445-8667)

★★★

THREE-STAR HOTELS

Diamond Head Beach Hotel $$ NW

On beach at foot of Diamond Head. Small, sixty-five-room pink gem, European style, continental breakfast. Studio and suite units. Sunning beach, swimming beach. Reciprocal charges for Michel's Restaurant. 2947 Kalākaua Avenue 922-1928 (800 367-6046)

Hawaiian Regent $$$

Two towers, 1346 newly decorated rooms, across from Kuhio Beach, ocean front and ocean view. Garden lobby bar and cafe, fine dining, dancing club, swimming pools, tennis, shopping. Large meeting space. 2552 Kalakaua Avenue 922-6611 (800 367-5370)

The Ilikai at Waikiki Beach $$

Next to Ala Wai Yacht Harbor. 791 rooms total with oversize rooms, glorious views, particularly from 'Top of the I' Sunday brunch. Two pools, complete tennis facilities and water sports, two restaurants and lounges, thirty shops. Ample meeting spaces. 1777 Ala Moana Blvd 949-3811 (800 367-8434)

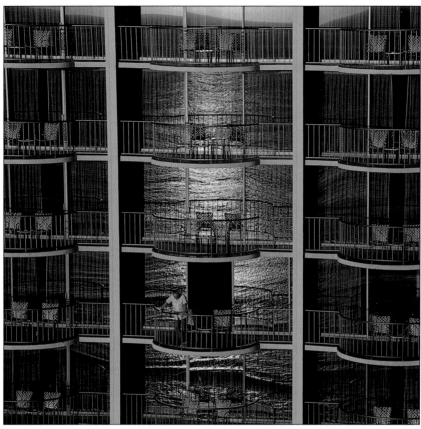

Honolulu sunset multiplied by myriad hotel rooms.

New Otani Kaimana Beach Hotel $$ NW

Across from Kapi'olani Park on lovely Sans Souci Beach, this newly modernized version of an old Hawaiian favorite has kept most of its traditional charm. Hau Tree Lanai, one of the last on-the-beach al fresco dining spots has the best view of offshore Waikīkī. Japanese restaurant is pricey; 138 newly renovated rooms, twenty-four garden apartments. 2863 Kalākaua Ave. 923-1555 (800 657-7949)

Outrigger Prince Kuhio $$$

Modern, marble elegance at this 620-room hotel one block from Kuhio Beach. Keyed elevator access to top three floors, Kuhio Club service. Tenth floor recreation deck and pool, two specialty restaurants, lounges and entertainment. 2500 Kuhio Avenue 922-0811 (800 733-7777)

Sheraton-Waikiki $$$

Front and center on Waikiki Beach with 1885 rooms. Three specialty restaurants, two coffee shops, lounges and entertainment. Two pools, an array of shops. Spectacular views from rooftop Hanohano Room. Major meeting hotel. Just completed $50 million redecoration project. 2255 Kalakaua Avenue 922-4422 (800 325-3535)

Waikiki Parc $$

One of Waikīkī's newest hotels; 298-room, twenty-two-story affordable luxury hotel adjacent to sister hotel, the Halekulani. Sophisticated accoutrements, two fine restaurants, lounges, recreation area and swimming pool. 2233 Helumoa Road 921-7272 (800 422-0450)

TWO-STAR HOTELS

Aston at the Waikiki Banyan $$

Provides both the convenience of a condominium and advantages of a hotel in 876 units. Each one-bedroom suite has fully-equipped kitchen and hotel services. Tennis court, pool, sauna, snack shop and mini-mart. One block from beach. 201 'Ohua Avenue 922-0555 (800 922-7866)

Aston Waikiki Sunset $$$

Four hundred thirty-five-unit resort of one- and two-bedroom apartments on the Diamond Head side of Waikīkī one block from beach. Heated pool, paddle tennis, sauna and barbecue, plus restaurant and lounge. 229 Paoakalani Street 922-0511 (800 922-7866)

Waikiki Beach Hotel $$

Across from Kūhiō Beach, one block from Kapi'olani Park; 714 rooms, most with ocean views. Specialty dining room, restaurant, coffee house, Captain's Lounge with nightly entertainment. Pub and swimming pool on upper sundeck. 2570 Kalākaua Avenue 922-2511 (800 877-7666)

Outrigger Waikiki $$ NW

Waikīkī beachfront, 530 rooms newly renovated, multiple dining and entertainment choices, swimming pool and all beach activities. Sixteenth floor is Kuhio Club; keyed elevator, concierge services, weight room. Full shopping, escalator entrance. 2335 Kalākaua Avenue 921-9747 (800 733-7777)

Pacific Beach Hotel $$

Busy, friendly, 850-room hotel across from Kūhiō Beach. Has amazing four-story 'oceanarium', the focal point of several restaurants, lounges and the nightclub. Tennis, shuffleboard, pool and Jacuzzi, shops. Some rooms with kitchens. 2490 Kalākaua Avenue 922-1233 (800 367-6060)

Princess Kaiulani $$

Across the street from Waikīkī Beach; 1156 rooms, three international restaurants and lounges, Polynesian showroom, large pool and restaurant in cool garden, spacious lobbies, varied shops. 120 Kai'ulani Avenue 922-5811 (800 325-3535)

ACCOMMODATION

Ala Moana Hotel $$$

Twelve hundred-room hotel has walkway overpass to Ala Moana Shopping Center; popular with business clients. Two blocks to Ala Moana Beach. Big pool, sunning area, several restaurants and lounges, showroom. Fine dining with highest view in town. 410 Atkinson Drive 955-4811 (800 367-6025)

☆

ONE-STAR HOTELS

Aston Island Colony $ NW

Seven hundred forty-unit property on Ala Wai Canal, choice of hotel rooms, studios or one-bedroom suites with full hotel amenities. Open-air lobby, pool, Jacuzzi, sauna, restaurant and lounge. 445 Seaside Avenue 923-2345 (800 922-7866)

Discovery Bay $$ NW

Across from Ilikai Hotel, two blocks to beach, same to Ala Moana Shopping Center; thirty-eight-story towers with one- and two-bedroom condominium units, fully equipped. Pool, sauna, spa, shopping complex and five ☆ restaurant. 1778 Ala Moana Blvd 944-8555 (800 367-7040)

Outrigger Reef Hotel $$ NW

Right on Waikīkī Beach, 885-room hotel sporting a $10 million renovation, Island hospitality in an informal atmosphere. Pool forms glass wall of Harry's Underwater Bar, one of five bars and lounges, six restaurants, shops galore. Young-at-heart property. 2169 Kālia Road 923-3111 (800 733-7777)

Sheraton Makaha Resort & Country Club $$

Championship golf course, tennis courts, riding stables, swimming pool, shuttle to beach; 200-room cottage-type, secluded hotel. Restaurants and lounges. Mākaha, Leeward O'ahu 695-9511 (800 325-3535)

Waikiki Shores $$

One hundred fifty-nine-unit apartment hotel on Waikīkī Beach and Fort DeRussy Park. Studios, one- and two-bedrooms, spacious, modern, with charming views. In the midst of all Waikīkī activity. 2161 Kālia Road 926-4733 (800 367-2353)

UNRATED HOTELS

Aloha Surf $

Newly renovated, 197 rooms on Ala Wai Canal, well-known Won Kee Chinese restaurant, swimming pool, shops. 444 Kānekapōlei Street 923-0222 (800 423-4514)

ACCOMMODATION

UNRATED HOTELS

Ambassador Hotel $ NW

Two hundred twenty-five-room highrise at Kūhiō and Kalākaua gateway to Waikīkī; two blocks from Fort DeRussy Beach; pool, coffee shop, lounge. 2040 Kūhiō Avenue 941-7777

Breakers Hotel $

A bit of old Waikīkī tucked away inside walls and gardens with pool and kitchenettes; one block from beach. 250 Beach Walk 923-3181

The Coconut Plaza Hotel $$$ NW

A European style all-suite style hotel fronting the Ala Wai Canal. Pool, complimentary continental breakfast. 2171 Ala Wai Blvd. 923-8828

Foster Tower $$

Across from Kūhiō Beach, 141 studios, one- and two-bedroom condominium units. Super views, swimming pool, shops, restaurant. 2500 Kalākaua Avenue 923-6883 (800 367-7040)

Hawaii Dynasty $

Two hundred relatively spacious rooms, queen-sized beds, excellent Chinese/American restaurant, Dynasty I; pool, shops, one block to beach. 1830 Ala Moana Blvd 955-1111 (800 367-5122)

Hawaiiana Hotel $

Ninety-five Hawaiian-style studio rooms, one block from beach; two swimming pools set among flowers and trees; kitchenettes. 260 Beach Walk 923-3811 (800 367-5123)

Ilima Hotel $ NW

One hundred studio and one-bedroom suites; kitchens, recently redecorated, two blocks to beach; Sergio's Italian Restaurant, lounge, pool. 445 Nohonani Avenue 923-1877 (800 367-5172)

Imperial Hawaii Resort $$ NW

Across from the Halekulani, 270 condominium units: studios, one- and two-bedrooms; pool, sauna, shops, coffee shop, one block to beach. 205 Lewers Street 923-1827 (800 367-8047)

Miramar at Waikiki $$

Three hundred seventy newly redecorated rooms, beautiful Chinese restaurant, cafe, lounges, swimming pool, shops. 2345 Kuhio Avenue 922-2077 (800 227-4320)

Outrigger East $ NW

Action-oriented hotel with 444 rooms, two blocks from beach; pool, shops, three restaurants, lounges, some kitchenettes, escalator entrance. 150 Ka'iulani Avenue 922-5353 (800 733-7777)

Outrigger Maile Court $$

Forty-three floors, 200 hotel rooms and suites with kitchenette and full hotel service. Pool, spa, shuffleboard, views. 2058 Kūhiō Avenue 947-2828 (800 733-7777)

Outrigger Malia $

Busy, friendly hotel, 328 rooms, well-known restaurant, lounges, shops, tennis court; two blocks to beach. 2211 Kūhiō Avenue 921-4804 (800 733-7777)

Park Shore $$ NW

On corner between Kūhiō Beach and Kapi'olani Park, friendly 227-room hotel, good views, restaurants, pool, shops. 2586 Kalākaua Avenue 923-0411 (800 367-2377)

Pleasant Holiday Isle $ NW

Two hundred sixty-four-room highrise smack in the center of Waikīkī, one block to the beach; pool, shops, cocktail lounge. 270 Lewers Street 923-0777

Queen Kapiolani $$ NW

Three hundred fifteen rooms, some with views, pool, shops, lounge with Hawaiian entertainment; Peacock Restaurant has Hawaiian buffets. 150 Kapahulu Avenue 531-5235 (800 367-5004)

Waikiki hotels overlooking Ala Wai Yacht Harbor.

UNRATED HOTELS

Royal Kuhio $ NW

Three hundred eighty-five one- and two-bedroom condominium units, full kitchen; swimming pool, paddle tennis, no in-room telephone service. 2240 Kūhiō Avenue 923-2502 (800 367-5205)

Waikiki Beachcomber $$ NW

Across Kalākaua from Royal Hawaiian; 498 redecorated rooms; escalator entrance, pool, shops, restaurants, lounges. 2300 Kalākaua Avenue 922-4646 (800 622-4646)

Waikiki Gateway Hotel $ NW

Two hundred-room hotel shaped like Mayan pyramid; pool, coffee shop, lounge, award-winning Nick's Fishmarket Restaurant. 2070 Kalākaua Avenue 955-3741 (800 367-5124)

Waikiki Grand Hotel $ NW

Across from Kapi'olani Park, 175 studio units, half-block to beach; full hotel service, Zen Restaurant, pool, shops. 134 Kapahulu Avenue 923-1511 (800 729-4726)

Waikiki Parkside Hotel $ NW

Across from Hilton Hawaiian Village, one block to beach, 250 rooms, some with kitchenettes, pool, restaurant, lounge. 1850 Ala Moana Blvd 955-1567 (800 237-9666)

GUEST HOUSES AND MORE

There are only two of these on O'ahu, in fact in the whole State. Indeed, there are not many of them left anywhere. By 'guest house' is meant a grand old home that has been converted to exclusive use as an inn and, though it does provide beds and breakfasts, it can hardly be placed in the same category as the popular budget bed-and-breakfast operations run from an increasing number of private homes.

Manoa Valley Inn $$$

Formerly called *John Guild Inn*, this lovely inn is a splendid example of excellence on a small scale. The setting, the decor and the service are all superb, and the small size of the place—there are only six rooms and a suite—allow a level of special, personal service and a feeling of intimacy and privacy that is not possible in the finest of large hotels. If you are at all interested in pampering yourself with luxuries characteristic of a bygone era, contact the inn for further details. 2001 Vancouver Drive 947-6019 (800 634-5115)

The Plantation Spa $$$

This is the island's only stand-alone spa, and it couldn't be located in lovelier area for rest and relaxation—amid the lush jungle of the island's Windward side. The spa handles only 14 guests at one time, and offers a one-week fitness program. 51-550 Kamehameha Hwy, Kaaawa 237-8685

BED AND BREAKFAST

An increasingly popular travel option is bed-and-breakfast lodging in private residences. This type of accommodation is more wide-spread on outer islands than on O'ahu, and on O'ahu is more common on the windward side of the island where there are only a couple of hotels. A broad range of living quarters—from modest to luxurious and rural to urban—can be arranged, with the median price at roughly thirty-five dollars a day. **Bed & Breakfast Honolulu** (3242 Kā'ohinani Drive 595-7533), **Bed & Breakfast Hawai'i** (196 Nenue Street 536-8421) and **Pacific-Hawai'i Bed & Breakfast** (19 Kai Nani Place 262-6026) can provide information and reservations.

ACCOMMODATION

179

The Royal Hawaiian, now dwarfed by countless hotels.

HOSTELS

Located in Mānoa Valley near the University of Hawaiʻi, **Honolulu International Youth Hostel** (2323A Sea View Avenue 946-0591) is a quiet, convenient, super-cheap place to stay. Some of its amenities include a kitchen, TV room and ping pong table; books and information on sightseeing, camping and outer island jaunts are available. **Hale Aloha** (926-8313) at 2417 Prince Edward St., and **Inter-Club Hostel Waikiki** (924-2636) at 2413 Kūhiō Ave. also have facilities.

VACATION HOMES

Extended vacations often call for a private 'home away from home'.

With a 'Kailua-style' attitude (informal), **Kailua Beachside Cottages** (262-4128) has a range of accommodations, from cottages to spacious homes, available on or near Kailua Beach. The following companies also cater to the vacation rental market: **Aston Hotels & Resorts** (922-3368, 800 922-7866), **Colony Resorts** (523-0411, 800 367-6046) and **Hawaiian Island Resorts** (531-7595, 800 367-7042).

CABINS AND CAMPSITES

Adventurous souls with a taste for the outdoor life favor more rustic lodging. Tent camping is permitted at some parks on Oʻahu, though some visitors at some campsites have experienced theft and other unpleasantness from time to time. A safer option is rental cabins—especially fun for families with teenage children.

Private camps

Rural accommodations are inexpensive; rates for cabins and camping depend on the size of the group.

Beachfront **Camp Mokuleia** (68-729 Farrington Hwy 637-6241) has cabins for four to six people and a campground.

Camp Hauula (55-017 Kamehameha Hwy 293-5390), run by the Catholic Youth Organization has dormitory-like rooms; theirs is a casual atmosphere, located right on the beach.

YWCA's **Camp Kokokahi** (45-035 Kāneʻohe Bay Drive 247-2124) on Kāneʻohe Bay rents cabins and has a larger complex with more rooms to accommodate bigger groups.

City and county beach parks

Like the State Parks, for camping purposes the beach parks are only open from Friday through Tuesday, with two exceptions. There are no camping fees, but permits must be obtained two weeks prior to camping at the City and County of Honolulu's Parks and Recreation Department (650 S King Street ground floor 523-4525). All parks have restroom facilities and showers. A map of the parks, available at the Department, lists the following camping areas open to the public: Makapu'u, Waimānalo, Bellows Field (weekends only), Ho'omaluhia Botanic Garden, Kualoa, Kahana Bay and Swanzy (weekends only) on the Windward side; Hale'iwa and Mokulē'ia on the North Shore and Ke'eau, Lualualei and Kahe Point on the Leeward side.

All of the above sites are described under BEACHES except Ho'omaluhia, which is under Parks and Gardens in SIGHTSEEING.

181

State parks

Permits are required for camping in State Parks, and these may be obtained at the Division of State Parks' district office on O'ahu (1151 Punchbowl Rm 310 M-F 8am-4:15pm). There are no fees, but applications must be submitted in person at the counter one week in advance of stay. Campgrounds are open from Friday through Tuesday on O'ahu. The sites where camping is permitted include Keaīwa Heiau State Recreation Area (see *Heiau* under SIGHTSEEING), the Kalanai Point section of Mālaekahana State Recreation Area and Mālaekahana Beach, and Sand Island State Recreation Area (see BEACHES).

ACCOMMODATION

NOTES

ET CETERA

Traveling with children
Other services
Handicapped travelers
Cautionary notes

TRAVELING WITH CHILDREN

H awai'i is an ideal destination for family vacations. Our relaxed, easygoing lifestyle, boundless outdoor activities and attention-getting, wholesome local entertainment provide children (and parents) with an enormous variety of diversions, many of them also educational.

AMUSEMENTS

O'ahu holds many delights for children. The **Honolulu Zoo**, in addition to its regular exhibits of fascinating creatures, has a mini-zoo of farm-type livestock especially for children where they can handle and interact with the animals.

Sea Life Park, an outstanding example of this genre, offers spectacular viewing of undersea creatures and the environments in which they live, as well as displaying the high intelligence of marine mammals such as dolphins and sea lions. The **Waikīkī Aquarium** also provides a closer look at the marine world, and many of its activities, such as guided walks along reef and shore, are ideal for curious youngsters. You can bring a lunch and enjoy the **Hawaiian Humane Society's Bird Park**, a restful wooded glade with an aviary as well as a turtle pond and other natural wonders.

Another memorable visit for the children would be to the **Kahala Hilton Hotel** to watch the dolphin feeding, every day at 11am, 2pm and 4pm; this delightful spectacle is open to the public and free of charge.

The **Polynesian Cultural Center** and **Waimea Falls Park** are excellent places for families to spend a full afternoon, and their rural locations provide the opportunity for swimming and picnicking enroute. There are also a number of easy hiking trails that are suitable for families with older children.

Kids and adults might be amused by a spin on the ice at the **Ice Palace** in the Pearl City area, after a day at the beach.

There is a small **children's playground** on the *mauka* side of **Kapi'olani Park** with swings and a conglomerate of walkways and tunnels.

For details about Parks and Popular Attractions see SIGHTSEEING. For descriptions and ratings of beaches, see BEACHES. Many other activities suitable for family excursions are detailed under SPORTS & RECREATION. Worthwhile spectator events, carnivals and such are listed under LOCAL FESTIVALS/CALENDAR OF EVENTS.

FAMILY RESTAURANTS

Most restaurants happily accommodate diminutive young diners; many prefer advance notice if you are bringing very young children.

Kids always enjoy **Showbiz**

Pizza Place, which has various amusements to occupy them while the pizza bakes. A great eating place for youngsters is the **Oceanarium** family restaurant at the Pacific Beach Hotel where diners are seated around the curve of a three-story, 280,000-gallon aquarium filled with fascinating fishes. Teens will enjoy the upbeat, trendy atmosphere at the new **Hard Rock Café**. Everyone in the family can choose a different cuisine at the **Makai Market** food court at Ala Moana Center. The **Yum Yum Tree, Tony Roma's, Marie Callendars, The Old Spaghetti Factory** and the Hyatt's **Terrace Grille** are also favored family restaurants. For local-style family dining, try **Zippy's** or **Bea's**. Also see FINE AND FUN DINING and the Appendix at the back of this book.

TENDER TOTS

Keep in mind the sensitive skin of a child when doling out the sunscreen. It cannot be stressed enough how potentially hazardous the sun can be in a tropical environment, and nothing ruins a vacation quicker than an afflicted youngster. Use total sun block for the first few days, then doses of gradual protection for the duration of your visit, but protection should be used at all times. For burns, calamine lotion and lotions with aloe are helpful.

In the event of a medical emergency, **Kapi'olani Women's and Children's Medical Center** (1319 Punahou Street 947-8511) should be contacted immediately.

Their **Poison Center** number is 941-4411.

California sea lion, Sea Life Park.

ET CETERA

186

ACTIVITY PROGRAMS

The **Hawai'i Nature Center** runs an environment education program aimed primarily at schools, but it has fascinating weekend programs and workshops in Hawaiiana—such as making ancient Hawaiian toys like kukui nut tops and jacks, and bamboo nose flutes—and an extensive nature-oriented summer program for children and families. Twice each month the Center sponsors guided hikes along the nature trails in the Ko'olaus near Honolulu (2131 Makiki Heights Drive 973-0100).

Some hotels offer daily programs for children during summer and holiday seasons, when they employ junior hostesses to coordinate the activities. These might include hula lessons, lei making and building sandcastles.

BABYSITTING

Many hotels also offer babysitting services; contact your concierge or information desk.

If you want a night out without the children and your hotel doesn't have an in-house babysitter, call **Aloha Babysitting Service** (732-2029); this reliable operation has been providing visitors in the Waikīkī area with fully licensed and bonded sitters, twenty-five years of age or older, for many years. Sitters travel to the hotels with books and toys in tow for a modest hourly rate plus a small additional charge per additional child. The service has a four-hour minimum and a minimal charge for transportation to the hotel.

OTHER SERVICES

Here we cover a miscellany of other services that did not lend themselves to appropriate inclusion in other sections of the guidebook—everything from typists to luggage repair to specialists in the arrangement of tropical nuptials.

Luggage repair

There are numerous cobblers capable of this type of repair; for your convenience, we looked for those in the Waikīkī area. As it happens there are four of them at 1630 Kalākaua Avenue, which is a couple of blocks *mauka* of Kapi'olani Boulevard: **A-1 Luggage Repair Company** (949-4527), and **Luggage Doctor** (947-6666). A-1 also has a shop at Ala Moana Center, and **AA Kim's Shoe 'n' Luggage Repair** (see below) is a few blocks *mauka* of Waikīkī on McCully.

Shoe repair

Offering either one-day or on-the-spot shoe repairs—depending on the problem and the workload—are: **AA Kim's Shoe 'n' Luggage Repair** (946-6008), **K & S Shoe Repair** (735-0057) and **Joe Pacific Shoe Repair** (946-2998), all located near Waikīkī.

Dry cleaning

Handy Waikīkī dry cleaning services are: **Happy Cleaners** (955-5866), **Al Phillips the Cleaner** (923-1971) and **Caesar's Cleaners** (734-0052). Some hotels will also handle this service for guests.

Laundromats

The need for a laundromat can be urgent. These facilities are available at the **Outrigger Hotel Arcade** (923-0711), the **Outrigger East** and **Outrigger West Hotels** (923-2057), at the **Coral Seas Hotel**, the **Edgewater Hotel** and at the **Waikiki Ena Road Laundry** (942-3451), next door to 7-Eleven on 'Ena Road. Many hotels have coin-operated laundromat facilities for the exclusive use of their guests.

Nuptials

An activity popular among visitors to the Islands is either getting married or renewal of vows. Most couples who do this were acquainted before they arrived.

Numerous enterprises are engaged in the business of making people's romantic dreams of tropical settings and ceremonies come true. We have so many spots that are splendidly suited to the purpose that the difficulty is in choosing. Some of the most favored locations are Waikīkī Beach, Hanauma Bay, Haiku Gardens, Waimea Falls Park, Moanalua Gardens and Foster Botanic Gardens; there are also, of course, many lovely indoor settings, but outdoor ceremonies are overwhelmingly preferred. Some of the companies that arrange or assist in wedding ceremonies and celebrations are **A Hawaiian Wedding Experience** (926-6689), **Weddings In Paradise** (941-7515), **Waimea Falls Park** (638-8511), **Aloha Wedding Planners** (523-1441) and the **Damien Waring Estate** (373-2141). An option that's a little different is a ceremony at sea, offered by **Tradewinds Sailing Charters** (533-0220 or 533-7734) and **Windjammer Cruisers** (926-1566).

For information on marriage licenses see Permits and Licenses under GETTING HERE.

Notaries

Few visitors need the services of a notary public during their stay but, in the event that you do, one in Waikīkī is **Budget Typing & Notary Service** (947-6636), who also make out-calls. Not far from Waikīkī is **Kenneth Kawada** (732-3737). **Robert Lee** (732-2955) operates from Kaimuki during the day and, from 6pm-12m nightly, can be found Downtown (523-5979).

Business services

Increasingly, business visitors in particular have need of secretarial and other executive services while on O'ahu. Handy to hotel-based business people are: **Best Secretarial Service of Oahu** (946-2440), **Business Services Center** (955-9555), **Executive Secretarial Services** (521-6383), and **Ditto's Photocopy and Typewriter Rentals** (943-0005 open twenty-four hours).

Clothing repair

There are lots of tailors in town who will custom make garments to your specifications as well as mend what you've torn. The most conveniently located clothing repair artists for Waikīkī-based visitors are **Ann's Dress Hospital** (949-5775), which also services men's clothing, and **A-1 Cleaning by DeMello** (941-7576) at the Hilton Hawaiian Village.

Civic clubs

A lot of visitors who belong to civic clubs back home inquire with tourist service desks about local chapters; most frequently sought are **Lions Club International** (*District 50* 524-7025) and **Rotary International** (*District 500* 734-5698); visiting members from other districts are welcome to telephone for information about local meetings and activities.

Libraries

O'ahu's libraries offer lending rights to visitors who obtain a local library card during their stay. The **Waikīkī-Kapahulu** (732-2777) branch of the public library system is conveniently located at the Diamondhead end of the Ala Wai Canal. The **Hawai'i State Library** (548-4775), worth visiting for the building alone, is located on the edge of the downtown 'capital district', at the corner of King and Punchbowl Streets, adjacent to 'Iolani Palace.

ET CETERA

Post offices

Last but not least is your friendly neighborhood post office. Post office hours are: **M-F 8:00am-4:30pm Sa 8:00am-12noon.** The **Waikīkī** branch (330 Saratoga Road 941-1062) is located right next to Fort DeRussy, in the same block. Another convenient branch is at **Ala Moana Center** (946-2020) on the *mauka* side just 'Ewa of the central mall. The **Downtown** station (546-5625) is located at the corner of Merchant and Richards Streets, opposite 'Iolani Palace, in the beautiful Old Federal Building. Honolulu's **Main Post Office** is at the Airport (3600 Aolele Street 423-3930).

HANDICAPPED TRAVELERS

T he environment of O'ahu is great for handicapped travelers, and many do visit our shores. A lot of attention has begun to be paid to the needs of our handicapped visitors (as well as residents), and the Hawai'i Commission on the Handicapped has published a brochure titled 'The Oahu Travelers Guide for Physically Handicapped Persons', which contains full details of access and facilities for a number of O'ahu points of interest, beaches and parks, shopping centers, hotels, restaurants and entertainment establishments that serve the tourist industry. Copies are available from the Commission on the Handicapped (Old Federal Building 335 Merchant Street Rm 353 548-7606). The internationally recognized wheelchair access symbol (W) is used in the ACCOMMODATION and DINING sections of this book to denote those establishments that do not have wheelchair access.

TRANSPORTATION AND TOURS

The City and County provides curb-to-curb service through **Handi-Van Service** (1585 Kapi'olani Blvd Suite 1554 833-2222). To obtain a free pass, apply at the Department of Transportation Services-MTL Office (725 Kapi'olani Blvd 524-4626 7:30am-4pm). Reservations must be made twenty-four hours in advance. The vans run from 6am-4pm, and fares are one dollar each way for all distances. Visitors who have obtained a pass during their stay may use this service to return to the Airport.

Handicabs of the Pacific (50 S Beretania Street 524-3866), a private taxi company, has vans with ramps to accommodate wheelchairs and provides special tours for disabled persons. Airport transfers to Waikīkī hotels are available for a slightly expensive but reasonable charge, including attendants.

Tours include: a half-day City Tour of Honolulu, an all-day Circle Island Tour, a half-day Little Island Circle Tour from Waikīkī to Sea Life Park, a day and evening Polynesian Cultural Center package including admission to the show and a Sunset Dinner Sail on the Ali'i Kai. Each van seats four wheelchairs plus attendants, and charters are available per hour with a minimum time of two hours. All reservations should be made a day in advance.

For handicapped persons with a valid driver's license, **Avis Rent-a-Car** (836-5511) can install hand controls at no additional cost with one week's advance notice.

CAUTIONARY NOTES

ET CETERA

There are few worries in our Island paradise, but the wise traveler should be aware of a few things that could possibly cause annoyance or difficulty.

Unfortunately, theft tops the list. Anyone leaving belongings unattended on the beach is inviting their removal by unscrupulous passersby. Parked cars are particularly preyed upon, especially rental cars. Camping areas may also be subject to hostile invasion, so camping alone is not recommended.

The streets are thronged with Mainland youth handing out flyers for cruises, dinners and other tourist-oriented commercial enterprises. Sometimes you will also be approached by members of the Hare Krishna sect offering to sell you books, incense and such. There is nothing wrong with the products they are selling—in fact the quality is usually high—but you needn't

buy. The adherents of this sect are generally quite polite about taking no for an answer because they get so much practice at it. They are perfectly harmless.

You'll find booths along Waikiki's streets offering incredible bargains for dinner shows, tours, car rentals and other attractive propositions. The bargains are real, but in exchange for the savings, you are required to attend a sales presentation for timeshare condominium vacation units in Hawai'i. Most of these take an hour to an hour and a half, and the saving is often well worth the time spent, but be warned that this is a *very* high pressure sales pitch. Don't be intimidated into buying something you don't want.

Drug peddlers are amazingly audacious in Waikiki. They approach people on the streets and offer deals of drugs, usually marijuana or cocaine. Even if you are interested in buying, be cautious as the quality and purity of

The exotic anthurium is one of Hawai'i's most popular tropical

the product is usually inferior and may be dangerous; inexperienced shoppers may even get oregano or baking soda.

Very often, fanatical Christian 'evangelists' are found along Kalākaua Avenue preaching loudly from impromptu pulpits. They are usually not selling anything; they just want to be heard.

NEIGHBOR ISLANDS

Each of our principal islands has its own special magic, and each deserves a book of its own. *The Essential Guide to Maui, The Essential Guide to Kaua'i* and *The Essential Guide to Hawai'i, the Big Island* provide the same in-depth coverage of those islands as that provided in this *Essential Guide to O'ahu*. We hope you can visit all our islands and discover for yourself the unique charm—past and present—of each.

Those wishing to visit islands other than O'ahu will find that the interisland air service is frequent and excellent; there are no boats providing regular passenger service. Flights are short, the longest taking only around half an hour. Prices are kept reasonable by a high level of traffic. Oahuans alone make half a million trips to the outer islands each year.

The island closest to O'ahu is **Moloka'i**, nearly twenty-six miles across the Kaiwi Channel. It is serviced by Air Molokai, Hawaiian Airlines and Princeville Airways.

Only nine miles from Moloka'i,

Hanalei Bay, Kaua'i.

across the Kalohi Channel is **Lāna'i**, mostly owned by the Dole company and mostly planted with pineapples. There are two new luxury resorts now on the island along with the original traditional Lanai Lodge. You can get there by Hawaiian Airlines, Aloha Island Air, or Air Molokai.

The not-quite-nine-mile Pailolo Channel separates Moloka'i from **Maui**, which is only a twenty-five minute flight from O'ahu. Air service from O'ahu is provided by Aloha Airlines, Hawaiian Airlines, Air Molokai, and Princeville Airways, and by Hawaiian and Aloha Island Air to Kapalua-West Maui Airport. United Airlines and American Airlines offer direct flights to Maui from the US mainland.

Tiny **Kaho'olawe**, not quite seven miles off the southern coast of Maui, and nearly eighteen miles southeast of Lāna'i is inaccessible. Since 1941 it has been used by the military as a target for bombing practice, and any landing on the island by unauthorized people is prohibited by law.

Nearly thirty miles southeast of Maui, across the 'Alenuihāhā Channel is the island of **Hawai'i**, usually referred to as **'the Big Island'**. It has two main airports, one at Hilo, on the east coast, and one on the Kona (southwest) coast, both serviced by Aloha Airlines and Hawaiian Airlines. Hilo and the Kona coast's Kailua are the island's two principal towns; there are also major resort developments on the Kohala (northwest) Peninsula, which are serviced through the Kona Airport. United Airlines offers direct flights daily to Kona from the US mainland. Princeville Airways also runs daily flights to the small airstrip at Kamuela on the island's north coast.

Northeast of O'ahu, more than seventy-two miles across the Ka'ie'ie Channel, is **Kaua'i**, the oldest of the archipelago's major islands. Aloha Airlines and Hawaiian Airlines fly to the main airport at Lihu'e on the southeast coast, and Princeville Airways services the small Princeville airstrip on the north coast. United Airlines offers daily direct service from the US mainland to Lihu'e.

Just over seventeen miles west of Kaua'i, across the Kaulakahi Channel is the small, privately owned island of **Ni'ihau**. Except for short helicopter tours, access to this island has been restricted to residents for well over a century.

APPENDIX

RENTAL AGENCIES

CAR & TRANSPORTATION

Alamo Rent A Car
Honolulu Int'l Airport 834-4080
142 Uluniu Ave 924-4444 Worldwide Reservations 800 327-9633

Aloha Funway Rentals
1984 Kalākaua Ave 942-9696
(and other locations)

Alohamenities
955-3886

Americabs
1314 S. King St 521-6680

Avis
Honolulu Int'l Airport 834-5536
148 Ka'iulani Ave 924-1688 Worldwide Reservations 800 831-8000

Budget Rent-A-Car
2379 Kūhiō Ave 922-3600 Worldwide Reservations 800 527-0700

Dollar Rent A Car
Central Reservations 926-4200
Honolulu Int'l Airport 926-4251
Hilton Hawaiian Village 926-4240
(and other locations)

Executive Limousine
1720 Ala Moana Blvd 941-1999

Hertz
Central Reservations 836-2511
Honolulu Int'l Airport 836-1091
Hilton Hawaiian Village 947-3329
Worldwide Reservations 800 654-
3131 (and other locations)

National Car Rental
Honolulu Int'l Airport 831-3800
1778 Ala Moana Blvd 922-3331
Worldwide Reservations 800 227-
7368

Odyssey Rentals
1922 Kalākaua Ave 947-8036

Thrifty Rent-A-Car
Honolulu Int'l Airport 836-2388
2164 Kālia Rd 923-7383
Outer Island Reservations 833-0046
(and other locations)

Tropical Rent-A-Car
Central Reservations 836-1041
Honolulu Int'l Airport 836-1176
2002 Kalākaua Ave 949-2002
(and other locations)

University Cyclery
1728 Kapi'olani Blvd 944-9884

OTHER RENTALS

Adventure Kayaking International
2463 Kūhiō Ave 924-8898

Aaron's Dive Shop
602 Kailua Rd 261-1211
46-216 Kahuhipa St, Kane'ohe
235-3877

Aloha Beach Service
Surfrider Hotel 922-3111

Aloha Dive Shop
Koko Marina 395-5922

Aloha Parasail
521-2446

Aloha Windsurfing
2239 Aloha Dr. 926-1185

Bob Twogood Kayaks Hawaii
171 Hamakua Dr 262-5656

Haleiwa Surf 'n' Sea
62-595 Kamehameha Hwy 637-9887

Jetski Hawaii
1130 N. Nimitz 943-8938

Kailua Sailboard Company
130 Kailua Rd 262-2555

Local Motion
1714 Kapi'olani Blvd 955-7373

Naish Hawaii
160 Kailua Rd 261-6067
2335 Kalākaua Ave 924-8600

Outrigger Beachboy Service
Outrigger Main Hotel 923-0711

Sea Breeze Parasailing
377 Keahole 396-0100
Seaction
Hilton Hawaiian Village 946-6133
South Sea Aquatics
1050 Ala Moana Blvd 538-3854
Steve's Diving Adventures
1860 Ala Moana Blvd 947-8900

Suyderhoud Water Ski Center
Koko Marina 395-3773
Tropical Kayaking
Laie 293-5339
Waikiki Beach Services
Reef Hotel 924-4941
Sheraton-Waikiki 922-4422
Windsurfing Hawaii
156C Hāmākua Dr. Kailua

HOTELS & CONDOMINIUMS

Aloha Surf
444 Kānekapōlei St 923-0222
Ambassador Hotel
2040 Kūhiō Ave 941-7777
Aston Island Colony
445 Seaside Ave 923-2345
Aston Waikiki Banyan
201 'Ōhua Ave 922-0555
Aston Waikiki Beach Tower
2470 Kalākaua Ave 342-1551
Aston Waikiki Sunset
229 Paoakalani St 922-0511
Breakers Hotel
250 Beach Walk 923-3181
Coconut Plaza Hotel
2171 Ala Wai Blvd 923-8828
Colony Surf Hotel
2895 Kalākaua Ave 923-5751
Diamond Head Beach Hotel
2947 Kalākaua Ave 922-1928
Discovery Bay
1778 Ala Moana Blvd 944-8555
Foster Tower
2500 Kalākaua Ave 923-6883
The Halekulani
2199 Kālia Rd 923-2311
Hawaii Dynasty
1830 Ala Moana Blvd 367-5122
Hawaii Prince Hotel
100 Holomoana St 956-1111
Hawaiian Regent Hotel
2552 Kalākaua Ave 922-6611
Hawaiiana Hotel
260 Beach Walk 923-3811

Hilton Hawaiian Village
2005 Kālia Rd 949-4321
Holiday Inn Waikiki
3570 Kalākaua Ave 877-7666
Hyatt Regency Waikiki
2424 Kalākaua Ave 923-1234
Ilikai at Waikiki Beach
1777 Ala Moana Blvd 949-3811
Ilima Hotel
445 Nohonani Ave 923-1877
Imperial Hawaii Resort
205 Lewers St 923-1827
The John Guild Inn
2001 Vancouver Dr 947-6019
Kahala Hilton
5000 Kāhala Ave 734-2211
Miramar at Waikiki
2345 Kūhiō Ave 922-2077
New Otani Kaimana Beach Hotel
2863 Kalākaua Ave 923-1555
Outrigger East
150 Ka'iulani Ave 922-5353
Outrigger Maile Court
2058 Kūhiō Ave 947-2828
Outrigger Malia
2211 Kūhiō Ave 921-4804
Outrigger Prince Kuhio
2500 Kūhiō Ave 922-0811
Outrigger Reef Hotel
2169 Kālia Rd 923-3111
Outrigger Waikiki
2335 Kalākaua Ave 921-9747
Pacific Beach Hotel
2490 Kalākaua Ave 922-1233

Park Shore
  2586 Kalākaua Ave 923-0411
Pleasant Holiday Isle
  270 Lewers St 923-0777
Princess Kaiulani
  120 Kaʻiulani Ave 922-5811
Queen Kapiolani
  150 Kapahulu Ave 531-5235
Ramada Renaissance Ala Moana
Hotel
  410 Atkinson Dr 955-4811
Royal Hawaiian Hotel
  2259 Kalākaua Ave 923-7311
Royal Kuhio
  2240 Kūhiō Ave 923-2502
Sheraton Makaha Resort
  Mākaha 695-9511
Sheraton-Waikiki

  2255 Kalākaua Ave 922-4422
Sheraton Moana Surfrider Hotel
  2365 Kalākaua Ave 922-3111
Turtle Bay Hilton & Country Club
  Kahuku 293-8811
Waikiki Beachcomber
  2300 Kalākaua Ave 922-4646
Waikiki Gateway Hotel
  2070 Kalākaua Ave 955-3741
Waikiki Grand Hotel
  134 Kapahulu Ave 923-1511
Waikiki Parkside Hotel
  1850 Ala Moana Blvd 955-1567
Waikiki Parc
  2233 Helumoa St 921-7272
Waikiki Shores
  2161 Kālia Rd 926-4733

PLACES OF INTEREST

ʻAʻala Park
  King and Beretania Sts
Alexander & Baldwin Building
  822 Bishop St 525-6611
Aliʻiolani Hale
  417 S King St 548-6424
Aloha Tower
  Ala Moana Blvd & Bishop St
  536-6373 or 548-5713
Arizona Memorial
  Arizona Memorial Dr. 422-0561
Bishop Estate Building
  1000 Bishop St 523-2111
Bishop Museum & Planetarium
  1525 Bernice St 848-4129
Byodo-In Temple
  Valley of the Temples
C. Brewer Building
  827 Fort St 536-4461
Coronation Pavilion
  ʻIolani Palace Grounds
Courts of the Missing
  Natʼl Mem. Cem. of the Pacific

Damien Museum and Archives
  130 ʻŌhua Ave 923-2690
Del Monte Pineapple Variety Garden
  junction of Hwys 99 and 80
Dillingham Transportation Building
  735 Bishop St 523-3022
Dole Cannery Square
  650 Iwilei Rd 536-3411
Dole Pineapple Pavilion
  64-1550 Kamehameha Hwy
  621-8408
Father Damien Statue
  State Capitol Building
First Hawaiian Bank Building
  165 S King St 525-7000
Foster Botanic Gardens
  180 N Vineyard Blvd 531-1939
Friend Building
  Bethel St
Golden Pavilion
  Honolulu Memorial Park
Haiku Gardens
  46-336 Haʻikū Rd Kāneʻohe

247-6671
Hawai'i Maritime Center
Aloha Tower
Hawai'i Nature Center
2131 Makiki Heights Dr. 942-0990
Hawai'i State Archives
'Iolani Palace Grounds 548-2356
Hawai'i State Capitol Building
415 S Beretania St 548-5420
Hawai'i State Library
478 S King St 548-4775
Hawaiian Electric Building
900 Richards St 548-5662
He'eia State Park
Kāne'ohe Bay
Helemano Plantation
64-1510 Kamehameha Hwy
622-3929
Hemmeter Building
250 S Hotel St 524-5600
Hilo Hattie's Fashion Center
700 N Nimitz Hwy 537-2926
Honolulu Academy of Arts
900 S Beretania St 538-1006
Honolulu Contemporary Arts Museum
2411 Makiki Heights Dr. 526-1322
Honolulu Hale
530 S King St 523-4111
Honolulu Memorial Park
22 Craigside Pl. 538-3925
Honolulu Zoo
Kapahulu and Monsarrat Aves
923-7723
Honpa Hongwanji Temple
1727 Pali Hwy 536-7044
Ho'omaluhia
off Kamehameha Hwy between
Kailua and Kāne'ohe 235-6636
Hsu Yun Temple
42 Kawānanakoa Pl 536-8458
'Iolani Barracks
'Iolani Palace Grounds
'Iolani Palace
King and Richards Sts 538-1471
Izumo Taishakyo

215 N Kukui St 538-7778
Judd Block
corner Fort and Merchant Sts
Kahana Valley State Park
Kahana Bay, off Kamehameha Hwy
Kamaka Inc.
550 South St 531-3165
Kamehameha V Post Office
corner Bethel and Merchant Sts
Kāne'ākī Heiau
Mākaha Valley
Kapi'olani Park
Monsarrat, Pākī Aves and
Ponimō'ī Rd
Kaumakapili Church
766 N King St 845-0908
Kawaiaha'o Church
King and Punchbowl Sts 538-6267
Keaīwa Heiau
end of 'Aiea Heights Dr., 'Aiea
Kekūanaō'a Building
465 S King St
King Kamehameha I Statue
Ali'iōlani Hale
Kuan Yin Temple
170 N Vineyard Blvd 533-6361
Kodak Hula Show
Waikīkī Shell, Kapi'olani Park
833-1661
Kū'īlioloa Heiau
Pōka'ī Bay
Lili'uokalani Gardens
Waikahalulu Ln
Lion Coffee
831 Queen St 521-3479
Lum Sai Ho Tong
1315 River St 536-6590
Lyon Arboretum
3860 Mānoa Rd 988-3177
Makiki Japanese Christian Church
829 Pensacola St 538-6664
Melchers Store
corner Bethel and Merchant Sts
Mission Houses Museum
553 S King St 531-0481
Mission Memorial Buildings

corner King and Punchbowl Sts
Moanalua Gardens
1350 Pineapple Pl. 833-1944
Mormon Temple
55-600 Naniloa Lp, Lāi'e 293-2427
Nat'l Mem. Cemetery of the Pacific
(Punchbowl), 2177 Pūowaina Dr.
Old Federal Building
corner King and Richards Sts
Old O'ahu Railway Station
King and Iwilei Sts
Our Lady of Peace Cathedral
Fort Street Mall 536-7036
Pacific Whaling Museum
Sea Life Park, Makapu'u 259-5177
Paradise Park
3737 Mānoa Rd 988-6686
Polynesian Cultural Center
Kamehameha Hwy, Lā'ie 293-3333
Pu'uomahuka
off Pūpūkea Rd above Waimea
Bay
Pu'u 'Ualaka'a State Wayside
Round Top Dr.
Queen Emma Summer Palace
2913 Pali Hwy 595-3167
Queen Lili'uokalani Statue
between 'Iolani Palace and State
Capitol Building
Richards Street YWCA
1040 Richards St 538-7061
Royal Mausoleum
2261 Nu'uanu Ave 537-1716
Sacred Falls State Park
Hau'ula, off Kamehameha Hwy
St Andrew's Cathedral
corner Queen Emma and Beretania
Sts 524-2822
Sanju Pagoda
Honolulu Memorial Park
Sea Life Park
Kalaniana'ole Hwy at Makapu'u Pt
259-7933
Soto Zen Temple
1708 Nu'uanu Ave
Stagenwald Building

119 Merchant St
T.R. Foster Building
corner Merchant St and
Nu'uanu Ave
Tennent Gallery
203 Prospect St 531-1987
Tenrikyo Mission
2236 Nu'uanu Ave 595-6523
Tenrikyo Temple
2920 Pali Hwy 595-6523
Thomas Square
King, Beretania, Victoria Sts and
Ward Ave
Ulupō Heiau
off Kailua Rd near Kailua YMCA
US Army Museum of Hawai'i
Kālia Rd 543-2639
USS _Bowfin_
11 Arizona Memorial Dr. 423-1341
Valley of the Temples Memorial Park
47-200 Kahekili Hwy, Kāne'ohe
239-8811
Wa'ahila Ridge State Recreation Area
off Wai'alae Ave
Waikīkī Aquarium
2777 Kalākaua Ave 923-9741
Waimea Falls Park
59-864 Kamehameha Hwy, Waimea
638-8511
War Memorial Natatorium
Kalākaua Ave, near Waikīkī
Aquarium
Washington Place
320 S Beretania St 538-3113
Waterhouse Warehouse
corner Merchant St and Nu'uanu
Ave
Wing Wo Tai Building
Nu'uanu Ave
Wo Fat
115 N Hotel St 537-6260
Yokohama Specie Bank
corner Bethel and Merchant Sts

Tube coral.

Looking toward Ka'ena Point from the leeward coastline.

RESTAURANTS

AMERICAN

Buzz's Original Steakhouse
413 Kawailoa Rd 261-4661
2533 Coyne St 944-9781
98-751 Kuahao Pl 487-6465
Captain's Galley
2365 Kalākaua Ave 922-3111
Guiltless Gourmet
593 Kam Hwy 456-2288
Hard Rock Café
corner Kalākaua Ave and
Kapi'olani Blvd
Il Fresco
Ward Centre 523-5191
Kemoo Farm
1718 Wilikina Dr 621-8481
Plumeria Cafe
Kahala Hilton 734-2211
Rainbow Lanai
Hilton Hawaiian Village 949-4321
Surf Room
Royal Hawaiian Hotel 923-7311
Terrace Grille
Hyatt Regency Waikiki 922-9292
Tony Roma's
1792 Kalākaua Ave 942-2121
4230 Wai'alae Ave 735-9595 (and
other locations)
Tripton's American Café
449 Kapahulu Ave 737-3819
Windows of Hawaii
1441 Ala Moana Blvd 941-9138
Yum Yum Tree
Ward Ctr 523-9333 Kahala Mall
737-7938 (and other locations)

CHINESE

Dynasty II
1050 Ala Moana Blvd 531-0208
Golden Dragon
Hilton Hawaiian Village 949-4321
King Tsin
1110 McCully St 946-3273

Wo Fat
115 North Hotel St 533-6393
Woodlands
1289 S King St 526-2239

CONTINENTAL

Alfred's
1750 Kalākaua Ave 955-5353
Bagwell's
2424 Hyatt Regency Waikiki
922-9292
Bali by the Sea
Hilton Hawaiian Village 949-4321
Black Orchid
Restaurant Row 521-3111
The Cove
Turtle Bay Hilton 293-8811
Hanohano Room
Sheraton-Waikiki 922-4422
La Mer
Halekulani Hotel 923-2311
Maile Restaurant
Kahala Hilton 734-2211
Nicholas Nickolas
Ala Moana Americana Hotel
955-4466
Oceanarium Restaurant
Pacific Beach Hotel 922-1233
Rose City Diner
Restaurant Row 525-ROSE
Roy's Restaurant
6600 Kalanianaole Hwy 396-7697
Ruth's Chris Steak House
Restaurant Row 599-3860
The Secret
Hawaiian Regent Hotel 922-6611

FRENCH

Bon Appetit
Discovery Bay 942-3837
Chez Michel
Eaton Square 955-7866

Michel's at the Colony Surf
3895 Kalākaua Ave 923-6552

ITALIAN

Baci Ristorante
Waikiki Trade Ctr 924-2533
Matteo's
Marina Surf Hotel 922-5551
Sergio's
445 Nohonani St 926-3388

JAPANESE

Musashi
Hyatt Regency Waikiki 922-9292
Pagoda Floating Restaurant
1525 Rycroft St 941-6611
Restaurant Suntory
Royal Hawaiian Ctr 922-5511
Shirokiya's
Ala Moana Ctr 941-9111
Shogun Japanese Steak & Seafood
Restaurant
2863 Kalākaua Ave 922-1233

MEXICAN

Compadres Mexican Bar & Grill
Ward Ctr 523-1307
Hernando's Hideaway & Cantina
2139 Kūhiō Ave 922-7758
La Salsa
Restaurant Row 536-4828
Peppers
Outrigger East Hotel 926-4374

SEAFOOD

Jameson's by the Sea
62-540 Kamehameha Hwy
Hale'iwa 637-4336
John Dominis
43 'Āhui St 523-0955
Lobster Tank
2139 Kūhiō Ave 924-4455

Nick's Fishmarket
2070 Kalākaua Ave 955-6333
Orson's
1050 Ala Moana Blvd 521-5681
Seafood Emporium
Royal Hawaiian Ctr 922-554

MISCELLANEOUS

Bavarian Beer Garden
Royal Hawaiian Ctr 922-6535
Keo's Thai Cuisine
625 Kapahulu Ave 737-9250
Ward Ctr 533-0533
Swiss Inn
5730 Kalaniana'ole Hwy 377-5477
The Willows
901 Hausten St 946-4808

BAKERIES

Bakery Kapiolani
1517 Kapi'olani Blvd 949-3111
(and other locations)
Croissanterie
222 Merchant St 533-3443
Dee Lite Bakery
1930 Dillingham Blvd 847-5396
(and other locations)
King's Bakery
1936 S King St 941-5211
444 Hobron Ln 955-8899
(and other locations)
Leonard's Bakery
933 Kapahulu Ave 737-5591
Mary Catherine's
Ward Ctr 521-3525
Napoleon's
(see Zippy's under Fast Foods)
Old Vienna Bake Shoppe
952 North King St 845-9907
The Patisserie
2115 S Beretania St 941-3055
Edgewater Hotel 922-4974
2330 Kūhiō Ave 922-9752
(and other locations)

St. Germain
Shirokiya's at Ala Moana Ctr
955-1711 (and other locations)
Yum Yum Tree
Ward Ctr 523-9333 Kahala Mall
737-7938 (and other locations)

SWEETS

Baskin-Robbins
2500 Kalākaua Ave 922-1192
Royal Hawaiian Ctr 924-7844
(and other locations)
**Bubbie's Homemade Ice Cream &
Desserts**
1010 University Ave 949-8984
The Chocolate Lady
1411 Kalākaua Ave 949-7658
Chikaramochi Store
1341 River St 533-4744
The Cookie Corner
1001 Bishop St 536-9543
3221 Wai'alae Ave Ste 225
734-7557
(and other locations)
Crackseed World
870 Kapahulu Ave 737-6486
Dairy Queen
Ala Moana Ctr 949-4075
Ward Warehouse 536-1241
(and other locations)
Dave's Ice Cream Parlors
2077 Kūhiō Ave 942-2485
Ward Warehouse 523-3692
1901 Kapi'olani Blvd 955-7609
(and other locations)
Famous Amos
2301 Kalākaua Ave 922-3400
670 Halekauwila St 537-5507
(and other locations)
The Fudge Works
62-540 Kamehameha Hwy
Hale'iwa 637-9464
Häagen Dazs
2330 Kalākaua Ave 923-6877
2356 Kalākaua Ave 924-9336
2586 Kalākaua Ave 923-5177

(and other locations)
Hawaiian Holiday
2200 Kalākaua Ave 923-9811
2430 Kalākaua Ave 922-5306 (The
MacNuttery)
2098 Kalākaua Ave 942-7798
(and other locations)
Honolulu Chocolate Co.
Ward Center 531-2997
Restaurant Row 528-4033
2908 E Manoa Rd 988-4999
Island Snow
International Market Place (two)
922-8480, 926-0353
Royal Hawaiian Ctr 926-3067 (and
other locations)
Lappert's
2124 Kalākaua Ave 924-0116
1450 Ala Moana Blvd 942-0320
Matsumoto's M. Store
66-087 Kamehameha Hwy
Hale'iwa 637-4827
Morrow's Nut House
Royal Hawaiian Ctr 923-9687
Ala Moana Ctr 947-7477 (and other
locations)
Mrs. Field's
116 Ka'iulani Ave 926-9186
Ala Moana Ctr 949-1475 (and other
locations)
Nisshodo
1095 Dillingham Blvd 847-1244
Penguin's
1035 University Ave 941-1446
1960 Kapi'olani Blvd (corner
McCully and Kapi'olani) 947-5011
See's
Ala Moana Ctr 943-1960
1475 Kapi'olani Blvd 947-7555
Kahala Mall 737-9592 (and other
locations)
Swensen's Ice Cream Factory
909 Kapahulu Ave (and other
locations)
TCBY (The Country's Best Yogurt)
2700 S King St 946-6644

1613 Nuʻuanu Ave 521-2301 (and other locations)

White Mountain Creamery
2145 Kūhiō Ave 922-7791
819 Kapahulu Ave 734-8754

Yami Yogurt
Ala Moana Ctr 955-4144 (and other locations)

FAST FOODS

Bea's
2840 Kapiʻolani Blvd 732-6685

Bob's Bar-B-Que
1860 Kalākaua Ave
1108 12th Ave 732-2479 (and other locations)

Burger King
131 Kaʻiulani Ave 923-2974
2186 Kalākaua Ave 922-2979
2255 Kūhiō Ave 924-1040 (and other locations)

Church's
2310 Kūhiō Ave 922-9653
1202 S Beretania St 531-5465 (and other locations)

Domino's
corner Kapiʻolani Blvd and McCully St 942-9600
3298 Campbell Ave 737-0888 (and other locations)

Grace's Inn
1192 Alakea St 537-3302
2227 S Beretania St 946-8020

Harpo's
Ward Warehouse 521-6748
477 Kapahulu Ave 735-8593 (and other locations)

Healthy's
2525 S King St 955-2479

Hippo's
468 ʻEna Rd 944-8466

Jack-in-the-Box
2424 Kalākaua Ave 923-4483
Waikiki Grand Hotel 922-2235
633 Kapahulu Ave 735-2696 (and other locations)

KC Drive-Inn
1029 Kapahulu Ave 737-5581

Kentucky Fried Chicken
647 Kapahulu Ave 732-2454
1470 Kapiʻolani Blvd 949-2855 (and other locations)

Kozo Sushi
2334 S King St 946-5666 (and other locations)

Kua ʻAina
66-214 Kamehameha Hwy
Haleʻiwa 637-6067

Magoo's
3435 Waiʻalae Ave 732-2838
1239 Wilder Ave 521-5005

Makai Market Food Court
Ala Moana Ctr 946-2811

McDonald's
2204 Kalākaua Ave 923-8678
2301 Kalākaua Ave 922-5634
2164 Kālia Rd 924-7177 (and other locations)

Pizza Hut
2154 Kalākaua Ave 923-1181
Kuhio Mall 926-5025
Kahala Mall 735-9788 (and other locations)

Pizzeria Uno
2256 Kūhiō Ave 926-0646

Popeye's
720 Keʻeaumoku St 944-8508 (and other locations)

Round Table
315 Lewers St 923-0077
2615 S King St 942-7666
641 Keʻeaumoku St 941-5051
(and other locations)

Ruffage Natural Foods
2443 Kūhiō Ave 922-2042

Shiro's
2494 S Beretania St 942-3126 (and other locations)

Showbiz Pizza Place
Aina Haina Ctr 373-2151

Taco Bell
1960 Kapiʻolani Blvd 947-9595

1345 S King St 949-6069
717 Kapahulu Ave 737-7337 (and
other locations)
Taco House
225 Queen St 536-1443
750 Kailua Rd 262-9559
(and other locations)
Ted's Kal-Bi Ribs
2020 S King St 946-0364
Vim & Vigor
Ala Moana Ctr 955-3600

Kahala Mall 734-8990 (and other
locations)
Washington Saimin Stand
1117 S King St 533-3524
Zippy's
Ala Moana Ctr 942-7766
1725 S King St 955-5948
601 Kapahulu Ave 737-5535
Zorro's
2310 Kūhiō Ave 926-5555
2126 Kalākaua Ave 924-8808

SHOPS & CENTERS

SHOPPING CENTERS
Ala Moana Center
1450 Ala Moana Blvd 946-2811
Dole Cannery Square
650 Iwilei St 536-3411
Duke's Lane
between Kalākaua and Kūhiō Aves
near Seaside
Eaton Square
444 Hobron Ln 544-1850
Atrium Shops
Hyatt Regency Waikiki
2424 Kalākaua Ave 922-9292
International Market Place
2330 Kalākaua Ave 923-9871
Kahala Mall
4211 Wai'alae Ave 732-7736
Kilohana Square
1016 Kapahulu Ave 735-4503
King's Village
131 Ka'iulani Ave 922-1288
Kuhio Mall
2301 Kūhiō Ave 922-2724
Pearlridge Center
1005 Moanalua Rd 'Aiea 488-0981
Rainbow Bazaar
Hilton Hawaiian Village
2005 Kālia Rd 949-4321
Royal Hawaiian Shopping Center
2201 Kalākaua Ave 922-0588

Waikiki Shopping Plaza
2250 Kalākaua Ave 923-1191
Waikiki Trade Center
2255 Kūhiō Ave 922-7444
Ward Centre
1200 Ala Moana Blvd 531-6411
Ward Warehouse
1050 Ala Moana Blvd 531-6411
Windward Mall
46-056 Kamehameha Hwy
Kāne'ohe 235-1143

SHOPS
A to Z
2370 Kūhiō Ave 922-0027
ABC Discount Stores
Hyatt Regency Waikiki 926-5241
923-7635 Ala Moana Ctr 941-3374
Royal Hawaiian Ctr 923-2069
Kuhio Mall 923-2009 (and other
locations)
The Academy Shop
Honolulu Academy of Arts
900 S Beretania St 523-1493
Adopt-a-Book
222 Merchant Basmt 523-3772
Alion
Kahala Mall 735-7878
Ala Moana Ctr 946-5075
Sheraton Moana Surfrider 922-5070

Aloha Swap Meet
Aloha Stadium
99-500 Salt Lake Blvd 488-7731

Altillo
2139 Kūhiō 926-1680
Kahala Mall 734-3000

Andrade & Company
Royal Hawaiian Ctr 926-1211
Ala Moana Ctr Men's 926-1380
Ala Moana Ctr Women's 926-1382
Atrium Shops 926-1388
King's Village 926-1394

Antiques Pacifica
Royal Hawaiian Hotel 923-5101

The Art Loft
186 N King St 523-0489

Bernard Hurtig's Orientwest
Kahala Hilton 732-0721

Blair Ltd
404A Ward Ave 536-4907

Blue Ginger
Ward Warehouse 526-0398

Blue Jeans 'n' Bikinis
1724 Kapi'olani Blvd 941-1313

Carol & Mary's
Ala Moana Ctr 946-5075
Kahala Mall 946-5075

Carriage House
Kilohana Square 737-2622

Cartier
Ala Moana Center 955-5533

Cathedral Gift Shop
Ala Moana Ctr 949-3436

Chapman's
Ala Moana Ctr 941-4330
Atrium Shops 923-7010
Sheraton-Waikiki 923-4657
(and other locations)

Cherry Blossom
2184 Kalākaua Ave 923-6844

Chocolates for Breakfast
Ala Moana Ctr 947-3434
Waikiki Shopping Plaza 923-4426

Cielo
Kahala Mall 732-2660

Circle-K Stores

45-596 Kamehameha Hwy
Kāne'ohe 235-5096
95-280 Kipapa Dr. Mililani 623-6801

Conrad Jewelers
Ala Moana Ctr 949-0005

Coral Grotto
Ala Moana Ctr 955-6760
Atrium Shops 923-3454
Royal Hawaiian Ctr 923-7534
Rainbow Bazaar 941-1122
(and other locations)

Crazy Shirts
Ala Moana Ctr 941-0135
Atrium Shops 923-0025
Int'l Market Place 922-4791
King's Village 923-5966
Kuhio Mall 923-6678
(and other locations)

Creative Fibres
450 Piikoi St 537-3674

Diamond Head Market
3058 Monsarrat Ave 735-3541

Down to Earth
2525 S King St 947-7678

Elephant Walk
Ala Moana Ctr 949-4011

Especially For You
535 Ward Ave 533-0681

Ethel's Dress Shoppe
Ala Moana Ctr 946-5047
119 Merchant St 538-3627
Pearlridge Ctr 487-1591

Eurasian Antiques
580 Nimitz Hwy 533-7274

Jeffrey Barr
Kahala Mall 735-7622

Following Sea
Kahala Mall 734-4425

The Food Pantry
2211 Ala Wai Blvd 922-2818
2370 Kūhiō Ave 923-9831
444 Hobron Ln 947-3763

Foodland
Ala Moana Ctr 949-5044
1460 S Beretania St 944-9046
2939 Harding Ave 734-6303

(and other locations)
Fort Ruger Market
  3585 Alohea Ave 737-4531
Foster Botanic Gardens Gift Shop
  180 N Vineyard Blvd 533-6335
Froggies
  1521 S King St 942-8686
Fumi's
  Ala Moana Ctr 955-5767
  Int'l Market Place 923-2473
Galerie St Martin
  Eaton Square 945-7791
Gem
  333 Ward Ave 531-2642
Granat Bros
  Kahala Mall 732-1408
  Pearlridge Ctr 488-0977
  Windward Mall 247-8777
Haimoff & Haimoff Creations in Gold
  The Halekulani 923-8777
  Ward Ctr 523-8043
  (Carol & Mary's)
  Ala Moana Ctr 949-2719
Hawaiian Etc
  2424 Kalākaua Ave 923-0591
  2370 Kūhiō Ave 923-1325
Hildgund at Dawkins Benny
  119 Merchant St 536-8778
  Windward Mall 235-5120
Hilo Hattie's Fashion Center
  700 Nimitz Hwy 537-2926
Honolulu Bookshops
  Ala Moana Ctr 941-2274
  1001 Bishop St Gnd Flr 537-6224
  Pearlridge Ctr 487-1548
  (and other locations)
House of Music
  Ala Moana Ctr 949-1051
Huckleberry Farms
  1613 Nu'uanu Ave 524-7960
Island MuuMuu Works
  650 Iwilei Rd 536-4475
Interlude Books
  1427 Kalākaua Ave 949-2666
'Iolani Palace Shop

'Iolani Palace 545-2326
Irene's Hawaiian Gifts
  Ala Moana Ctr 946-6818
The Island Heritage Collection
  533-0500
Island Shells
  Ala Moana Ctr 947-3313
J.C. Penney
  Ala Moana Ctr 946-8068
  Pearlridge Ctr 488-0961
  Windward Mall 235-0011
The Jade Tree
  King's Village 923-2768
Kam Super Swap Meet
  Kam Drive-In
  98-850 Moanalua Rd 488-5822
Kuhio Pharmacy
  2330 Kūhiō Ave 923-4466
Kula Bay
  Hilton Hawaiian Village 943-0771
  Royal Hawaiian 923-0042
Lanakila Crafts
  1809 Bachelot St 531-0555
Laura Ashley
  Ala Moana Ctr 942-5200
Liberty House
  Ala Moana Ctr, Kahala Mall, Royal Hawaiian Ctr and all locations 941-2345
Little Hawaiian Craft Shop
  Royal Hawaiian Ctr 926-2662
Local Motion
  1714 Kapi'olani Blvd 944-8515
Longs Drugs
  Ala Moana Ctr 941-4433
  1330 Pali Hwy 536-7302
  Kahala Mall 732-0784
  (and other locations)
Louis Vuitton
  Ala Moana Ctr 955-2218
  Royal Hawaiian Ctr 926-0621
Mamo
  Ward Warehouse 522-0616
Mandalay
  The Halekulani 922-7766

APPENDIX

Manoa Gallery
2733 E Mānoa Rd 988-4386
Martin and MacArthur
841 Bishop St 524-4434
Max H. Davis
Kilohana Square 735-2341
McInerny's
Royal Hawaiian Ctr 926-1351
Mills Gallery
701 Bishop St 536-3527
Miko Oriental Art Gallery
Kilohana Square 735-4503
Mitsukoshi
Atrium Shops 926-8877
Nautilus of the Pacific
2005 Kālia Rd 947-4755
Hawaiian Regent Hotel 924-9335
Otaheite Shoppe
Ala Moana Ctr 941-5470
Atrium Shops 922-8768
Ilikai Hotel 946-1391
(and other locations)
Outrigger Pharmacy
2335 Kalākaua Ave 923-2529
Pacific Book House
Kilohana Square 737-3475
Past Era
701 Bishop St 533-6313
Pauahi Nuuanu Gallery
1 N Pauahi St 531-6088
Pearl Factory
Rainbow Bazaar 942-9857
Atrium Shops 922-1329
Int'l Market Place 922-4244
(and other locations)
The Pegge Hopper Gallery
1164 Nu'uanu Ave 524-1160
The Pocketbook Man
Ala Moana Ctr 945-7555
Pomegranets In The Sun
Ward Warehouse 531-1108
R. Field Wine Company
Ward Ctr 521-4043
Restaurant Row 528-4043
Rafael
Ward Ctr 521-7661

Ramsay Galleries
119 Merchant St
1128 Smith St 732-5700
Reyn's
Ala Moana Ctr 949-5929
Kahala Mall 737-8313
Kahala Hilton 737-3785
Robyn Buntin
Eaton Square 945-3959
Ross Sutherland
Ala Moana Ctr 946-2888
Ruffage Natural Foods
2443 Kūhiō Ave 922-2042
Safeway
1121 S Beretania St 538-7315
1360 Pali Hwy 538-3953
(and other locations)
Sandwich Island Books
125 Merchant St Ste 1 528-2312
Sears
Ala Moana Ctr
Pearlridge Ctr
Windward Mall 947-0211
Security Diamond
Ala Moana Ctr 949-6432
7-Eleven Food Stores
1323 Kalākaua Ave 946-3382
1901 Kalākaua Ave 944-8001
2299 Kūhiō Ave 924-7470
(and other locations)
Shellworld Hawaii
Royal Hawaiian Ctr 923-2214
2381 Kalākaua Ave 923-2685
Kahala Hilton 732-3800
Shirokiya
Ala Moana Ctr 941-9111
2552 Kalākaua Ave 922-2711
Pearlridge Ctr 941-9111
Shop Pacifica
Bishop Museum & Planetarium
1525 Bernice St 848-4158
Slow Poke' Fish Market
4210 Wai'alae Ave 735-4532
45-1048 Kamehameha Hwy
Kāne'ohe 235-3011

Splash!
New Otani Kaimana Beach Hotel
923-6064 Ala Moana Ctr 942-1010
Splash! for Men
New Otani Kaimana Beach Hotel
922-2427
Star Market
2470 S King St 941-0913
Kahala Mall 734-0284
(and other locations)
Susan Marie
Ward Ctr 536-3811
Tahiti Imports
Ala Moana Ctr 941-4539
Tamashiro Market
802 N King St 841-8047
Tiffany & Co.
Sheraton Moana Hotel 922-2722
Times
1290 S Beretania St 524-5711
1776 S King St 955-3388
1173 21st Ave 732-6677
(and other locations)

Tower Records
611 Ke'eaumoku St 941-7774
98-199 Kamehameha Hwy 486-4966
Tuli's Grocery
951 North King St 841-4065
Tres Sea
150 Hamakua Kailua Dr 263-3572
Tropical Clay
470 N Nimitz Hwy 537-2492
Waikiki A-1 Superette
2228 Kalākaua Ave 923-4580
Waldenbooks
Waikiki Shopping Plaza 922-4154
Royal Hawaiian Ctr 926-3200
Kahala Mall 737-9550
Waterfall Gallery
1160A Nuuanu 521-6863
Zales
Kahala Mall 734-0213
Pearlridge Ctr 487-5573
Windward Mall 247-8787

TOUR COMPANIES

Akamai Tours
2270 Kalākaua Ave Ste 1702
922-6485

American Hawaii Cruises
550 Kearny St San Francisco CA
94108 800 227-3666

Atlantis Submarines
Hilton Hawaiian Village 949-4321

Cloud 9 Limousine Service
PO Box 15773 Honolulu 96815
524-7999

E Noa Tours
1110 University Ave Rm 306
599-2561

Elite Limousine Service
1059 12th Ave Ste E 735-2431

Executive Limousine Services
1777 Ala Moana Blvd 941-1999

Gray Line Hawaii
PO Box 30046 Honolulu 96820
834-1033

Handicabs of the Pacific
50 S Beretania St 524-3866

Hawaiian Cruises
150 Ka'iulani Ave 923-2061

Islands in the Sky
Hawaiian Airlines 1164 Bishop St
Ste 800 537-5100

Kaneohe Bay Cruises
PO Box 1604 Honolulu 96744
235-2888

Leahi Catamaran
2255 Kalākaua Ave 922-5665

Panorama Air Tour
214 Lagoon Dr. 836-2122

Papillon Helicopters
228 Lagoon Dr Ste 207, Waikīkī
836-1566, Turtle Bay 293-2155

Paradise Cruises
210 Ward Ave Ste 330 536-3641

Polynesian Adventure Tours
2200 Kūhiō Ave Rm 109M
922-0888

Roberts Hawaii
444 Hobron Ln 5th Flr
947-3939

Royal VSP Services
905 Ahua St 839-4499

Scenic Air Tour Hawaii
266 Lagoon Dr. 836-0044

Tradewinds Sailing Charters
350 Ward Ave Ste 206 533-0220
533-7734

Trans Hawaiian Services
3111 Castle St 735-6467

Pineapple harvest in central O'ahu.

Waimea Bay, North Shore.

PLACES OF WORSHIP

BAHA'I
Honolulu Community
3264 Allan Pl. 235-4121

BUDDHIST - CHINESE
Hsu Yun Temple
42 Kawānanakoa Pl. 536-8458
Kwan Yin Temple
170 N Vineyard Blvd 533-6361

BUDDHIST - NICHIREN
Honolulu Myohoji Mission Temple
2003 Nu'uanu Ave 595-3517

BUDDHIST - SHINSU
Honpa Hongwanji Temple
1727 Pali Hwy 536-7044

BUDDHIST - ZEN
Soto Mission Temple
1708 Nu'uanu Ave 538-6429

BUDDHIST - KOREAN
Dae Won Sa Temple
2559 Wai'ōma'o Rd 735-7858

APOSTOLIC
Apostolic Faith Church
1043 Middle St 847-5902

ASSEMBLY OF GOD
South Pacific Assembly of God
2330 Kūhiō Ave Ste 204 926-3677

AMERICAN BAPTIST
First Baptist Church of Honolulu
1313 Pensacola St 521-4708

CONSERVATIVE BAPTIST
International Baptist Church
20 Dowsett Ave 595-6351

BAPTIST - INDEPENDENT
Ohana Baptist Church
839-6992

SOUTHERN BAPTIST
Waikiki Baptist Church
424 Kuamo'o St 955-3525

BYZANTINE CATHOLIC
Maria-Sophia Chapel
86-660 Lualualei Hmstd Rd
696-2244

ROMAN CATHOLIC
St Augustine
130 'Ōhua Ave 923-7024
Star of the Sea
4470 Ali'ikoa St 734-0396

CHARISMATIC
Word of Life Christian Center
1270 Queen Emma St 528-4044

CHRISTIAN
International Christian Church
2322 Kāneali'i Ave, Pauoa 536-5730

CHRISTIAN SCIENCE
First Church of Christ Scientist
1508 Punahou St 949-8403

CHURCH OF CHRIST
Church of Christ at Honolulu
1732 Ke'eaumoku St 536-7952

CHURCH OF GOD
Honolulu Church of God
949-4995

EPISCOPAL
St Andrew's Cathedral
Queen Emma Sq. 524-2822

GREEK ORTHODOX
Saints Constantine and Helen
17 Old Pali Pl. 595-7088

JEHOVAH'S WITNESSES
Jehovah's Witnesses
1228 Pensacola St 531-2990

LUTHERAN
Prince of Peace Lutheran-Waikiki
333 Lewers St PH 922-6011

METHODIST
Christ United Methodist Church
1639 Ke'eaumoku St 536-7244
First United Methodist Church
1020 S Beretania St 533-1774
Pacific Islanders United Methodist
2106 Pālolo Ave 737-2042

MORMON
Kahala-Kaimuki Chapel
4849 Kīlauea Ave 734-1254

NAZARENE
Honolulu Kaimuki
959 12th Ave Kaimukī 737-8827

NON-DENOMINATIONAL
Waikiki Beach Chaplaincy
Hilton Hawaiian Village 923-3137

PENTECOSTAL
Door of Faith Church & Bible
School
1161 Young St 538-1339

PRESBYTERIAN
First Presb. Church of Honolulu
1822 Ke'eaumoku St 537-3321

SEVENTH DAY ADVENTIST
Diamond Head Seventh Day
Adventist Church
828 18th Ave 737-1234

SPIRITUALIST
Aquarian Foundation
2440 Kūhiō Ave 926-8134

UNITARIAN
First Unitarian Church Of Honolulu
2500 Pali Hwy 595-4047

UNITED CHURCH OF CHRIST
Central Union Church
1660 S Beretania St 941-0957
Kaumakapili Church
766 N King St 845-0908

UNITY
Unity Church of Hawaii
3608 Diamond Head Cir. 735-4436

JEWISH
Congregation SofMa'Arav
PO Box 11154 Honolulu 923-5726
Temple Emanu-El
2550 Pali Hwy 595-7521

MEDITATION CENTERS
Siddha Meditation Ashram
1925 Makiki St 942-8887

MOSLEM
Muslim Students' Association
1935 'Ale'o Pl. 947-6263

SHINTO
Daijingu Temple
61 Pū'iwa Rd 595-3102
Izumo Taishakyo Mission
215 N Kukui St 538-7778

RELIGIOUS SCIENCE
Religious Science Church
4819 Kīlauea Ave 537-1729

TAOIST
Lum Sai Ho Tong Temple
1315 River St 536-6590

HAWAIIAN WORDLIST

S ome of these words may be seen without the markings that alter pronunciation (and meaning), as explained in the INTRODUCTION. In the pronunciation guides given here, typical English syllables which most closely
approximate the Hawaiian vowel sounds are used; a precise rendition would
require long and complex explanations. The *'okina* (glottal stop) has been
retained to show where adjacent vowels should *not* slide from one to the other.
The *kahako* (macron) shows where the vowel is held a little longer. Stress is
indicated by capitalization.

a'ā [AH-'AH] a rough, crumbly type of lava
aikāne [aye-KAH-neh] friend
akamai [ah-kah-my-ee] smart, wise, on the ball
ali'i [ah-LEE-'ee] chief, nobility
aloha a nui loa [ah-LO-ha ah NOO-ee LO-ah] much love
aue, auwē [ah-oo-EH-EH] alas!, oh dear!, too bad!, goodness!
'awa [AH-vah] traditional Polynesian drink wrung from the roots of the
pepper plant (kava)
'Ewa [EH-vah] toward 'Ewa Plantation
hana hou [hah-nah HO-oo] encore, do it again
hanohano [hah-no-HAH-no] distinguished, magnificent
haole [HAH-oh-leh] originally foreigner; now Caucasian
hapa [HAH-pa] half, part
hapa-haole [HAH-pa HAH-oh-leh] half Caucasian
Hau'oli Makahiki Hou [ha-oo-'oh-lee mah-ka-hee-kee ho-oo] Hawaiian
translation of Happy New Year (now used, but not a traditional greeting)
haupia [ha-oo-PEE-ah] coconut pudding
heiau [HEH-ee-ah-oo] ancient Hawaiian place of worship
hele [HEH-leh] go, walk around
holoholo [ho-lo-HO-lo] to visit about, make the rounds
holoku [ho-LO-koo] a fitted, ankle-length dress, sometimes with train
ho'olaule'a [ho-'oh-lah-oo-LAY-'ah] celebration
hui [HOO-ee] club, association
hukilau [HOO-kee-lah-oo] community net-fishing party
hula [HOO-lah] Hawaiian dance
huli [HOO-lee] turn over, turn around
humuhumunukunukuapua'a [hoo-moo-hoo-moo-noo-koo-noo-koo-ah-poo-
AH-'ah] Hawai'i's State Fish; a small triggerfish famous for its long name
iki [EE-kee] little (size)
imu [EE-moo] ground oven
imua [ee-MOO-ah] forward, onward
kāhili [kah-ah-HEE-lee] a royal feathered standard
kahuna [kah-HOO-nah] priest, expert
kai [KY-ee] sea, sea water
kala [KAH-lah] money (literally dollar)
kama'aina [kah-mah-AYE-nah] native born, longtime Hawai'i resident, old
established family
kanaka [kah-NAH-kah] originally 'man' or person; now a native Hawaiian
kāne [KAH-neh] boy, man, husband

kapa [KAH-pah] tapa cloth (made from mulberry bark)
kapakahi [kah-pah-KAH-hee] crooked, lopsided
kapu [KAH-poo] forbidden, sacred, taboo, keep out
kaukau [KAH-oo-kah-oo] food
keiki [KAY-kee] child
kiawe [kee-AH-vay] mesquite tree
kokua [ko-KOO-ah] help, assistance, aid
kona [KO-nah] winds 'that blow against the trades', lee side of an island
kukui [koo-KOO-ee] 'candlenut'
kumu [KOO-moo] teacher
lānai [lah-NY-ee] porch, terrace, veranda
lani [LAH-nee] heaven, heavenly, sky
lauhala [lah-oo-HAH-lah] leaf of the pandanus tree (for weaving)
laulau [LAH-oo-lah-oo] bundled food in ti leaves
lei [LAY-ee] garland of flowers, shells or feathers, wreath
lilikoi [lee-lee-KOH-ee] passion fruit
loa [LO-ah] long
lomi [LO-mee] rub, press, massage, type of raw salmon (usually lomilomi)
lua [LOO-ah] toilet, restroom
lū'au [LOO-'ah-oo] feast, party, taro leaf
mahalo [mah-HAH-loh] thank you
mahimahi [mah-hee-MAH-hee] dorado or dolphin fish
mahu [MAH-hoo] gay, homosexual
makai [mah-KY-ee] toward the sea
make [MAH-keh] dead
makule [mah-KOO-leh] elderly, old (of people)
malihini [mah-lee-HEE-nee] newcomer, visitor
malo [MAH-lo] man's loincloth
mauka [MAH-oo-ka] toward the mountains, inland
mauna [MAH-oo-nah] mountain
Mele Kalikimaka [meh-leh kah-lee-kee-MAH-ka] Merry Christmas
Menehune [meh-neh-HOO-neh] legendary race of dwarfs
moemoe [mo-eh-MO-eh] sleep
mu'umu'u [moo-'oo-moo-'oo] long or short loose-fitting dress
nui [NOO-ee] big
ohana [oh-HAH-nah] family, extended family
'ōkole [oh-oh-KO-lay] buttocks, bottom, rear
'ōkolemaluna [oh-oh-ko-lay-mah-LOO-nah] Hawaiian translation of 'bottoms up' (a bit crude)
'ono [OH-no] delicious
pakalolo [pah-kah-LO-lo] marijuana
pake [PAH-keh] Chinese
pali [PAH-lee] cliff, precipice; *the* Pali=the Nu'uanu Pali
paniolo [pah-nee-OH-lo] cowboy
pau [PA-oo] finished, done
pau hana [pa-oo HAH-nah] finish work
pahoehoe [pah-ho-eh-HO-eh] type of lava with smooth or ropy surface
pikake [pee-KAH-keh] jasmine flower, named after 'peacock'
poi [POY] pasty food made from pounded taro
puka [POO-kah] hole, door
pūpū [POO-poo] hors d'oeuvres (literally 'shells')

tūtū [TOO-too] grandmother, affectionate term for old people—relatives or friends—of grandparents' generation (According to the rules of language set down by the missionaries, there is no 't' in the Hawaiian language, but hardly anyone ever says *kuku*.)

'uku [OO-koo] fleas, head lice

'ukulele [oo-koo-LAY-leh] small, stringed instrument from Portugal

wahine [va-HEE-neh, wah-HEE-neh] girl, woman, wife

wikiwiki [wee-kee-WEE-kee] fast, in a hurry, quickly

he pronunciation of pidgin is self-evident, and its spelling is phonic rather than fixed. In most cases, the derivation is also obvious. The lilt that is peculiar to this local lingo cannot be adequately described; it must be heard. This list is

PIDGIN ENGLISH WORDLIST

given as a guide to listening only. Do not try to speak pidgin. You could inadvertently say something offensive or insulting, and the response might be exceedingly unpleasant. Everyone who speaks pidgin also understands correctly spoken English.

an den? So? What next? What else? [and then]

any kine anything [any kind]

ass right you are correct [that's right]

bambucha big

bambula big

beef fight

blalah heavy set, Hawaiian man, may be looking for a fight

bradah friend [brother]

brah short for bradah

buggah guy, friend, pest

bumbye after awhile, [by and by]

bummahs too bad, disappointed expression [bummer]

cockaroach rip off, steal, confiscate

cool head main ting keep calm, relax

da the

da kine anything being discussed, used as either noun or verb when the speaker can't think of the right word

dat that

dem them, guys, folks

eh? you know, do you understand?; also used at the beginning of a statement

garans guaranteed, for sure

geevum go for it! [give them]

grind eat

grinds food

had it destroyed, wrecked

haaah? what? I didn't hear you

haolefied like a haole

hele on go, leave, 'with it', 'hip'

high mucka mucka arrogant, conceited, elite

ho! exclamation used before a strong statement

how you figga? how do you figure that, makes no sense
howzit hi, hello, how are you doing, what's happening [how is it]
junk lousy, terrible
kay den okay then, fine
li'dat like that, short cut for lengthy explanation
li'dis like this
humbug trouble, bother
make 'A' make a fool of yourself [make ass]
make house make yourself at home, act like you own the place
mama-san local Japanese equivalent of 'mom' at 'mom and pop' stores
Maui wowie potent marijuana (from Maui)
minors no big thing, minor
mo' more
mo'bettah better, good stuff
moke heavy set Hawaiian male, often looking for a fight
nah just kidding (often **nah, nah, nah**)
no can cannot, I can't do it
o' wot? (added on to most questions, usually when the speaker is fed up)
poi dog mutt, person made up of many ethnic mixtures
popolo black, negro
shahkbait white-skinned, pale [shark bait]
shaka all right, great, well done, perfect, okay, right on
sleepahs flip flops, thongs [slippers]
stink eye dirty look, evil eye
talk story rap, shoot the breeze, gossip
tanks eh? thank you
tita heavy set Hawaiian woman, may be looking for a fight [sister]
try used at beginning of a command
we go let's leave
yeah? added on to end of sentences
yeah yeah yeah yeah yes, all right, shut up

RECOMMENDED READING

T
here are countless books—of varying quality and accuracy—detailing the many aspects of Hawaiian history and culture, both ancient and modern. It has been impossible to detail any of these fascinating areas in a guidebook small enough to be handy. We recommend the following:

Atlas of Hawaii, by The Department of Geography, University of Hawai'i, University of Hawai'i Press, 1983. This book provides text on Hawai'i's natural environment, culture and economy along with maps.

The Beaches of O'ahu, by John R.K. Clark, University of Hawai'i Press, 1977. A complete guide to all of O'ahu's beaches, including recreational facilities and water sports, with maps, photographs, and details of ancient lore.

The Best of Aloha, Island Heritage Publishing, 1990. This full-color coffee table gift book features the best articles and photographs of the people, places, arts, and events that have been a part of *Aloha Magazine* and Hawaii over the last 12 years. It is a timeless collection which reflects the heritage, life-style, and geographic richness of the islands.

Bird Life in Hawaii, by Andrew J. Berger, Island Heritage, 1987. The story of the bird life of Hawai'i, including exotic birds and species which have become rare and endangered, each illustrated in full color accompanied by text written by the world's leading authority on Hawaiian birds.

Entertaining Island Style, by Lavonne Tollerud and Barbara Gray, Island Heritage, 1987. Menu planning is made simple in this colorful book. From lu'aus and beach parties to elegant Hawaiian suppers, there are many creative ideas for entertaining.

Favorite Recipes from Hawaii, by Lavonne Tollerud and Barbara Gray, Island Heritage, 1987. A collection of Hawai'i's most popular recipes. It includes Hawaiian cocktails, hors d'oeuvres, soups, salads, breads, main dishes, condiments, rice and noodles, vegetables and desserts.

Flowers of Hawaii, photography by Allan Seiden and Loye Gutherie, Island Heritage, 1987. A beautifully photographed guide to Hawai'i's colorful flowers, such as hibiscus, orchids and lilies, and their origins.

A Guide to Hawaiian Marine Life, by Les Matsura, Island Heritage, 1987. Written by a marine educator at the Waikīkī Aquarium, this guide highlights the marine life in Hawai'i through description and color photographs.

Hanauma Bay – An Island Treasure, by Liysa and Don King, Island Heritage Publishing, 1990. Hundreds of color photographs and descriptions of tropical fish included in this soft-cover book enhance the reader's experience at this famous Marine Preserve and create a greater appreciation of the ocean environment.

Hawaii, **by James Michener,** Random, 1959. A novel about Hawai'i from its geological birth to the present, by this renowned author.

Hawaii: A History, **by Ralph S. Kuykendall,** Prentice, 1961. A good and readable overall history of Hawai'i from the first Polynesian voyages to statehood.

Hawaii: The Aloha State, **by Allan Seiden,** Island Heritage, 1987. Visit exciting Waikīkī, colorful Lahaina, majestic Waimea Canyon, historic Kona—all the Hawaiian islands are brought to life in this beautifully photographed book.

Hawaii—Tides of Change, **by Bob Krauss,** Island Heritage, 1989. A witty, introspective essay on Hawai'i's island culture, with beautiful photography by long-time nature photographer Rick Golt.

Hawaiian Dictionary, **by Mary Kawena Pukui and Samuel H. Elbert,** University of Hawai'i Press, 1986. Hawaiian-English, English-Hawaiian dictionary, regarded as the definitive reference for Hawaiian vocabulary. It contains folklore, poetry and ethnology compiled by the leading authorities of Hawaiiana and Polynesian languages.

Hiking O'ahu, **by Robert Smith,** Wilderness Press, 1983. This accurate guidebook lists hiking trails on O'ahu, with descriptions of the route, the highlights, rating of difficulty, driving instructions, distance and average hiking time.

The Illustrated Atlas of Hawaii, **by Gavan Daws, O.A. Bushnell & Andrew Berger,** Island Heritage, 1987. Illustrations of the Hawaiian island chain, native plants, birds and fish by Joseph Feher with a concise history.

The Journal of Prince Alexander Liholiho, **Jacob Adler, ed.,** University of Hawai'i Press, 1967. Young Alexander Liholiho and his brother Lot visited the United States, England and France on a diplomatic mission with Dr Judd. This diary records the impressions of the future king.

Kaaawa: A Novel About Hawaii in the 1850's, **by Oswald Bushnell,** University of Hawai'i Press, 1972. An historical novel set on O'ahu about the missionary period.

Ka'ahumanu: Molder of Change, **by Jane Silverman,** Friends of the Judiciary History Center of Hawaii, 1987. A biography of the most powerful woman in Hawaiian history and the vast changes she wrought in the social and political life of the kingdom she ruled.

Kahuna La'au Lapa'au: The Practice of Hawaiian Herbal Medicine, **by June Gutmanis,** Island Heritage, 1987. Authoritative and definitive work on Hawaiian herbs and the secrets of Hawaiian herbal medicine with colorful illustrations.

Kalakaua: Hawaii's Last King, **by Kristin Zambucka,** Mana Publishing Co. and Marvin/Richard Enterprises, Inc., 1983. This pictorial biography with more than 180 old photographs recounts the colorful reign of Hawai'i's last king.

Maui: The Demigod, by Steven Goldsberry, Poseidon Press, 1984. This work about a universal figure in Polynesian folktales is remarkable for its utter originality and beauty of its language. The story is wise and funny, erotic and terrifying, and filled with humanity, folly and fate.

Molokai, by Oswald Bushnell, World Publishing Company, 1963. A novel about a group of people sent to a leper colony on Moloka'i and the shocking details of their lives.

Na Pule Kahiko: Ancient Hawaiian Prayers, by June Gutmanis, Editions Limited, 1983. This collection of traditional Hawaiian prayers, in both Hawaiian and English, is annotated with fascinating detail about the contexts in which these prayers, and prayers in general, were used in the lives of ancient Hawaiians.

An Ocean in Mind, by Will Kyselka, University of Hawai'i Press, 1987. The extraordinary story of a 6000-mile trip from Hawai'i to Tahiti and back, the 1980 voyage of the *Hokule'a,* without the use of modern navigational aid. Navigator Nainoa Thompson, of Hawaiian descent, studied the stars, winds and currents to explore his Polynesian past.

Our Hawaii - The Best of Bob Krauss, Island Heritage Publishing, 1990. Author of more than a dozen books, this well-known kama'aina columnist for The Honolulu Advertiser has masterfully assembled over 70 of his finest stories in 12 captivating chapters, which includes "You Can Always Tell A State By Its Food", "Aloha Shirts & Panty Hose" and "Ghosts, Gods & Hawaiian Spirits."

Pearl Harbor: The Way it Was, by Scott C.S. Stone, Island Heritage, 1987. A largely photographic essay relating to the attack, particularly from the Japanese view. Some previously unpublished photos of the attack are included. Stone, a former Naval officer and foreign correspondent, holds major writing prizes.

Place Names of Hawaii, by Mary Kawena Pukui, Samuel H. Elbert & Esther T. Mookini, University of Hawai'i Press, 1974. Place names listed with pronunciation and translation where known. Includes names of valleys, streams, mountains, land sections, surfing areas, towns, villages and Honolulu streets and buildings. Pukui and Elbert also compiled the *Hawaiian Dictionary.* Mookini has taught the Hawaiian language at the University of Hawai'i.

Princess Kaiulani: Last Hope of Hawaii's Monarchy, Kristin Zambucka, Mana Publishing Co., 1982. Pictorial biography of Hawai'i's beautiful and tragic princess. Niece of Queen Lili'uokalani, Hawai'i's last reigning monarch, Princess Ka'iulani was next in the line of succession to the throne.

Pua Nani, by Jeri Bostwick, photographs by Douglas Peebles, Mutual Publishing, 1987. Stunning color photography of the myriad blossoms—both native and introduced—that festoon these islands with their glorious hues and intricate structures.

Punchbowl, **by Doug Carlson,** Island Heritage, 1982. This book traces the extinct volcano crater's prominence as a site of human sacrifice in prehistoric Hawai'i to today's use as the final resting place for thousands of American war casualties and veterans.

The Return of Lono, **by Oswald Bushnell,** University of Hawai'i Press, 1971. A fictional reconstruction of the discovery of the Hawaiian Islands by Captain Cook.

Reflections of Kauai, **by Penny Pence Smith,** Island Heritage Publishing, 1990. The lush beauty and charm of Hawaii's oldest island are featured in both the photographic images and the text of this coffee table book.

Shoal of Time, **by Gavan Daws,** University of Hawai'i Press, 1974. An excellent and authoritative history of Hawai'i from earliest times to statehood, 1959.

The Story of James Dole, Island Heritage Publishing, 1990. Penned by his grandson Richard Dole and eldest daughter Elizabeth Dole Porteus, this biography of James Drummond Dole not only provides the reader insight into the private life of Hawaii's "Pineapple King," but the workings behind the establishment of the Dole Foods empire.

The Story of Pineapple in Hawaii, **by Kenneth Nagata and Lyon Arboretum,** Island Heritage Publishing, 1991. Vivid color photographs and condensed, easy-to-read text provide readers with factual information of the cultivation of the pineapple and its historic significance to Hawaii. The book also features favorite local recipes using this popular fruit.

Target: Pearl Harbor, **by Scott C.S. Stone,** Island Heritage, 1986. The story of the attack on Pearl Harbor using fictional characters and told for young readers by this prize-winning author.

Tropical Drinks and Pupus from Hawaii, **by Lavonne Tollerud and Barbara Gray,** Island Heritage, 1987. Delicious island cocktails and fruit drinks are complimented with a wide range of Hawaiian-style hors d'oeuvres.

Under A Maui Sun, **by Penny Pence Smith,** Island Heritage Publishing, 1990. The finest work from Hawaii's leading photographers showcase Maui's sunny disposition in this 200-page coffee table gift book.

The View from Diamond Head, **by Don Hibbard and David Franzen,** Editions Limited, 1986. Illustrated with more than 500 historical and contemporary photographs, this landscape format book tells the story of Waikiki, from the days before European arrival when it was a center of power and government on O'ahu, through its transition to rural outpost, to its renaissance as a world-class tourist resort.

Waikiki/Oahu: The Gathering Place, **by Allan Seiden,** Island Heritage, 1986. The excitement and beauty that have made O'ahu the hub of the Pacific, come to life in this beautiful book with vivid photography.

INDEX

APPENDIX

224

PHOTO CREDITS

APPENDIX

1	Scott Rutherford	47	Camera Hawaii	111	Scott Rutherford
3	Scott Rutherford	49	Scott Rutherford	113	Camera Hawaii
4	Bob Abraham	53	Bob Abraham	115	Steve Rawls
7	Bob Abraham	56	Scott Rutherford	117	Bob Abraham
9	Monte Costa	57	Scott Rutherford	119	Bob Abraham
11	Monte Costa	57	Scott Rutherford	123	Monte Costa
12	Bob Abraham	59	Camera Hawaii	137	Bob Abraham
13	Mike Tsukamoto	60	Monte Costa	140	Monte Costa
14	Monte Costa	61	Monte Costa	141	Mark Stephenson
15	Monte Costa	62	Monte Costa	143	Ward Centre
17	Scott Rutherford	63	Monte Costa	147	Monte Costa
18	Bob Abraham	64	Monte Costa	149	Monte Costa
20	Monte Costa	65	Monte Costa	151	Monte Costa
22	Scott Rutherford	66	Monte Costa	155	Bob Abraham
23	Monte Costa	68	Camera Hawaii	156	Hyatt Regency Waikiki
24	Camera Hawaii	69	Camera Hawaii	161	Hyatt Regency Waikiki
25	Mike Tsukamoto	71	Polynesian Cultural Ctr	161	Bob Abraham
27	Bob Abraham	76	Monte Costa	165	Monte Costa
28	Monte Costa	76	Mike Tsukamoto	168	Monte Costa
29	Bob Abraham	77	Bob Abraham	169	Hyatt Regency Waikiki
31	Camera Hawaii	77	Monte Costa	170	Bob Abraham
33	Bob Abraham	79	Bob Abraham	173	Bob Abraham
35	Bob Abraham	82	Mike Tsukamoto	177	Bob Abraham
36	Bob Abraham	93	Monte Costa	179	Mike Tsukamoto
37	Monte Costa	95	Mike Tsukamoto	183	Monte Costa
38	Bob Abraham	96	Mike Tsukamoto	185	Monte Costa
39	Bob Abraham	97	Mike Tsukamoto	190	Mike Tsukamoto
40	Camera Hawaii	99	Camera Hawaii	191	Scott Rutherford
41	Bob Abraham	100	L. Guthrie	193	Bob Abraham
42	Scott Rutherford	101	Vince Cavataio	199	Mike Tsukamoto
43	Scott Rutherford	102	Monte Costa	200	Scott Rutherford
44	Camera Hawaii	104	Phil Uhl	211	Camera Hawaii
45	Camera Hawaii	107	Camera Hawaii	212	Scott Rutherford
46	Camera Hawaii	109	Bob Abraham		